The
Elephant
Whisperer

ALSO BY LAWRENCE ANTHONY
WITH GRAHAM SPENCE

*Babylon's Ark: The Incredible Wartime
Rescue of the Baghdad Zoo*

The Last Rhinos

The Elephant Whisperer

Learning about Life, Loyalty and
Freedom from a Remarkable
Herd of Elephants

LAWRENCE ANTHONY

With Graham Spence

PAN BOOKS

First published 2009 by Sidgwick & Jackson

First published in paperback 2010 by Pan Books

This updated edition first published 2017 by Pan Books
an imprint of Pan Macmillan
The Smithson, 6 Briset Street, London EC1M 5NR
Associated companies throughout the world
www.panmacmillan.com

ISBN 978-1-5098-3853-0

9 8

A CIP catalogue record for this book is available from the British Library.

Printed and bound by CPI Group (UK) Ltd, Croydon, CR0 4YY

Visit www.panmacmillan.com to read more about all our books
and to buy them. You will also find features, author interviews and
news of any author events, and you can sign up for e-newsletters
so that you're always first to hear about our new releases.

To my beautiful, caring Françoise,
for allowing me to be who I am.

acknowledgements

To Mom for a lifetime of encouragement, Jason, Dylan and Tanny for their care, and for my wonderful grandsons Ethan and Brogan, Gavin, Mandy, 'The Chosen One', Jackie, and Laurie and Wilkie from Cambodia. Terrie, Paul, Cameron, and Graham for his insight and skill. The Malby family. Hilary and Grant. Jonno and Stan for fun friendships, and refusing to agree on anything, ever. Nkosi Nkanyiso Biyela for his wisdom, Ben and the Ngubane family for their wonderful friendship, Nkosi Phiwayinkosi Chakide Biyela for his foresight and leadership. Barbara, Yvette and all the Earth Org staff for taking up the challenge. Ian Raper for his leadership. Mehdy and the Zarrabeni family, Dave Cooper the game rangers' game ranger. Bella. Elmien. Marion Garaï. The Bruwer boys. Jabu, Promise, Winnie, Tom, Cindy, Fortunate, Zamu, Mkwanazi, Mabona, Vusi, Ngwenya, Bheki, Bonisiwe, Biyela, Zelda, Brigitte and all the incredible Thula Thula staff. David and Brendan for being there and doing it, and to Peter Joseph, Ingrid Connell, and Lisa Hagan for their confidence and support.

Picture Acknowledgements

Page 1: photographs © Françoise Malby-Anthony apart
  from top left © *Sarie* Magazine
Page 2: photographs © Dylan Anthony

prologue

In 1999, I was asked to accept a herd of troubled wild elephants on my game reserve. I had no inkling of the escapades and adventures I was about to embark upon. I had no idea how challenging it would be or how much my life would be enriched.

The adventure has been both physical and spiritual. Physical in the sense that it was action from the word go, as you will see in the following pages; spiritual because these giants of the planet took me deep into their world.

Make no mistake, the title of this book is not about me for I make no claim to any special abilities. It is about the elephants – it was they who whispered to me and taught me how to listen.

How this happened was purely at a personal level. I am no scientist, I am a conservationist. So when I describe how the elephants reacted to me, or I to them, it is purely the truth of my own experiences. There are no laboratory tests here, but through trial and error, I found out what worked best for me and my herd in our odyssey together.

Not only am I a conservationist, I am an extremely lucky one for I own a game reserve called Thula Thula. It consists of 5,000 acres of pristine bush in the heart of Zululand, South Africa, where elephants once roamed freely. No longer. Many rural Zulus have never seen an elephant. My elephants were the first wild ones to be reintroduced into our area for more than a century.

Thula Thula is a natural home to much of the indigenous wildlife of Zululand, including the majestic white rhino, Cape buffalo, leopard, hyena, giraffe, zebra, wildebeest, crocodile, and many species of antelope, as well as lesser-known predators such as the lynx and serval. We have seen pythons as long as a truck and we have possibly the biggest breeding population of white-backed vultures in the province.

And, of course, we have elephants.

The elephants came to us out of the blue, as you will read. Today, I cannot visualize a life without them. I don't want a life without them. To understand how they taught me so much, you have to understand that communication in the animal kingdom is as natural as a breeze. That in the beginning it was only self-imposed human limitations that impeded my understanding.

In our noisy cities we tend to forget the things our ancestors knew on a gut level: that the wilderness is alive, that its whispers are there for all to hear – and to respond to.

We also have to understand that there are things we cannot understand. Elephants possess qualities and abilities well beyond the means of science to decipher. Elephants cannot repair a computer, but they do have communication, physical and metaphysical, that would make Bill Gates's mouth drop open. In some very important ways they are ahead of us.

Some unexplained occurrences are quite evident throughout the plant and animal kingdom and there is nothing like looking at what is actually going on around you, to turn a lot of what you always thought to be true on its head.

For instance, any game ranger will tell you that if you decide to dart rhino for relocation to other reserves, the day you go out to do so there will not be a rhino around for love or money. Yet the day before, you saw them all over the place. Somehow they knew you were after them and they simply vanished. The next week when you only want to dart buffalo, the rhino you couldn't find will be standing by watching you.

Many years ago I watched a hunter stalking his prey. He had a permit to target only an impala ram from a bachelor herd. Yet the only males he encountered that day were those with breeding herds of females. And even more incredibly, these non-shootable studs stood nonchalantly within range, eyeing him without a care in the world, while in the background bachelor herds were running for their lives.

How is this so? None of us know. The more prosaic rangers among us just say it's Murphy Law – that whatever can go wrong, will. When you want to shoot or dart an animal they are never around. Others, like me, are not so sure. Maybe it's a bit more mystical. Maybe the message is in the wind.

This less conventional view is supported by a wise old Zulu tracker I know well. A vastly experienced man of the bush, he told me that whenever monkeys near his village got too brazen at stealing food, or threatening or biting children, they would decide to shoot one to scare the troop off.

'But those monkeys are so clever,' he said, tapping his temple. 'The moment we decide to fetch the gun they disappear. We have learned not even to say the name "monkey" or "gun" out loud among ourselves because then they will not come out of the forest. When there is danger they can hear without ears.'

Indeed. But amazingly this transcends even to plant life. Our guest lodge on Thula Thula is about two miles from our home in a grove of indigenous acacias and hardwoods that have been there for centuries. Here in this ancient woodland, the acacia tree not only understands it's under attack when browsed by antelope or giraffe, it quickly injects tannin into its leaves making them taste bitter. The tree then releases a scent, a pheromone, into the air to warn other acacias in the area of the potential danger. These neighbouring trees receive the warning and immediately start producing tannin themselves in anticipation of an attack.

Now a tree has no brain or central nervous system. So what is making these complex decisions? Or more pertinently – why? Why would a seemingly insentient tree care enough about its neighbour's safety to go to all that trouble to protect it? Without a brain how does it even know it has family or neighbours to protect?

Under the microscope, living organisms are just a soup of chemicals and minerals. But what about what the microscope doesn't see? That life force, the vital ingredient of existence – from an acacia to an elephant – can it be quantified?

My herd showed me that it can. That understanding and generosity of spirit is alive and well in the pachyderm kingdom; that elephants are emotional, caring and extremely intelligent; and that they value good relations with humans.

This is their story. They taught me that all life forms are important to each other in our common quest for happiness and survival. That there is more to life than just yourself, your own family, or your own kind.

chapter one

In the distance, the percussive shot of a rifle sounded like a giant stick of firewood cracking.

I jumped out of my chair, listening. It was a sound wired into a game ranger's psyche. Then came a burst . . . *crack-crack-crack*. Flocks of squawking birds scrambled, silhouetted in the crimson sunset.

Poachers. On the west boundary.

David, my ranger, was already sprinting for the trusty old Land Rover. I grabbed a shotgun and followed, leaping into the driver's seat. Max, my brindle Staffordshire bull terrier, scrambled onto the seat between us. With all the excitement buzzing he was not going to be left behind.

As I twisted the ignition key and floored the accelerator, David grabbed the two-way radio.

'Ndonga!' he bellowed. 'Ndonga, are you receiving? Over!'

Ndonga was the head of my Ovambo guards and a good man to have on your side in a gunfight, having served in the military. I would have felt better knowing him and his team were on their way but only static greeted David's attempts to contact him. We powered on alone.

Poachers had been the scourge of our lives since my fiancée Françoise and I bought Thula Thula, a magnificent game reserve in central Zululand. They had been targeting us for almost a year now. I couldn't work out who they were or where they were coming from. I had talked often with the *izinduna* – headmen – of the surrounding rural Zulu tribes and they were adamant that their people were not involved. I believed them. Our employees were mainly local and exceptionally loyal. These thugs had to be from somewhere else.

Twilight was darkening fast and I slowed as we approached the western fence and killed the headlights. Pulling over behind a large anthill, David was first out as we eased through a cluster of acacia trees, nerves on edge, trigger fingers tense, watching and listening. Tightly choked pump-action scatterguns with heavy pellets were our weapons of choice against poachers, for in the dark, in the bush, things are about as close and personal as you can get. As any game ranger in Africa knows, professional poachers will shoot first and shoot to kill.

The fence was just fifty yards away. Poachers like to keep their escape route open and I made a circling motion with my arm to David. He nodded, knowing exactly what I meant. He would keep watch while I crawled to the fence to cut off the retreat if a firefight erupted.

An acrid whiff of cordite spiced the evening air. It hung like a shroud in the silence. In Africa the bush is never willingly mute; the cicadas never cease. Except after gunshots.

After a few minutes of absolute stillness, I knew we had been set up. I switched on my halogen torch, sweeping its beam up and down the fence. There were no gaps revealing where a poacher could have cut his way in. David flicked on his torch as well, searching for tracks or blood spoor indicating if an animal had been killed and dragged off.

Nothing. Just an eerie silence.

With no tracks inside the reserve I realized the shots must have been fired from just outside the fence.

'Damn, it's a decoy.'

As I said that, we heard more shots – muffled but distinctive 'crumps' on the far side of the reserve, at least forty-five minutes' drive on dirt tracks that often are little more than quagmires in the spring rains.

We jumped back into the Land Rover and sped off, but I knew it was hopeless. We had been taken for suckers. We would never catch them. They would be off the reserve with a couple of slain nyala – one of Africa's most beautiful antelopes – before we got near.

I cursed my foolhardiness. If I had only sent some rangers to the far side instead of charging off blindly, we could have caught them red-handed.

But this proved one thing. I now knew for certain the *izindunas* who had been claiming my problems were internal – someone operating within the reserve – were spot on. This was not the local community's work. It was not a few hungry tribesmen and scrawny dogs hunting for the pot. This was a well-organized criminal operation led by someone who followed our every move. How else could they have timed everything so perfectly?

It was pitch-dark when we arrived at the eastern perimeter of the reserve and we traced the scene with our torches. The tracks told the story. Two nyala had been taken with high-velocity hunting rifles. We could see the flattened bloodstained grass from where their carcasses were dragged to a hole in the fence, which had been crudely hacked with bolt cutters. About ten yards outside the fence were the studded muddy tracks of a 4x4 bush vehicle that by now would be several miles away. The animals would be sold to local butchers who would use them for biltong, a dried meat jerky that is much prized throughout Africa.

The light of my torch picked up a bloody tuft of charcoal-grey fur fluttering on the cut fence wire. At least one of the dead bucks was a male – the female nyala is light brown with thin white stripes on her back.

I shivered, feeling old and weary. Thula Thula had been a hunting ranch before I had bought it and I had vowed that would end. No animal would be needlessly killed again on my watch. I didn't realize how difficult that vow would be to keep.

Despondently we drove back to the lodge. Françoise greeted us with mugs of dark, rich coffee. Just what I needed.

I glanced at her and smiled my thanks. Tall, graceful and very French, she was just as beautiful as the day I had first met her catching a taxi on a freezing London morning twelve years ago.

'What happened?' she asked.

'A set-up. There were two groups. One fired some shots on the far boundary, then watched our Land Rover lights. As soon as we got there, the others bagged two buck on the eastern side.'

I took a gulp of coffee and sat down. 'These guys are organized; someone's going to get killed if we're not careful.'

Françoise nodded. Three days ago the poachers had been so close it felt as if their bullets were whistling a fraction above our heads.

'Better report it to the cops tomorrow,' she said.

I didn't reply. To expect the police to pay much attention to two murdered antelope was pushing it a little.

Ndonga was furious the next morning when I told him that more animals had been shot. He admonished me for not calling him. I said we had tried but failed to get a response.

'Oh . . . sorry, Mr Anthony. I went out for a few drinks last night. Not feeling too good today,' he said, grinning sheepishly.

I didn't feel like discussing his hangover. 'Can you make this a priority?' I asked.

He nodded. 'We'll catch these bastards.'

I had barely got back to the house when the phone rang. A woman introduced herself: Marion Garaï from the Elephant Managers and Owners Association (EMOA), a private organization comprised of several elephant owners in South Africa that takes an interest in elephant welfare. I had heard of them and the good work they did for elephant conservation before, but as I was not an elephant owner, I had never dealt with them directly.

Her warm voice instantly inspired empathy.

She got straight to the point. She had heard about Thula Thula and the variety of magnificent indigenous Zululand wildlife that we had. She said she had also heard of how we were working closely with the local population in fostering conservation awareness and wondered . . . would I be interested in adopting a herd of elephant? The good news, she continued before I could answer, was that I would get them for free, barring capture and transportation costs.

You could have knocked me over with a blade of grass. Elephant? The world's largest mammal? And they wanted to give me a whole herd? For a moment I thought it was a hoax. I mean how often do you get phoned out of the blue asking if you want a herd of tuskers?

But Marion was serious.

OK, I asked; what was the bad news?

Well, said Marion. There was a problem. The elephants were considered 'troublesome'. They had a tendency to break out of reserves and the owners wanted to get rid of them fast. If we didn't take them, they would be put down – shot. All of them.

'What do you mean by troublesome?'

'The matriarch is an amazing escape artist and has worked out how to break through electric fences. She just twists the wire around her tusks until it snaps or takes the

9

pain and smashes through. It's unbelievable. The owners have had enough and now asked if EMOA can sort something out.'

I momentarily pictured a five-ton beast deliberately enduring the agonizing shock of 8,000 volts stabbing through her body. That took determination.

'Also, Lawrence, there are babies involved.'

'Why me?'

Marion sensed my trepidation. This was an extremely unusual request.

'I've heard you have a way with animals,' she continued. 'I reckon Thula Thula's right for them. You're right for them. Or maybe they're right for you.'

That floored me. If anything, we were exactly 'not right' for a herd of elephant. I was only just getting the reserve operational and, as the previous day had spectacularly proved, having huge problems with highly organized poachers.

I was about to say 'no' when something held me back. I have always loved elephants. Not only are they the largest and noblest land creatures on this planet, but they symbolize all that is majestic about Africa. And here, unexpectedly, I was being offered my own herd and a chance to help. Would I ever get an opportunity like this again?

'Where're they from?'

'A reserve in Mpumalanga.'

Mpumalanga is the north-eastern province of South Africa where most of the country's game reserves – including the Kruger National Park – are situated.

'How many?'

'Nine – three adult females, three youngsters, of which one was male, an adolescent bull, and two babies. It's a beautiful family. The matriarch has a gorgeous baby daughter. The young bull, her son, is fifteen years old and an absolutely superb specimen.'

'They must be a big problem. Nobody just gives away elephants.'

'As I said, the matriarch keeps breaking out. Not only does she snap electric wires, she's also learnt how to unlatch gates with her tusks and the owners aren't too keen about jumbos wandering into the guest camps. If you don't take them, they will be shot. Certainly the adults will be.'

I went quiet, trying to unravel all this in my head. The opportunity was great, but so was the risk.

What about the poachers – would the promise of ivory bring even more of them out of the woodwork? What about having to electrify my entire reserve to keep these giant pachyderms in when I could barely keep thieves with high-velocity rifles out? What about having to build an enclosure to quarantine them while they got used to their new home? Where would I find the funds . . . the resources?

Also Marion didn't shy away from saying they were 'troublesome'. But what did that really mean? Were they just escape artists? Or was this a genuine rogue herd, too dangerous and filled with hatred of humans to keep on a game reserve in a populated area?

However, here was a herd in trouble. Despite the risks, I knew what I had to do.

'Hell yes,' I replied. 'I'll take them.'

chapter two

I was still reeling from the shock of becoming an instant elephant-owner, when I got another: the current owners wanted the herd off their property within two weeks. Or else the deal would be off. The elephants would be shot as the owners regarded them as too much of a liability. Unfortunately, when an animal as large as an elephant is considered 'troublesome', it is almost always shot.

Two weeks? In that time we had to repair and electrify twenty miles of big game fencing and build from scratch a quarantine *boma* – a traditional holding pen – strong enough to hold the planet's most powerful animal.

When I bought Thula Thula, in 1998, it was 5,000 acres of primal Africa, the only improvement being an old hunters' camp with outside ablutions. But its history is as exotic as the continent itself. Thula Thula is the oldest private game reserve in the province of KwaZulu-Natal in South Africa and thought to be once part of the exclusive hunting grounds of King Shaka, the near-deified warrior who founded the Zulu nation in the early nineteenth century. In fact it was so exclusive that anyone caught hunting there without the king's express permission was put to death.

From Shaka onwards, for most of its existence Thula Thula's teeming wildlife has made it a hunting magnet, attracting wealthy clients seeking trophy antelope. In the 1940s the owner was a retired Governor General of Kenya,

12

who used it as an upmarket shooting lodge for the gin and tonic set.

That's all in the past. Hunting was scrapped the moment we took over. The characterful but dilapidated old biltong and brandy camp was demolished, and in its place we built a small luxury eco-lodge set on expansive lawns leading down to the Nseleni River. The beautiful Old Dutch gabled farmhouse overlooking the reserve became home and offices for Françoise and me.

But to get there has been a personal odyssey. I grew up in 'old' Africa, before the days of mass urbanization, running barefoot under big skies in Zimbabwe, Zambia and Malawi. My friends were rural African kids and together we ranged the wild world that was our backyard.

During the early 1960s my family moved to the sugar-cane-growing coastal belt of Zululand, South Africa. The hub of the area at the time was a hamlet out in the boondocks called Empangeni. It was a tough town with character. Stories of leathery farmers partying all night and skidding their tractors through the main street swigging 'spook 'n diesel' (cane spirit mixed with a smidgen of Coca-Cola) are still told to this day. For us teenagers, you had to hold your own and play a hard game of rugby to earn respect.

My shooting skills, honed in the deep African bush, also stood me in good stead and farmers sent me out on their lands to bag guinea fowl and grouse for the pot. The backwoods was my home; I could hit a can thrown into the air at twenty paces with a .22 rifle and think little of it.

After finishing school I left for the city, establishing a real-estate company. But my youthful memories of wild Africa followed me. I knew one day I would return.

That happened in the early 1990s. I was poring over a map of the area west of Empangeni and was struck by the profusion of unutilized tribal land, far too feral for even the hardiest cattle. These trust lands gallop right up to the borders of the famous Umfolozi-Hluhluwe reserve, the first game sanctuary established anywhere in Africa and where the southern white rhino was saved from extinction.

The trust land, a massive tract of gloriously pristine bush, belonged to six different Zulu clans. An idea light-bulbed in my head: if I could persuade them to join in conserving wildlife instead of hunting or grazing, we could create one of the finest reserves imaginable. But to do this I would have to convince each tribal leader to agree individually to lease the land to a single trust. It would be called the Royal Zulu, and benefits such as job creation would go straight back into the struggling local communities.

Thula Thula, with solid infrastructure already in place was the key to the project. It was a natural wedge abutting the tribal lands and forming a crucial eastern gateway to the reserves. And for the first time in fifty years it was on the market. Destiny? Well . . . who knows?

I took a deep breath, spoke nicely – very nicely – to my bank manager and Françoise and I ended up as the new owners.

I fell in love with it from the moment I went walkabout. It's something I still do, jump in the Land Rover and drive out onto the open savannahs or into the thickest, most thorn-scrubbed veldt I can find, and go for a walk. There is nothing more energizing than inhaling the tang of wilderness, loamy after rain, pungent with the richness of earth shuddering with life, or taking in the brisk dry cleanness of winter. In the outback, life is lived for the instant. The land thrums with exuberance when everything is green and lush and is stoically resilient when it isn't. In the bush, simple acts give intense atavistic pleasures, such as sliding a sprig of grass into the tiny slot of a scorpion hole and feeling a tug that pound for pound would rival a game fish. Even today that triggers memories of my born-free adolescence as vividly as a lovelorn youth recalling his first heart-thudding kiss.

So too does the chime of songbirds, the tunesmiths of the planet, where even a panicked warning call is perfectly in pitch. Or watching life's endlessly fascinating passing show, the brutal poetry of the food chain where life is so precarious yet pulses so powerfully in every shape, colour and form.

Those solitary hikes in Thula Thula evoked the path I first walked as a child in untamed places. Now decades later I was bringing a herd of elephants, to me the definitive symbol of wild Africa, back to an ancient Zululand home. Thula Thula's landscape is an elephant's paradise: woodlands leading to sweet savannah, riverbanks choked with nutritious grasses and waterholes that never run dry, even in the bleakest of winters.

But we had to get cracking, electrifying the fences and building a sturdy *boma*. The word *boma* means stockade and with antelope it's a simple matter of erecting barriers high enough to stop them from leaping over. However, with elephants, which are stronger than a truck, it's a different ballgame altogether. You have to spike the fences with enough mega-volts to hold a five-ton juggernaut.

The electrical force is designed not to injure the animals; it's only there to warn them off. Thus it's vital that the *boma* is a replica of the reserve's outer border so once they have learned that bumping into it is not much fun, they will later steer clear of the boundary.

There was no way we were going to be able to do all that in just two weeks but we would certainly give it a damn good try and wing it from there.

I radioed David and Ndonga to come to the office.

'Guys, you're looking at the owner of a herd of elephants.'

Both stared for a moment as if I had gone loopy. David spoke first. 'What do you mean?'

'I've been given nine elephants.' I scratched my head, still hardly believing it myself. 'It's a one-off deal – if I don't take them they'll be shot. But the bad news is that they're a bit of a problem. They've broken through fences before – electric ones.'

David's face lifted in a massive grin.

'Elephants! Fantastic!' He paused for a moment and I could see he was mulling over the same concerns that I had. 'But how are we gonna hold them here? Thula's fences won't stop ellies.'

'Well, we've got two weeks to fix them. And to build a *boma*.'

'Two weeks? For twenty miles of fence?' Ndonga spoke for the first time, giving me a doubtful look.

'We've got no choice. The current owners have given me a deadline.'

David's unfettered enthusiasm was gratifying and I instinctively knew he would be my right-hand man on this project.

Tall and well built with handsome Mediterranean features, David was a natural leader with a sense of purpose about him that belied his nineteen years. Our families have ties stretching back decades and it was, I believe, fate that brought him to Thula Thula during this pivotal period. A fourth-generation Zululander, he had no formal game-ranger credentials but that didn't worry me. He could do a hard day's work and was in tune with the natural world, which I have found to be one of the best recommendations for anyone, regardless of vocation. He also had been a top rugby player, a flank forward with a reputation for almost kamikaze tackles. This tenacity would certainly be tested at Thula Thula.

I then called in the Zulu staff and asked them to put the word out among the local community that we needed labourers. The nearest village to us is Buchanana where

16

unemployment runs at 60 per cent. I knew there would be no problem finding able bodies, the problem would be the skill factor. A rural Zulu can build a decent shelter out of sticks, a puddle of mud and a handful of grass, but we were talking of constructing an electrified elephant-proof stockade. The gangs would have to be heavily supervised at all times, but they would develop skills which would stand them in good stead when job hunting later.

Sure enough, over the next two days there were hordes of people outside Thula Thula's gates clamouring for work. Hundreds of thousands in rural Africa live close to the brink, and I was glad to be able to contribute to the community.

To keep the *amakhosi* – local chieftains – on our side, I made appointments to explain what we were doing. Incredibly, most Zulus have never set eyes on an elephant as nowadays the giants of South Africa are all in fenced sanctuaries. The last free roaming jumbos in our part of Zululand were actually killed almost a century ago. So the main aim of visiting the chiefs was to explain that we were bringing these magnificent creatures 'home' again, as well as providing assurances that the fences were electrified on the inside and thus wouldn't harm any passers-by.

However, the fact that none of the locals had seen an elephant before did not stop them from voicing 'expert' opinions.

'They will eat our crops,' said one, 'and then what will we do?'

'What about the safety of our women when they fetch water?' another asked.

'We're worried about the children,' said a third, referring to the young herd boys who do a man's work looking after cattle alone. 'They do not know elephant.'

'I heard they taste good,' piped up another. 'An elephant can feed all the village.'

OK, that was not quite the reaction I wanted. But generally the *amakhosi* seemed well disposed to the project.

Except one. I was away for a day and asked one of my rangers to discuss the issue with an interim chief. Sadly all he succeeded in doing was antagonizing the man. The chief kept repeating 'these are not my elephant; I know nothing about this' to anything said.

Fortunately Françoise was there and took over. She did so reluctantly as rural Zulu society is polygamous and uncompromisingly masculine. No man wants to be seen listening to a woman.

Chauvinism? Sure, but that's the way it is out in the sticks. It took skill and charm for Françoise to hold her ground. Eventually the chief relented, admitting he had no real concerns.

With approval from the *amakhosi* secured, we selected seventy of the fittest-looking recruits and in record time were up and running. Singing ancient martial songs, the Zulu gangs started work and despite the impossible deadline, as the fence slowly crept across the countryside, I began to breathe easier.

Then just as we started to see progress we ran up against a wall.

David came sprinting into the office. 'Bad news, boss. Workers on the western boundary have downed tools. They say they're being shot at. Everyone's too scared to work.'

I stared at him, uncomprehendingly. 'What do you mean? Why would anyone shoot at a gang of labourers?

David shrugged. 'I dunno, boss. Sounds like it has to be a cover for something else, perhaps a strike for more money . . .'

I doubted that, as the workers were paid a decent rate already. The reason for the strike was more likely to be *muthi*, or witchcraft.

In rural Zululand belief in the supernatural is as common

as breathing, and *muthi* is all-powerful. It can either be benevolent or malevolent, just as *sangomas* – witchdoctors – can be both good and evil. To resist bad *muthi* you need to get a benign *sangoma* to cast a more potent counter spell. *Sangomas* charge for their services, of course, and sometimes initiate stories of malevolent *muthi* for exactly that purpose – and that's what could be happening here.

'What do we do, boss?'

'Let's try and find out what's going on. In the meantime we don't have much choice. Pay off those too spooked to work and let's get replacements. We've got to keep moving.'

I also gave instructions for a group of security guards to be placed on standby to protect the remaining labourers.

The next morning David once more came running into the office.

'Man, we've got real problems,' he said, catching his breath. 'They're shooting again and one of the workers is down.'

I grabbed my old Lee–Enfield .303 rifle and the two of us sped to the fence in the Land Rover. Most of the labourers were crouching behind trees while a couple tended to their bleeding colleague. He had been hit in the face by heavy shotgun pellets.

After checking that the injury was not life-threatening, we started criss-crossing the bush until we picked up the tracks – or spoor as it is called in Africa. It belonged to a single gunman – not a group, as we had initially feared. I called Bheki and my security *induna* Ngwenya, whose name means crocodile in Zulu, two of our best and toughest Zulu rangers. Bheki is the hardest man I have ever met, slim with quiet eyes and a disarmingly innocent face, while Ngwenya, thickset and muscular, had an aura of quiet authority about him which influenced the rest of the rangers in his team.

'You two go ahead and track the gunman. David and I will stay here to protect the rest of the workers.'

They nodded and inched their way through the thornveld until they believed they were behind the shooter. They slowly cut back and waited . . . and waited.

Then Ngwenya saw a brief glint of sunlight flash off metal. He signalled to Bheki, pointing to the sniper's position. Lying low in the long grass, they rattled off a volley of warning shots. The sniper dived behind an anthill, fired two blasts from his shotgun, then disappeared into the thick bush.

But the guards had seen him – and to their surprise, they knew him. He was a 'hunter' from another Zulu village some miles away.

We drove the shot labourer to hospital and called the police. The guards identified the gunman and the cops raided his thatched hut, seizing a dilapidated shotgun. Amazingly, he confessed without any hint of shame that he was a 'professional poacher' – and then heaped the blame on us, saying that erecting an electric fence would deprive him of his livelihood. He no longer could break into Thula Thula so easily. He denied trying to kill anyone, he just wanted to scare the workers off and stop the fence being built. Not surprisingly, that didn't cut much ice with the authorities.

I asked to see the shotgun and the cops obliged. It was a battered double-barrel 12-bore, as ancient as its owner. The stock, held together with vinyl electrical tape, was scratched and chipped from thousands of scrapes in the bush. The barrel was rusted and pitted. There was no way this was the person responsible for our major poaching problem.

So who was?

With that disruption behind us the construction continued from dawn to dusk, seven days a week. It was back-breaking work, sweaty and dirty with temperatures soaring to 110 degrees Fahrenheit. But mile by torturous mile, the electric fence started to take shape, inching northwards, then cutting east and gathering momentum as the workers' competency levels increased.

Building a *boma* was equally gruelling, albeit on a far smaller scale. We measured out 110 square yards of virgin bush and cemented 9-foot-tall, heavy-duty eucalyptus poles into concrete foundations every 12 yards. Then coils of tempered mesh and a trio of cables as thick as a man's thumb were strung onto the poles, tensioned by the simple expedient of attaching the ends to the Land Rover bumper and 'revving' it taut.

But no matter how thick the cables, no bush fence will hold a determined elephant. So the trump card is the 'hot wires'. The electrification process is deceptively simple. All it consists of is four live wires bracketed onto the poles so they run inside the structure, while two energizers that run off car batteries generate the 'juice'.

Simple or not, the energizers pack an 8,000-volt punch. This may sound massive, which it is, but the shock is not fatal as the amperage is extremely low. But believe me, it is excruciating, even to an elephant with an inch-thick hide. I can vouch first-hand, having accidentally touched the wires several times during repairs, or while carelessly waving arms in animated conversation, much to the mirth of my rangers. It's most unpleasant as the electricity seizes and surprises you. Your body shudders and unless you let go quickly you sit down involuntarily as your legs collapse. The only good thing is that you recover quickly to laugh about it.

Once the fence was up, the final task was to chop down any trees that could be shoved onto it, as this is an elephant's favourite way of snapping the current.

The deadline passed in an eye-blink and of course we were nowhere near finished, even though I had employed more men and at the *boma* we slaved virtually around the clock, even working by car lights at night.

Soon the telephones started jangling with the Mpumalanga reserve managers wanting to know what was going on.

'Everything's fine,' I boomed cheerfully over the phone, lying through my teeth. If they knew the problems we had with unrealistic deadlines and workers being shot at by a rogue gunman they probably would have called the deal off. Sometimes I would put Françoise on the line to pacify them, which she did admirably with her entrancing French lilt.

Then one day we got the call I dreaded.

The herd had broken out again and this time damaged three of the reserve's lodges. We were bluntly told that unless we took the elephants immediately, the owners would have to make a 'decision'.

Françoise fielded the call and crossing her fingers said we only need to get our elephant proofing approved by KZN Wildlife – the province's official authority – and all problems would be over.

Somehow the owners bought that and reluctantly agreed to an extension. But just a few more days, they warned, or else there would be a 'decision'.

That word again.

chapter three

Exhausted teams were still hammering in the final fence nails when the Mpumalanga reserve manager phoned to say he could wait no longer and was sending them, ready or not. The elephants were being loaded as we spoke and would arrive at Thula Thula within eighteen hours.

I hurriedly called our Parks authority, KwaZulu-Natal Wildlife, to come and inspect the *boma*, stressing that the animals were already on their way. Fortunately they were able to respond instantly and said an inspector would be at Thula Thula within a couple of hours.

David and I sped down for a final look-see as I wanted everything to be perfect. But while we were double-checking that all vulnerable trees were beyond toppling distance from the fence, something suddenly struck me as being odd. Something didn't look right.

And then I saw the problem. Damn it! While the electric wires were bracketed on the inside, the fence itself, including the heavy-duty cables, had been strung up on the outside of the poles. This was a fatal flaw because if an elephant braved the power and leant on the mesh it would rip off like paper. The poles thus provided at best flimsy inner-lateral support, literally just holding the fence up. Once the inspector saw this he would instantly condemn it. That meant the truck would be turned and the herd sent back to certain death.

I clenched my fists in exasperation. How could we make such an elementary error? It was too late to do anything as the dust mushrooming above the savannah signalled the arrival of the inspector. I prayed we could bluff our way through, but inwardly I despaired. The project was doomed before it began.

The inspector jumped out of his bush-worn Toyota Land Cruiser and I began effusively thanking him for arriving at short notice, stressing that the elephants were already on the road. I hoped that adding a deadline edge might swing things our way.

He was a decent guy and knew his business, making particular note of a large tambotie tree with gnarled bark knotted like biceps that was close to the fence. Tambotie is an exceptionally hard wood that blunts the sharpest chainsaw and the inspector remarked wryly that not even an elephant could snap this particularly 'muscular' one. He deemed it safe.

Then he went to check the meshing and my mouth went dry. Surely he'd notice the wire was on wrong side.

The Gods were with us that day, and to my gut-churning relief, he – like us – didn't spot the obvious mistake. The *boma* was given the green light. I now had my crucial authorization and summoned every available hand to secure the fence correctly.

The 600-mile drive south from Mpumalanga to Thula Thula would take all day and much of the night as the eighteen-wheeler needed plenty of pit stops to feed and water the jumbos. I wasn't concerned about the journey as one of Africa's top elephant hands, Cobus Raath, was in charge.

It was only then I got the news from Françoise – that she had heard that the herd's matriarch and her baby had been shot during the capture. The justification was that she was 'bad news' and would lead breakouts at Thula Thula as

24

well. We learnt this via a telephone call after the animals had left and I was as stunned as if I had been hit in the spleen. This was exactly what we at Thula Thula were fighting against. While I understood the conventional reasoning behind the choice to kill the matriarch, I felt that decision should have been mine. As elephants are so big and dangerous, if they create problems and pose a risk to lodges and tourists it is quite usual for them to be shot out of hand. However, I was convinced that I would be able to settle the herd in their new home. Consequently I was prepared to take the risk of accepting the escape-artist matriarch and her baby and work with her. Even so, this killing cemented my determination to save the rest of the herd.

The Zulus who live close to the land have a saying that if it rains on an inaugural occasion, that event will be blessed. For those in step with the natural world, rain is life. That day it didn't just rain, it bucketed. The bruised skies sprayed down torrents and I wasn't too sure the Zulus had this 'blessed' story right. When the articulated truck arrived outside Thula Thula in thick darkness the deluge had turned the dirt tracks into streams of mud.

Barely had we opened the gates to the reserve when a tyre burst, the reinforced rubber cracking loud as a rifle shot. This panicked the elephants, who had just seen their leader gunned down and they started thumping the inside of the trailer like it was a gigantic drum, while the crews worked feverishly to change the wheel.

'This is *Jurassic Park*!' Françoise cried. We laughed, not necessarily in mirth.

Françoise and I first met some years back in London at the Cumberland Hotel. It was minus 17 degrees Celsius and I urgently needed to get to Earls Court for a meeting. There was a long queue snaking up to the taxi rank outside the hotel and the doorman, who knew I was in a hurry, said he would see if anyone would share a cab. As it happened, a gorgeous woman right at the front was also going to Earls Court. The doorman asked if she would mind sharing and pointed at me. She leaned forward to get a better look, and then shook her head. It was the most emphatic 'No' I had seen.

Well, that's life. Rather than hang around I decided to take the Underground and as I strode off, to my surprise, the same woman miraculously appeared next to me at the Tube station.

''Ello,' she said in a thick French accent, 'I am Françoise.'

She said she felt guilty about not agreeing to share a cab and to make amends offered to show me which train to take. To say I was smitten would be putting it blandly.

She knew London well and asked if I was interested in jazz. I wasn't, but I also wasn't stupid enough to say so. In fact, I professed undying love for the genre. Thank the stars she didn't ask for proof – such as my favourite musician – and instead suggested that as jazz lovers we go to Ronnie Scott's Jazz Club that night. I pondered this for a fraction of a nanosecond before answering 'Yes' with more enthusiasm than absolutely necessary.

Apart from wondering why I had never appreciated the bewitchment of jazz before, I spent much of that evening telling her of the magic of Africa – not hard in the middle of an English winter. Was there plenty of sun in Africa, she asked? I scoffed . . . was there sun? We invented the word.

Well, here we were twelve years later drenched to the marrow in the bush, wrestling with a gigantic wheel on a muddy rig loaded with elephants. I don't recall mentioning this could happen while piling on the charm during our first date.

The spare wheel had scarcely been bolted on when to the surprise of no one the truck slid just a few yards before it sank into the glutinous mud, its tyres spinning impotently and spewing muck all over the place. No amount of cajoling, swearing, kicking or packing branches underneath worked. And even worse, the elephants were becoming more and more agitated.

'We've got to sort this out quickly or we're going to have to release them right here,' said Cobus, his brow creased with worry. 'They cannot stay in the truck any longer. Let's just pray like hell the outer fence holds them.'

We both knew that with this hair-trigger herd, it wouldn't happen. We also both knew that if the elephants escaped they would be shot.

Fortunately the driver, sick of all the pontificating, took matters into his own hands. Without a word he slammed the truck into reverse, and somehow skidded the huge rig out of the bog and veered off the greasy road into the savannah that had marginally more grip. Dodging tyre-shredding thornbush and slithering past huge termite mounds he somehow kept momentum until he reached the *boma*.

The crew cheered as though he had scored a touchdown at the Superbowl.

Coaxing the animals from the truck was the next problem. Due to their massive size, elephants are the only animals that can't jump at all, and so we had dug a trench for the semi to reverse into so the trailer's floor would be level with the ground.

However, the trench was now a soggy pit brimming with brown-frothed rainwater. If we backed into it, we would have a major problem extracting the vehicle. Mud is like ice; what it seizes it keeps. But with a herd of highly disturbed elephants inside, it was a risk we had to take.

Disaster! Not because the truck got stuck – instead, the trench was too deep and the trailer's sliding door jammed into the ground. To compound matters it was 2 a.m., dark as obsidian and the rain was still sluicing down thick as surf. I put out an emergency wake-up call to everyone on the reserve and armed with shovels we slithered around in the sludge hacking a groove for the door. I was surprised that my staff didn't mutiny.

Finally the big moment arrived and we all stood well back, ready for the animals to be released into their new home.

However, as it had been an extremely stressful few hours, Cobus decided first to inject the herd with a mild sedative, using a pole-sized syringe. He climbed onto the roof of the trailer, which had a large ventilation gap, and David jumped up to give him a hand.

As David landed on the roof a trunk whipped through the slats as fast as a mamba and lashed at his ankle. David leapt back, dodging the grasping trunk with a heartbeat to spare. If the elephant had caught him he would have been yanked inside to a gruesome death. As simple as that. Cobus told me he had heard of it happening before; a person pulled into a confined space with seven angry elephants would soon be hamburger meat.

Thankfully all went smoothly after this and as soon as the injections had been administered and they had calmed down the door slid open and the new matriarch emerged. With headlights throwing huge shadows on the trees behind, she tentatively stepped onto Thula Thula soil, the first wild elephant in the area for almost a century.

The six others followed: the new matriarch's baby bull, three females – of which one was an adult – and an eleven-year-old bull. The last out was the fifteen-year-old, three-and-half-ton, teenage son of the previous matriarch. He walked a few yards and even in his groggy state realized there were humans behind. He swivelled his head and stared at us, then flared his ears and with a high-pitched trumpet of rage turned and charged, pulling up just short of slamming into the fence in front of us. He instinctively knew, even at his tender age, that he must protect the herd.

I smiled with absolute admiration. His mother and baby sister had been shot before his eyes; he had been darted and confined in a trailer for eighteen hours; and here he was, just a teenager, defending his family. David immediately named him 'Mnumzane' (pronounced nom-zahn) which in Zulu means 'Sir'.

The new matriarch we christened 'Nana', which is what all Anthony grandchildren call my mum Regina Anthony, a respected matriarch in her own right.

The second female in command, the most feisty, we called 'Frankie' after Françoise. For equally obvious reasons. The other names would come later.

Nana gathered her clan, loped up to the fence and stretched out her trunk, touching the electric wires. The 8,000-volt wires sent a jolt shuddering through her hulk. Whoa . . . she hurriedly backed off. Then, with her family in tow she strode the entire perimeter of the *boma*, her trunk curled fractionally below the wire to sense the current's pulse, checking for the weakest link as she must have seen her sister, the previous matriarch, do so often before.

I watched, barely breathing. She completed the check and smelling the waterhole, led her herd off to drink.

The crucial aspect of an electrified *boma* is fine-tuning how long you keep the animals inside. Too short, and they don't learn enough to respect the mega-volt punch the fence packs. But if it's too long, they somehow figure out that it's possible to endure the convulsions for the few agonizing seconds it takes to snap the strand – like the previous matriarch did. Once that happens they will never fear electricity again.

Unfortunately no one knows exactly what that 'perfect period' is. Opinions vary from a few days for more docile elephants to three months for wilder ones. My new herd was anything but docile, so how long I should pen them was anybody's guess. However, what the experts had told me was that during the quarantine period the animals should have no contact with humans. So once the gates were bolted I instructed everyone to move off except for two game guards who would watch from a distance.

As we were leaving I noticed the elephants lining up at a corner of the fence. They were facing due north, the exact direction of their former home, as if their inner compasses were telling them something.

It looked ominous.

Soaked and freezing with my personal magnetic needle pointing unwaveringly towards a warm bed, I left with a deep sense of foreboding.

chapter four

Hammering echoed like a drum roll in my head. I wondered hazily where it was coming from.

My eyes flickered open. It was no dream. The banging stemmed from a shuddering door. *Rat-a-tat. Rat-a-tat-a-tat.*

Then I heard yelling. It was Ndonga. 'The elephants have gone! They've broken out the *boma*! They've gone!'

I leapt out of bed, yanking on my trousers and stumbling like a pogo-dancer on one leg. Françoise, also awake and wide-eyed at the commotion, threw a nightgown over her shoulders.

'I'm coming. Hang on!' I shouted and shoved open the top half of the bedroom's stable door that led directly to the farmhouse's lush gardens.

An agitated Ndonga was standing outside, shivering in the pre-dawn chill.

'The two big ones started shoving a tree,' he said. 'They worked as a team, pushing it until it just crashed down on the fence. The wires shorted and the elephants smashed through. Just like that.'

Dread slithered in my belly. 'What tree?'

'You know, that *moersa* tambotie. The one that KZN Wildlife *oke* said was too big to pull down.'

It took me a few moments to digest this. That tree must have weighed several tons and was thirty feet tall. Yet Nana and Frankie had figured out that by working in tandem they

31

could topple it. Despite my dismay, I felt a flicker of pride; these were some animals, all right.

The last foggy vestiges of sleep vaporized like steam. We had to get moving fast. One didn't have to be a genius to grasp that we had a massive crisis on our hands as the herd was now stampeding towards the border fence. If they broke through that last barrier they would head straight into the patchwork of rural homesteads scattered outside Thula Thula. And as any game ranger will attest, a herd of wild elephants on the run in a populated area would be the conservation equivalent of the Chernobyl disaster.

I cursed long and hard, only stopping when I caught Françoise's disapproving glance. I had believed the electric *boma* was escape-proof. The experts had told me exactly that, and it never occurred to me that they might be wrong.

David's bedroom was across the lawn and I ran over. 'Get everyone up. The elephants have broken out. We've got to find them – fast!'

Within minutes I had scrambled to raise a search party and we gathered at the *boma*, astounded at the damage. The large tambotie tree was history, its toppled upper section tenuously connected to the splintered stump by a strip of its bark oozing poisonous sap. The fence looked as though a division of Abrams tanks had thundered through it.

Standing next to the shattered tree was the astounded Ovambo guard who had witnessed the breakout. He pointed us in the direction he had last seen the elephants heading.

Almost at running speed, we followed the spoor to the boundary. We were too late. The border fence was down and the animals had broken out.

My worst fears were confirmed. But even so, how on earth had the animals got through an electrified fence pushing 8,000 volts so effortlessly?

We soon found out. Judging by their tracks, they had reached the eight-foot fence, milled around for a while and then backtracked into the reserve until – uncannily – they found the energizer that powers the fence. How they knew this small, nondescript machine hidden in a thicket half a mile away was the source of current baffled us. But somehow they did, trampling it like a tin can and then returning to the boundary, where the wires were now dead. They then shouldered the concrete-embedded poles out of the ground like matchsticks.

Their tracks pointed north. There was no doubt that they were heading home to Mpumalanga 600 miles away. To the only home they knew; even though it was a home that no longer wanted them – and where, in all probability, they would be shot. That's assuming game rangers or hunters didn't get them along the way first.

As daybreak filled the eastern sky a motorist three miles away spotted the herd loping up the road towards him. At first he thought he was seeing things. Elephants? There aren't meant to be any elephants here . . .

Half a mile or so later he saw the flattened fence and put two and two together. Fortunately he had the presence of mind to call, giving us valuable updated information.

The chase was on. I gunned my Land Rover into gear as the trackers leapt into the back.

We had barely driven out of the reserve when, to my astonishment, we saw a group of men parked on the shoulder of the dirt road, dressed in khaki and camouflage hunting gear and bristling with heavy-calibre rifles. They were as hyped as a vigilante gang and their excitement was palpable. You could smell the bloodlust.

I stopped and got out of the vehicle, the trackers and David behind me.

'What're you guys doing?'

One looked at me, eyes darting with anticipation. He shifted his rifle, caressing the butt.

'We're going after elephants.'

'Oh yeah? Which ones?'

'They've bust out of Thula, man. We're gonna shoot them before they kill someone – they're fair game now.'

I stared at him for several seconds, grappling to absorb this new twist to my escalating problems. Then cold fury set in.

'Those elephants belong to me,' I said taking two paces forward to emphasize my point. 'If you put a bullet anywhere near them you are going to have to deal with me. And when we're finished, I'm going to sue your arse off.'

I paused, breathing deeply.

'Now show me your hunting permit,' I demanded, knowing he couldn't possibly have obtained one before dawn.

He stared at me, his face reddening with belligerence.

'They've escaped, OK? They can be legally shot. We don't need your permission.'

David was standing next to me, fists clenched. I could sense his outrage. 'You know, David,' I said loudly, 'just look at this lot. Out there is a herd of confused elephants in big trouble and we're the only ones here without guns. We're the only ones who don't want to kill them. Shows the difference in priorities, doesn't it?'

Fizzing with anger, I ordered my men back into the Land Rover. Revving the engine and churning up dust clouds for the benefit of the gunmen staring aggressively at us we sped up the road.

The acrimonious encounter shook me considerably. Technically the urban Rambos were correct – the elephants were 'fair game'. We had just heard on our two-way radios that the KZN Wildlife authorities, whom we had alerted as soon as the herd had broken out, were issuing elephant rifles to their staff. I didn't have to be told that they were considering shooting the animals on sight. Their prime concern was the safety of people in the area and no one could blame them.

For us, it was now a simple race against time. We had to

find the elephants before anyone with a gun did. That's all it boiled down to.

After another mile up the road the herd's tracks veered into the bush, exactly as the motorist had told us. Thula Thula is flanked by vast forests of acacia trees and *ugagane* bush, which grows thickly with interwoven thorn-studded branches that are as supple and vicious as whips. It's a riotous tangle of hostile thickets; lovely and wild to view, but torturous to track in. The wickedly sharp thorns scarcely scratch an elephant's hide, of course, but to us soft-skinned species it was the equivalent of running through a maze of fish hooks.

The forest spread north as far as the eye could see. Could we find the animals in this almost impenetrable wilderness?

I looked up to the heavens, squinting against the harsh yellow-white glare that indicated we were in for a savage scorcher of a day and found my answer – air support. For us to have a fighting chance of catching the elephants before some gunman did, we had to have a helicopter tracking above. But to get a chopper up would cost thousands of dollars, with no guarantee of success. Also, most commercial pilots wouldn't have a clue as to how to scout elephants hiding in such rugged terrain.

But there was one man I knew who could track from the sky – and, fortuitously, he was a family friend. Peter Bell was not only a technical genius at Bell Equipment, an international heavy-duty vehicle manufacturer, but also an expert game-capture pilot and a good man to have on your side in an emergency. I quickly drove back to Thula Thula and phoned him.

Peter didn't have to be told how serious the problem was and unhesitatingly agreed to help. While he got his chopper ready, we continued the chase on foot. But we had barely infiltrated the acacia jungle when our Ovambo game guards, staring at what appeared to me to be a flinty patch of dirt, shook their heads. After some deliberation, they proclaimed the elephants had turned back.

I had inherited the Ovambos from the previous owner, who thought highly of them. There are thousands of Ovambos in Zululand today, many of whom had fought in the South African Army during the apartheid wars. They're mostly employed in the security industry and are valued for courage and weapon skills. They seldom socialized with my Zulu staff.

Ndonga had told me his team were expert trackers, which was why we were used them now.

'Are you sure?' I asked the head tracker.

He nodded and pointed towards Thula Thula. 'They have turned. They are going that way.'

This was news I was desperate to hear. Perhaps they would voluntarily return to the reserve. I grinned and slapped David on the back as we headed back through the bush towards home.

However, after twenty minutes of some of the toughest going I have ever experienced, I began to have doubts. Sweat was cascading down my face as I called over the chief tracker.

'The elephants are not here. There is no spoor, no dung and no broken branches. No signs at all.'

He shook his head, as if patiently consulting with a child, and pointed ahead. 'They are there.'

Against my better judgement we carried on a bit further and then I had had enough. There was something wrong here. It was obvious there were no elephants around. An elephant, due to its massive size and strength, does not need to be furtive. It leaves very clear tracks, piles of dung and snapped branches. It has no enemies apart from man, thus stealth is not in its nature.

Also, every indication was that they were heading

towards their previous home. Why would they suddenly backtrack now?

I called David, Ngwenya and Bheki and told the Ovambos they were wrong; we were returning to the original tracks. The Ovambos shrugged but made no move to join us. I was too wrapped up in the intensity of the chase to think much about that at the time.

An hour later we picked up the spoor again – fresh and heading in completely the opposite direction. Why had the Ovambos chosen the wrong route? Had they deliberately led me the wrong way? Surely not . . . I could only surmise that they were scared of stumbling without warning upon the elephants in the wild terrain. There was no denying this was dangerous work.

In fact, a few years back in Zimbabwe, an experienced elephant hunter had been killed on a safari doing exactly what we were doing – tracking elephant in thick bush. Following what he thought to be a lone bull, he suddenly discovered that he had walked slap into the middle of a herd spread out in the heavy undergrowth. The first sign of this comes when one realizes in horror that there are elephants behind, that you walked right passed them without noticing. They had turned the tables and the enraged animals came at the hunter and his trackers. Completely surrounded, he and his men had no chance. They died grisly deaths.

We kept in radio contact with Peter who flew tight search grids over the bush ahead while John Tinley, a KZN Wildlife ranger from our neighbouring reserve called Fundimvelo, visited nearby settlements asking headmen if any of their people had seen the herd. The answer was negative, which was good news. Our biggest concern was that the animals would wander into a village and stomp thatched huts into floor mats or, worse, kill people.

Hot and scratched, shirts dark with sweat and nerves

jangling, we kept moving, every now and again finding signs confirming we were on the right track. I reckoned we were at least two hours behind, but who knows – they could have been just ahead, waiting in ambush as the Zimbabwean herd had for the hunter. That fear was always with us. More than once we froze, hearts in our mouths as a kudu or bush-buck burst from its hiding place in a crackle of snapping sticks, often barely yards away so thick was the bush. It really was dangerous work and I could feel tensions starting to surface as we became more and more irritable.

Although progress was torturous, it was impossible to move faster. Thorns parted as one man squeezed through a gap and then snapped back like a hornet at the man behind.

What I was banking on was the animals stopping at a watering hole to rest, allowing us to catch up precious miles. A factor in our favour was that they had Nana's two-year-old son, who we called Mandla, in tow. We named him Mandla, the Zulu word for 'power' in honour of his incredible stamina in staying with the herd during the long chase. He would slow them down significantly. Or so I hoped.

Eventually after a long, hot, thirsty and frustratingly empty day, the sun dipped below the horizon, and we stopped. Nobody looks for elephant stumbling around a thorn jungle at night. Tracking the animals in the thick stuff during daylight is bad enough; in the dark it's suicide.

Reluctantly I called off the search and Peter agreed to fly again the next day.

We arrived home bedraggled and despondent and flopped onto the lawn in front of the house. Françoise came out and took over, issuing instructions for food and handing out ice-cold beers.

We were exhausted. But a hearty meal followed by a soaking hot bath does wonders for morale, and an hour later I wandered out onto the open verandah, sitting beneath the stars, trying to make sense of it all.

My Staffordshire bull terrier Max followed me. He was a magnificent specimen of the breed, forty pounds of brawn and muscle. I had got him as a just-weaned puppy and from that first moment he had tottered after me with unconditional devotion. His pedigree name was Boehringer of Alfa Laval, but Max suited him just fine. He would have been a trophy winner at shows except for one physical flaw: he had only one testicle. Which I thought was ironic – Max had more cojones than any creature I knew, man or beast. He was absolutely fearless.

And yet, he was an absolute pushover with children, who could pull his ears and poke his eyes and get nothing but a sloppy lick in return.

Max flopped at my feet, tail thumping on the floor. He seemed to sense my dismay, nudging me with his wet nose.

Stroking his broad head, I mulled over the day. What had possessed the herd to smash through two electrified fences? Why had the Ovambos made such a careless mistake with their tracking? Why had they then abandoned the search?

There was something that didn't gel; some piece missing from the jigsaw.

Max's low growl jerked me out of my thoughts. I looked down. He was fully alert, head up, ears half-cocked, staring into the dark.

Then a soft voice called out: 'Mkhulu.'

Mkhulu was my Zulu name. It literally means 'grandfather', but not in the limited Western sense. Zulus venerate maturity and to refer to someone as an *Mkhulu* was a compliment.

I glanced up and recognized the shadowy figure squatting on his haunches a few yards away. It was Bheki.

'*Sawubona*,' I said, giving the traditional greeting. I see you.

'*Yehbo.*' Yes, he nodded and paused for a while, as if pondering what to say next.

'Mkhulu, there is a mystery here. People are making trouble,' he said, his tone conspiratorial. 'They are making big trouble.'

'*Kanjane?*' How so?

'A gun spoke next to the *boma* last night,' he continued, aware that he now had my full attention, 'and the elephants were shouting and calling.'

He stood up briefly and raised his arms, mimicking an elephant's trunk. 'They were crazy, maybe one was even shot.'

'*Hau!*' I used the Zulu exclamation for surprise. 'But how do you know such important things?'

'I was there,' he replied. 'I know the elephants are valuable, so I stayed near to the *boma* last night, watching. I don't trust the *amagweragwer*.' The word meant 'foreigners', but I knew he was referring to the Ovambo guards.

'Then the big females came together and pushed a tree onto the fence. There was much force and it fell hard and broke the fence and they went out, they were running. I was afraid because they came close past me.'

'*Ngempela?*' Really?

'*Ngempela.*' It is true.

'Thank you very much,' I replied. 'You have done well.'

Satisfied that his message had been delivered, he stood up and stepped back into the darkness.

I exhaled loudly. Now that would explain a lot, I thought, my mind racing. A poacher shooting next to the *boma* unaware of the elephants' presence would certainly have put the jitters into the herd, particularly as their previous matriarch and baby had been shot barely forty-eight hours ago.

But much as I liked Bheki, I had to treat his suspicions about the Ovambo guards with caution. Tribal animosity in Africa often runs deep and I knew there was little love lost

40

between the Zulus and the Namibians. There was a possibility that the indigenous staff may use the confusion surrounding the escape to implicate the Ovambos so locals could get their jobs.

However, Bheki had certainly provided food for thought.

As dawn glimmered we drove to where we had left off yesterday and saw Peter's helicopter coming in low, circling like a hawk to select the best landing spot on the ribbon of potholed road. Seeing the chopper landing in billowing dust a group of Zulu children came running up from the nearby village, gathering around the thudding machine and chattering excitedly.

The tracking team plunged back into the thorny bush to pick up the spoor on the ground, while I assisted Peter in tracking from the air. As we took off, I gazed out over the endless panorama of this charismatic stretch of Africa, so steeped in history. Originally home to all of Africa's once-abundant wildlife – now mostly exterminated – it was where conservationists like us were making a stand. The key was to involve local communities in all of the benefits and profits of conservation and eco-tourism. It was a hard, frustrating struggle but it had to be fought and won. Tribal cooperation was the key to Africa's conservation health and we neglected that at our peril. It was vital that those rural kids who had been clamouring around the helicopter – kids who lived in the bush but had never seen an elephant – became future eco-warriors on our side.

We flew north along the Nseleni River, scanning the spear-leafed reed beds for jumbo tracks and barely skimming the towering sycamore figs whose twisted roots clasped the steep banks like pythons. It was difficult to see much as the rains had been good and the lush growth could have hidden a tank.

Then at last some news. KZN Wildlife radioed in saying

they had a report of a sighting: the herd had chased a group of herd boys and their cows off a waterhole the previous afternoon. Fortunately there had been no casualties.

This underscored the urgency of the situation, but at least we now had a confirmed position. Peter dropped me near the team, lifted off and dipped the chopper as he altered course while I jumped into the waiting Land Rover.

Then we got another call from KZN Wildlife. The elephants had changed direction and were heading towards the Umfolozi game reserve, KZN Wildlife's flagship sanctuary about twenty miles from Thula Thula. They gave us an estimated bearing, which we radioed to the chopper.

Peter found them in the early afternoon, just a few miles from the Umfolozi reserve's fence and some distance from our position on the ground. They were moving along steadily and Peter knew it was now or never; he had to force them around before they broke into Umfolozi as he would be unable to get them back once they were within the reserve's fences.

There is only one way to herd elephants from the air, and it's not pretty. You have to fly straight at the animals until they turn and move in the opposite direction – in this case back towards Thula Thula.

Peter banked and then whirred down, blades clattering and coming straight at Nana, skimming just above her head and executing a tight U-turn, then coming back from the same angle again, hovering in front of the animals to block them going forward.

This is stomach-churning stuff, requiring top-level flying skills, rock-steady hands and even steadier nerves. If you fly too high, the elephants will slip through underneath and be gone; too low and you risk hitting trees.

At this stage the elephants had been on the run for more than twenty-four hours and were exhausted. They should have turned wearily away from the giant bird furiously buzzing them from above. That is what 99 per cent of animals – even a creature as mighty as an elephant – would have done.

The herd stood firm.

Again and again the chopper came at them, the rotor clapping with rhythmic thunder as it virtually kissed the treetops. Yet still Nana and her family refused to retreat, trunks curled in defiance whenever Peter came in low, judging his distance by inches. But they didn't budge. He radioed to us what was happening, and I realized that my herd was something else. Maybe I was biased, but they were special . . .

Eventually, through superb flying, Peter inexorably wore them down. Inch by inch he edged them around until they were finally facing Thula Thula. Then he got them moving, herding them from above, deftly manoeuvring his machine like a flying sheepdog.

I started to breathe easier, daring to believe everything was going to be all right. Back at Thula Thula workers had spent the day mending the ruined fences, both at the *boma* and the border, and they radioed me to say everything was ready. We would still have to cut open a section of fence to drive them through, but we wouldn't know where to cut until they arrived.

Finally after hours of tense aerial herding, we saw the helicopter hovering low on the far horizon. They were going to make it. I gave instructions to the fence team to drop a wide section of the fence to provide instant access into the reserve and prayed the frazzled matriarch would go straight in.

Then I caught sight of her for the first time, pushing slowly through the bush just below the thundering helicopter. All I could make out was just the tips of her ears and the hump on her back, but it was the most welcome thing I have ever seen.

Soon they all came into view, plodding on until they were

at the road. Just a tantalizing fifteen yards from the lowered fence, Nana tested the air with her trunk and halted.

The mood suddenly changed. From fatigued acceptance, the herd now was charged with defiance. Nana trumpeted her belligerence and drew her family up in the classical defensive position, bottoms together facing outwards like the spokes of a wheel and they held their ground with grim determination. Peter continuously buzzed them . . . goading them to make that last little sprint into the reserve. But to no avail.

Seeing he was getting nowhere Peter peeled off and put the helicopter down. Leaving the motor running he sprinted over to me.

'I don't like to do this,' he said, 'but the only thing left is to go up and fire shots behind them. Force them to move forward. Can I borrow your gun?'

'No, I don't like it . . .'

'Lawrence,' Peter interrupted, 'we have spent a lot of time on this and I can't come back tomorrow. It's now or never. You decide.'

Gunfire was last thing I wanted. It meant more shooting around the already traumatized creatures, causing more distress.

But Peter was right; I had run out of alternatives. I unholstered my 9-mm CZ pistol, checked that the 13-shot magazine was full, and handed it to him.

He took it without a word, lifted off and hovering just behind the animals he started firing rapid shots into the ground.

Crack, crack, crack . . . the shots rang out, again and again and again.

He might as well have used spitballs. Nothing would move them. This was where they were going to make their stand. They were saying no more. It was something I understood with absolute clarity; a line in the sand.

Dusk fell, and in the glow of the strengthening stars I could see the murky shapes of the elephants still holding firm with iron defiance.

I felt sick with despair. We had been so close to pulling it off. Peter banked and flew off radioing that it was too dark for him to land without lights and he would drop my gun off at Thula Thula.

Realizing their 'persecutor' had left, Nana turned her bone-tired family around and they melted into the thick bush.

I groaned. Now we would have to do it all again the next day.

chapter five

Once again I was up before my 4 a.m. alarm rang, gulping down coffee strong enough to float a bullet, desperate to get going. It hadn't been a good night.

David and the trackers were standing by and as the first shards of pink dawn pierced the darkness we picked up the spoor from where Nana and her family had made their determined stand against the helicopter last night. The tracks again pointed north towards the Umfolozi game reserve and we followed their new path through the thorny thickets, going as fast as we dared.

By now it was obvious we had some very agitated, unpredictable wild elephants on our hands, and I couldn't rid myself of the vision of them trampling through a village. The words 'conservation's Chernobyl' were etched on my mind as we picked our way through the dense bush.

Peter was unable to fly that day so the chase was pared down to the bones – an elemental race on foot between the herd and us. But with their ten-hour lead, the odds were definitely uneven.

Meanwhile Françoise, tired of pacing around the house in anticipation, decided to do some sleuthing of her own. As the elephants had been in the area last night, she jumped into her car with Penny our almost pure-white bull terrier, who was a couple of years younger than Max, and scoured the dirt tracks surrounding the reserve asking anyone in sight, 'Haf you zeen my elefans?'

Few rural Zulus can understand English, let alone navigate the intricacies of a rich Gallic accent. Even fewer have clapped eyes on an elephant in their lives. Yet here, way out in the sticks was a beautiful blonde stranger with an almost albino-white dog asking if there happened to be any strolling around. No doubt they thought the sun was frying foreign heads.

However, Françoise's search became quite famous as a local news agency picked it up and by the time the report reached the boulevards of Paris, it had been rehashed so extensively that Françoise was portrayed as single-handedly pursuing elephants down a multi-lane highway.

In fact the story of the elephants' escape and our chase was now being carried in local papers. People were following our progress and fortunately for us the media coverage focused on the plight of the elephants and the fact that there was a baby with the herd.

Later that morning with some relief I heard from KZN Wildlife that the elephants had broken into the Umfolozi reserve during the night at two different points several miles apart, crashing through the electric fence with ease as it was only live-wired from the inside. There in the reserve they would be safe, at least from the macho hunting brigade.

The herd had split into two groups during the night, with Nana, her two calves and Mnumzane in the one and Frankie and her son and daughter in the other. Only once they were deep in the sanctuary did they meet up again. How they did that defies human comprehension. It seems impossible to navigate in the dark so precisely without compasses or radios – yet the two groups had travelled up to seven miles apart and then came together in dense bush at a given point. When you consider that, there is no doubt that elephants possess incredible communication abilities. It's known they emit stomach rumblings at frequencies far below human hearing that can be detected even when they're many miles apart. The animals either pick up these sensory impulses through their vast ears, or – as a newer theory postulates – they feel the vibrations through their feet. But whatever it is, these amazing creatures have some senses far superior to ours.

Close to where the two groups had rendezvoused was a thatched rondavel, a circular Zulu hut used by KZN Wildlife anti-poaching units. The rangers inside were fast asleep when they felt the flimsy structure of the building shaking as if caught in an earthquake. Then the top half of the stable door burst open and in the moonlight they saw a trunk snake through. The elephants had smelt the rangers' stock of rations, sacks of maize meal, the Zulu staple, and were going to take their share, which of course meant all of it. The men scurried under their beds for protection as the trunk weaved like a super-sized vacuum cleaner around the hut and yanked the maize sacks out.

Several other twisting trunks shattered the windows and the elephants jerked the furniture around, smashing it as they searched for more food. One man's bush jacket was wrenched from his hands and peeking through the splintered door he saw shadowy figures of the young calves stomping on it and flipping it into the air in a game between them.

Not once did the men on the floor reach for their weapons. Their lives were devoted to saving animals; they would only kill as a last resort. Shaken as they were and watching their possessions being strewn around a hut about to cave in was not considered a last resort.

As soon as the rampaging behemoths left, the rangers radioed through to the game reserve's headquarters.

At dawn Umfolozi's vastly experienced conservation manager, Peter Hartley, decided to assess the situation first-hand. While driving off-road he spotted the animals in the distance and got out to approach on foot without disturbing them. He knew from the number and descriptions that this was the Thula Thula herd. Cautiously advancing, he was still some distance away when suddenly Frankie swivelled. She had nosed his scent.

Elephants seldom charge humans unless they get too close, but with a bellow of rage, Frankie came thundering at him. Hartley, caught by surprise, turned and ran for his life through the thornveld, cutting himself as he scrambled through the barbed foliage. He leapt into his 4x4 and fortunately the vehicle started instantly as he dropped the clutch and sped off with five tons of storming juggernaut just yards behind, verifying the old rangers' maxim that there is no dignity in the bush.

Charging the conservation manager – of all people – seriously blotted the herd's already spotty reputation. Grim-faced, Hartley arrived back at reserve's headquarters and told of his close escape. The senior rangers were now extremely worried. This was getting out of hand and Hartley suggested they contacted the former owners in Mpumalanga to get a more comprehensive background report. And what they heard they didn't like at all.

I was still in the bush when I got the radio call to come to Umfolozi to 'chat' about the situation. Urgently.

It sounded ominous and I drove despondently along the rutted dirt tracks through tribal areas to the sanctuary's headquarters. While I was relieved that the elephants were safe, I was fearful about what was going to happen next. I had a terrible foreboding that I was about to hear their death sentences.

There was a funereal mood as I walked into the office. I knew most of these honest men of the bush and despite warm greetings they didn't look happy.

After a few pleasantries they got to the point. They spoke the words I was dreading. If they had known about the elephants' troubled background, they said they would never have granted the Thula Thula permit. The fact the animals had broken through two electric fences, chased cattle, raided a guard's hut, refused to be cowed by a buzzing helicopter and had charged the conservation manager clearly indicated that this was a dangerous, unsettled herd. A rogue herd. The risk of letting them remain in an area with rural settlements was too high.

In conservation 'speak', that meant only one thing. The rangers were going to destroy the herd.

I interrupted, determined to deflect the ominous direction the discussion was going before it became irrevocable. 'Guys, you have to remember that there's been a ton of publicity surrounding this breakout. The news is everywhere and public sympathy is pretty much with the elephants. The matriarch's baby especially has attracted a lot of attention and people all over the country are following the chase and rooting for them. If you shoot them now that they're safe and haven't done any harm, all hell will break loose in the media.'

I then stressed that it was just bad luck the herd had escaped. We had done everything by the book. Even KZN Wildlife's resident expert had pronounced the *boma* safe. Even he had not believed the herd would have been able to muscle down that single tree in the *boma* that initiated the breakout.

Once free, it was only natural that they would attempt to return to their original home. That's wired into their psyche. But as soon as I could acclimatize them at Thula Thula, they would be OK. I also pointed out that they hadn't hurt any humans, despite being on the run for three days.

I paused, acutely aware that I was arguing for the animals' lives. 'Please, gentlemen; can you give them one more chance? This won't happen again.'

A sombre silence enveloped the room. There wasn't much more I could say.

The rangers were ethical men who did not want to kill any animal unless it was absolutely unavoidable. However, in this case they said they didn't think Nana and her family had much going for them. They said hard experience had shown any herd that refused to respect an electric fence had crossed the shadow line and that there was little hope of rehabilitation.

I knew what they were saying was true.

'Look, Lawrence,' said one, 'we understand how you feel, but you know as well as we do that this is going to end badly. This herd is beyond help. They have been badly interfered with too many times and now see humans purely as enemies. They nearly killed Peter Hartley, for God's sake. He's never even heard of an elephant charging from that distance before. We're going to have to put the adults down.'

'Well, I don't know how you're going to do it,' I said, grasping at straws. 'The media are going to be all over you and it will be a real PR mess.'

'We've thought about that. What we propose is we dart and capture the herd for return to Thula, but while doing so we quietly overdose the adult females and suckling baby, and send only the youngsters back to you.'

I was dumbfounded. 'The press will smell a rat,' I responded, trying to stonewall any talk of death. 'Or blame you for incompetence. Either way you lose. You guys are in the limelight right now so let's just let things settle down. I'll get them back to the *boma* at Thula and keep them locked up there. Let's watch them carefully and then make a decision. If they're still out of control in a couple of months then we'll have no choice. I'll take full responsibility.'

There was a long pause and I sensed that I had touched a nerve. After what seemed like an eternity, they said they would think about it.

I returned to Thula Thula, exhausted and forlorn, where I explained to David what had happened.

The next day out of nowhere I got a call from a stranger introducing himself as a wildlife dealer.

'Listen, man,' his voice boomed from the receiver, 'I've heard about your elephant problem.'

I grimaced. Who hadn't?

'Well, I may just have the perfect solution for you.'

My curiosity was instantly piqued. 'Like what?'

'I'll buy the herd off you. Lock, stock and barrel. Not only that, I'll give you another one as a replacement. A good herd. Normal animals that won't give you any hassles.'

'You mean circus elephants?' I couldn't keep the sarcasm from my voice.

'No, no, man. Nothing like that. These are wild animals; just not as aggressive as yours. And I'll give you $20,000.'

'Why would you do that?'

'If your animals stay here, one way or another they will be shot. If I take them, they will be relocated to a sanctuary in Angola where there are no humans to worry them. At least they will be allowed to live.'

That certainly shook me. Here was a man offering to solve my problems in one single stroke. I would recover my initial costs of trucking the elephants and building the *boma* – and I would get another herd for free. Considering that I also was about to be hit with more capture and transport costs to get my herd back from the Umfolozi reserve, it was quite an attractive proposition. If I didn't accept this offer I was going to have to fork out a lot of cash.

'Give me your number and I'll get back to you,' I said.

However, something niggled. Perhaps this was just too good to be true; just too pat. I have always followed my gut instinct and something didn't smell right.

In fact, the more I thought about the dealer, the more irritated I became. I should have been grateful for the lifeline being offered; that would have been the sane reaction. But instead of profound relief that a solution was in sight, I felt strangely annoyed.

It then dawned on me that something fundamental – something innate but indefinable had happened. That phone call triggered the startling revelation that I had unwittingly forged a bond with this delinquent herd, even though I barely knew them. The strength of this connection shocked me.

The experiences of the past days had illustrated for me that despite fashionable eco-tourism, elephants didn't really count for much in the real world. This was a group of desperate and bewildered animals who had been on the run. But to the brandy and bullets brigade they were target practice with a yield of ivory; to the local tribesmen they were a threat. No one gave a fig that these were sentient creatures whose ancestors had roamed this planet for eons.

It hasn't always been like that. Indeed, just a few decades ago Zulus revered elephants. They still roar 'Wena we Ndlovu' – You are the Elephant – as praise to their king at public gatherings. The crescendo of thousands of martial voices is haunting, evoking memories of a time when these iconic creatures were hugely esteemed.

No longer. In Africa today elephants are simply competitors in the race for the land. In the West, they are mere curiosities while the East values only their ivory.

Our desperate three-day chase had hammered home to me the reality that these immensely powerful giants were actually as vulnerable as babies. Wherever this lost and confused group went, they would be at risk without someone fighting in their corner. As it was, Nana and Frankie were in all likelihood about to be executed.

Once I grasped that, an almost irrational link was established, which would re-chart my life. Like it or not, I felt part of the herd. Life had dealt them a cruel hand and I was determined to rectify what I could. I owed them that at least.

Finally some good news arrived, something in short supply at Thula Thula during those depressing days. KZN Wildlife agreed to a stay of execution. The elephants would be captured and returned to the *boma* at Thula Thula. Nana and Frankie had been reprieved.

But if they escaped again, the entire herd would be shot on sight. There would be no encore of the last chase. There would be no further discussion. This was no casual threat. I was told Africa's infamous elephant gun, the .458 was now being issued as standard equipment to all rangers in the area.

This was to be both their and my last chance.

chapter six

With the strings-attached stay of execution, I felt as though I could breathe again, now that the stresses of the past few weeks had been eased. To my overwhelming relief, I had been given another chance.

This time I had to succeed. It was literally a matter of life or death; KZN Wildlife was not going to compromise on that. This was the final throw of the dice, and the price of failure was simply unthinkable.

The *boma* had been repaired and I now could only wait while KZN Wildlife prepared to capture the herd. I spent most of this time trying to figure out how we could get the animals to calm down when they were returned. Not only must this be done for their sakes, I also had to consider the implications of having an agitated, delinquent herd on the reserve. Before I let them out into the freedom of the greater reserve I had to be absolutely certain they were settled. But how?

While this was churning in my mind, I received another call from EMOA. It was good to hear Marion Garaï's voice, my only ally in this fiasco.

'Lawrence, I have an idea that may help.'

'I need all the help I can get. What's up?'

'I've heard of an animal psychic . . .' She paused and laughed nervously. 'But before you say "no" please hear me out.'

Hmmm . . . I was somewhat concerned that our situation seemed so desperate that she was considering paranormal solutions.

'Shoot,' I said, then bit my tongue. 'Sorry . . . wrong choice of words, go ahead.'

'Apparently this psychic's done good work with troubled animals and has a unique way of communicating with them. Maybe she'll reach out to the matriarch, perhaps get her to settle down and then the rest of the herd will follow. I know this sounds really unusual, and I really can't guarantee anything, but it may be worth a try.'

Well, OK. I know first-hand that communication with animals can defy normal comprehension. Orthodox behaviour is not always the answer in the bush. But bringing in a psychic seemed way over the top. But what else was on offer? And what harm could it do? At best it may work; at worst it was merely quixotic.

'OK. But tell her politely to stay out of my way. I'm going to have my hands full when the elephants return.'

The psychic arrived a couple of days later; a middle-aged Canadian woman with curly red hair.

The next day for lunch she ordered peanut-butter sandwiches.

Françoise was aghast. The mere mention of peanut-butter sandwiches in her French kitchen was sacrilege. They were sent back for not being properly prepared. 'How many ways can you make a peanut-butter sandwich?' Françoise protested.

We later went down to the *boma* where she spent several hours sniffing the bush and sprinkling what she called 'cerebral vibrations of family, love and respect' onto the fences.

'That,' she said, 'will keep them in.'

The next day she pointed to my favourite tree in the garden: a magnificent wild fig with half-submerged roots as thick as a man's leg stretching into the lawn.

'That tree,' she said with a shudder, 'it has an evil spirit. You can feel it, can't you? Come . . . I'll exorcize it.'

As we walked over I studied the grand, gnarled trunk closely. I always considered it a giant benign umbrella providing shelter for flocks of birds that chimed in perfect melody every morning. They were my bush alarm clock. I wondered what malignant ghosts were lurking in those branches . . . then quickly shook my head clear.

She began some sort of religious incantation. I stood by, hoping like hell she would finish soon.

'It's gone,' she said after a few minutes, obviously pleased with herself.

As we were about to walk off, she turned and pointed to the sky.

'See those clouds? They're not clouds at all. They're spaceships carrying evil aliens who are preventing the elephants from returning home.'

All I could see was some cotton-puffs of cumulus. She must have noticed my scepticism.

'I should know,' she said, patting her ample bosom and leaning in close. 'I have travelled in them.'

The next day she walked into the kitchen to order her staple diet of peanut-butter sandwiches. But this time her instructions were that our ranger David must deliver the meal to her room.

The sandwiches were made to her specification: loaded with peanut butter and placed on a tray. As directed, David took the food and knocked on the door. It swung open and there in front of him was the psychic. She was stark naked.

David put the tray down and muttered, 'Your sandwiches, ma'am.' Then he turned and fled, his face the colour of beetroot.

Finally something real happened. KZN Wildlife phoned to say the herd would be delivered the following day.

Elephant capture is done throughout South Africa, but

not in KwaZulu-Natal. In fact the team at Umfolozi, who had famously pioneered capturing white rhino, saving the species from extinction, did not have the heavy equipment required for loading family groups, elephant herds, which comprise only adult females and their young. Babies are never separated during capture. Adult bulls are always transported individually. However, a new dual-purpose heavy trailer designed for transporting both giraffe and elephant had recently been purchased and now was the time to put it to the test. Which begged the questions: Would it be strong and large enough to accommodate all seven elephants? And would the team be able to move the hefty creatures into the trailer without the specialized equipment and sleds used elsewhere in the country? My elephants were going to be guinea pigs, so to speak.

I was comforted by the fact that my good friend Dave Cooper, Umfolozi's internationally respected wildlife vet and probably the top rhino expert in the world, would be in charge of the welfare of the elephants.

Capture always takes place early in the day to avoid heat stress. At six o'clock a helicopter carrying an experienced marksman in the shooter's seat thudded off to where the herd was last sighted. Dave remained on the ground so that any problems could be confronted as quickly as possible. After a few false alarms, the elephants were spotted and the pilot swooped down, coming in just above the treetops in a tight bank and then dropping until he was hovering almost on the ground to turn the now-running animals.

This is where African bush pilots' famed flying skills come into their own. The pilot toyed with the chopper, swaying this way then that, first blocking then lifting then dropping, all while threatening, cajoling, and charging forward at the now frantic elephants, herding them towards a dirt track he could see scarring the plains several hundred yards ahead. That rudimentary road was pivotal as the ground crew needed to get the heavy transport truck as close as possible to where the animals went down.

The marksman loaded the dart gun and readied himself as the pilot radioed his position to the ground crews.

The herd was now in full flight, crashing through the bush with the clattering chopper blades egging them on.

Suddenly Nana, family in tow, broke through the tree cover and into open ground at the area chosen for darting.

The pilot deftly shifted to just behind the stampeding animals, offering a clear view of their broad backs.

Crack! The .22 shell fired a hefty aluminium dart filled with M99, a powerful anaesthetic customized for elephants and other large herbivores, into Nana's rump. The matriarch is always darted first followed by the other larger animals. The calves are darted last to prevent them from being trampled or smothered by the larger family members. Nana's calf was in fact too small to safely dart from the air and Dave was warned to make up a dart and immobilize the calf on the ground.

As soon as one dart hit another was rapidly loaded and fired. The fluffy bright red feathers of the dart stuck out of the rumps of the running animals like beacons. The shooter must work quickly. Any delay between shots would have comatose elephants spread out all over the bush complicating matters immeasurably.

Once the last dart struck true the marksman gave a thumbs-up and the pilot gained altitude and hovered as first Nana, then the others started to stagger and sink to their knees before collapsing in slow motion. It is surreal when these galloping giants suddenly lose momentum and their tree-trunk legs turn to jelly as they buckle in the dust.

The ground team's speeding trucks were now less than a mile away. The timing was spot on and the helicopter bumped gently down in a whirlwind of red dust.

Dave hurried to where Nana lay in the dirt. The baby,

Mandla, was standing nervously next to her fallen body. He flapped his ears and reared his tiny trunk, instinctively trying to protect his prostrate mother. Dave got into position and fired a light plastic dart loaded with the smallest effective dose into the baby's shoulder.

As Mandla's knees folded, the vet broke a twig off a nearby *guarri* tree and placed it inside the end of Nana's trunk to keep the airways open. He did the same to the other elephants, and then went back to Nana, squeezing ointment into her exposed pupil, pulling her huge ear over her eye to protect it from the blossoming sun.

The other slumbering beasts got the same treatment and he methodically checked each one for injuries. Fortunately none had fallen awkwardly, breaking bones or tearing ligaments.

The ground team arrived and immediately reversed up to Nana. As the matriarch, they wanted her loaded first. This is done by unceremoniously winching the animal up into the air feet first and depositing the body at the rear entrance of the huge purpose-built truck. Then it is pulled and pushed into the truck by teams of men where it is revived by Dave with an injection of M5050. A five-ton slab of meat, muscle, blood and bone, hanging upside down is not a pretty sight, but it was done as gently and rapidly as possible. However without the specialized equipment this process took much longer than normal. While the larger animals were laboriously being loaded the effects of the drug started to wear off in some of those waiting their turn. When a drugged elephant starts waking up, you don't waste time hanging around. As trunks started to twitch and elephants attempted to raise their heads, Dave was kept busy running from one to the next, administering additional drugs intravenously into a large vein pulsing in the ear. Once all were aboard and awake, the trucks revved off to Thula Thula. The animals recovered during the ninety-minute journey and although a little wobbly, Nana again led her family into the *boma*, followed by Frankie looking as defiant as ever. Their bid for freedom had, if anything, increased their resentment of captivity. I knew we would have a rough few months ahead of us.

As the capture team drove off, one game ranger shouted over his shoulder, 'See you soon!'

This was no polite goodbye. His meaning was clear. He was saying these animals were bad news. He had no doubt that the herd would break out again and he would be back; this time with bullets, not darts. I felt like making an angry retort but couldn't think of one quick enough.

The next day the wildlife dealer phoned, doubling his bid to $40,000 and repeating the offer of a tamer replacement herd. Again it sounded unreal, just too good to be true. Again I stalled, saying I would consider it. And again, I felt irritated by the offer. I couldn't shake the belief that fate had a hand in all of this. Fate had sent me these elephants – I hadn't asked for them. And maybe some things were meant to be.

Just before nightfall I took a drive down to the *boma*, parked some distance away and with great caution walked towards the fence. Nana was standing in thick cover with her family behind her, watching my every move, malevolence seeping from every pore. There was absolutely no doubt that sooner or later they were going to make another break for it.

Then in a flash came the answer. I decided there and then that contrary to all advice, I would go and live with the herd. I knew the experts would throw up their hands in horror as we had been repeatedly instructed that to keep them feral, human contact in the *boma* must be kept to the barest minimum. But this herd had already had too much human contact of the very worst kind, and their rehabilitation, if such a thing was even possible at all, called for

61

uncommon measures. If I was to be responsible for this last-ditch effort to save their lives, I should do things my way. If I failed, at least I would have done my best.

I would remain outside the *boma*, of course, but I would stay with them, feed them, talk to them, but most importantly, be with them day and night. These magnificent creatures were extremely distressed and disorientated and maybe, just maybe, if someone who cared about them was constantly with them, they would have a chance. There was no doubt that unless we tried something different, they would continue trying to break out and would die in the attempt.

It boiled down to this: we had to get to know each other or else all bets were off. We didn't have time for the 'stand-off' measures proposed by the experts. As I said to David one evening, we had to get the matriarch to trust at least one person. Unless that happened, the herd would always be suspicious of humans and would never settle down.

'That human will have to be you,' he said.

I nodded. 'We'll see.'

I discussed this with Françoise and she agreed that the conventional approach to settling in the animals didn't seem to be working. I asked David if he wanted to come along and was answered by his broad smile. The *boma* was about three miles away from our house and so we packed the Land Rover with basic supplies. The vehicle would be our home for as long as it took.

I also brought along Max, who was always great company outdoors. When he was young and got his first taste of the bush he tended to chase everything in sight. This is a problem on a sanctuary as you don't want dogs harassing animals or incessantly barking as it may attract predators. I had to show Max the errors of his youth fast.

He was a surprisingly quick learner, even though his first experience with wildlife had not been particularly pleasant.

A large troop of vervet monkeys had made their home in the trees surrounding our home and delighted in taunting Max. They would gather on low hanging branches just out of his reach, tumbling over one another and screeching primate insults, sometimes even urinating on him or throwing dung at him with remarkable accuracy. Max would go berserk but was unable to respond to them.

For over a year this torment continued until one day something almost unheard of happened. A big young male eager to lead the chorus of jeers slipped out of the tree, landing at Max's paws. For a moment both animals looked at each other, stunned. Max circled silently as the male bared his teeth, then they pounced on one another. By the time I managed to get them apart Max had wrought revenge for those months of abuse.

A little later I went back to remove the monkey's carcass. The troop was still there and as I approached they became extremely belligerent. I backed off and witnessed a strange ritual, something I had never seen before. The monkeys descended and silently gathered around their dead colleague. Then after a few moments they gently lifted the corpse and carried it from branch to branch, tree to tree, as a funeral procession into the distance. An hour or so later they were back. I had no idea what they did with the body.

However, it was a turning point for Max. From then on the vervets ignored him. A truce had been struck.

Max was a true bush dog. A hushed command from me would see him crouched by my side or on the Land Rover seat, fully alert but as silent as a gecko whenever an animal approached. I knew he would behave around the elephants.

To Max camping out with us at the *boma* would be another chapter in his adventurous life. We would be with the elephants around the clock, living in the bush, catnapping in the truck or stretching out under the stars with our wristwatch alarms set regularly to remind us to patrol the fences. We would share the cold nights with them and we would sweat together in the searing days. It would be mentally and physically exhausting, particularly as the herd had already let us know in no uncertain manner that they didn't want us around.

The first day we spent watching from a distance of about thirty yards. Each day we would get closer, but it would be a gradual exercise. Nana and Frankie watched us continuously, rushing up to the fence if they thought we were getting too close.

Night came, swiftly and silently as it does in Africa. There is perhaps half an hour of gloaming and then it is dark. But darkness can be your friend. The wilderness seethes with life as the nocturnal creatures scurry out from holes and trees and crevasses, brave in the knowledge that most predators are resting. The sky switches on its full power, untainted by urban electrical static. I never tire of watching the megawatt heavens, picking out the Zodiac signs and revelling in the glory of the odd shooting star.

David's whisper woke me. 'Quick. Something's happening at the fence.'

I threw off my blanket and blinked to adjust my eyes to night vision. We crept up to the *boma* through the bush. I could see nothing. Then an enormous shape morphed in front of me.

It was Nana, about ten yards from the fence. Next to her was Mandla, her baby son.

I strained my eyes, searching for the others. Despite their bulk, elephants are difficult enough to see in dense bush during the day, let alone at night. Then I saw them, they were all standing motionless in the dark just a little way behind her.

I quickly glanced at my watch; 4:45 a.m. Zulus have a word for this time of the morning – *uvivi* – which means the darkness before the dawn. And it's true. In the Zululand bush, the darkness is most intense just before the first shreds of haze crack the horizon.

Suddenly Nana tensed her enormous frame and flared her ears.

'Jeez! Look at her!' whispered David, crouching next to me. 'Look at the bloody size of her.'

Nana took a step forward. 'Oh shit! Here she goes,' said David, no longer whispering. 'That bloody electric wire better hold.'

Without thinking I stood and walked towards the fence. Nana was directly ahead, a colossus just a few yards in front.

'Don't do it, Nana,' I said, calmly as I could. 'Please don't do it, girl.'

She stood motionless but tense like an athlete straining for the starter's gun. Behind her the rest of the herd froze.

'This is your home now,' I continued. 'Please don't do it, girl.'

I felt her eyes boring into me, even though I could barely make out her face in the murk.

'They will kill you all if you break out. This is your home now. You don't have to run any more.'

Still she didn't move and suddenly the absurdity of the situation struck me. Here I was in thick darkness talking to a wild female elephant with a baby, the most dangerous possible combination, as if we were having a friendly chat.

Absurd or not, I decided to continue. I meant every word and meant for her to get what I was saying. 'You will all die if you go. Stay here, I will be here with you and it's a good place.'

She took another step forward. I could see her tense up again, preparing to go all the way. I too was ready. If she could take the pain and snap the electric wire the rest of the fence wouldn't hold and she would be out. Frankie and the rest would smash through after her in a flash.

I was directly in their path, something I was well aware of. The fence cables would hold them for a short while but I would still only have seconds to scramble out of their way and climb a tree, or else be stomped flatter than an envelope. The nearest tree, a big acacia robusta with wicked thorns was perhaps ten yards to my left. I wondered if I would be fast enough. Possibly not . . . and when had I last climbed a thorn tree?

Then something happened between Nana and me, some infinitesimal spark of recognition, flaring for the briefest of moments.

Then it was gone. Nana nudged Mandla with her trunk, turned and melted into the bush. The rest followed.

David exhaled like a ruptured balloon.

'Bloody hell! I thought she was going to go for it.'

We lit a small fire and brewed coffee. There was not much to say. I was not going to tell David that I thought I had connected for an instant with the matriarch. It would have sounded too crazy.

But something had happened. It gave me a sliver of hope.

Each day was the same. As the sun came up, the herd would start endlessly pacing up and down the length of the fence, turning on us and charging if we dared get too close, halting only at the electric cable. The naked aggression and agitation, the fiercest I have seen from any animal, blazed nonstop whenever we approached the fence. And they would glare ferociously as we backed off and watched from a distance.

As they were in a confined area we had to provide them with extra food. This posed a problem as whenever we attempted to get close to the fence to throw bales of alfalfa into the enclosure they ignored the food and erupted in paroxysms of rage.

The only alternative was to arrange bales at opposite

sides of the *boma*, and as I distracted the elephants at one end and they came at me, David – an immensely strong young man – would leap onto the back of the truck and toss more bulky bales over the fence on the other side.

Then they would spot him and turn and charge in his direction. As he backed off I would throw food over from my side. Then they would come at me, and David would continue. They would only eat when we moved well away.

The belligerence see-sawed back and forth until we finished. There was no doubt that in their fury they would have killed us were it not for the fence. The hatred was so concentrated that I began to wonder what had previously happened to these creatures, especially as Marion had told me that while still babies Nana and Frankie had had some human contact. As far as I knew, they hadn't been physically maltreated, so was it something deeper? Was it some learned fear passed down from their ancestors who had been hunted to the brink? Was it because they instinctively knew humans were responsible for their confinement? That because of us they could no longer stride the great migration trails across the continent as their forebears had? Or was it simply that the death of their matriarch was the final straw?

I spent the rest of the day just watching them, trying to pick up some vibe other than rage. It now seemed that Frankie, the second-in-command, was the main aggressor. Nana was fractionally calmer – although by no means settled. Could I get through to her? I didn't know; I just hoped.

David and I were pushing up to 2,000 pounds of food a day over the wire and we shed weight like a snake sloughs off its skin. In a week alone, we each lost ten pounds, most of it in sweat. If I hadn't been so worried, I would have relished being in such good shape.

But one thing was certain: the elephants always knew David and I were around. I would spend hours walking around the *boma*, checking the fence and deliberately speaking loudly so they heard my voice. Sometimes I would even sing, which David uncharitably remarked was enough to make even him want to jump straight onto the electric fence. If I ever caught Nana's attention I would look directly at her and focus on positive gentle communication, telling her time and time again that this was her family's new home and that everything she would ever need was here. Most of the time, though, I spent sitting or standing still at a chosen spot near the fence, purposefully ignoring them, just being there doing nothing, saying nothing, showing I was comfortable whether they were close by or not.

Slowly but surely we became an integral part of their lives. They began to 'know' us, but whether that was a good or bad thing, I wasn't sure.

However, the alarming ritual that took place during *uvivi*, when they seemed most determined to break out, continued. Every morning at precisely 4.45 – I could virtually set my watch by it – Nana would line up the herd facing their old home in Mpumalanga. She would then tense up, yards from the fence, and for ten adrenalin-soaked minutes I would stand up to her, pleading for their lives, telling her that this was now their home. The words I used were unimportant as Nana obviously didn't understand English; I just concentrated on keeping the tone as reassuring as I could. It was always touch-and-go and my relief as she ghosted back into the bush with her family was absolute.

When the sun eventually rose, David and I would retire to the truck, shattered by these tense stand-offs, saturated in sweat even in the early morning chill.

Silently David would start a small fire near the Land Rover and put the coffee pot on, each of us wondering what the day would bring. Why were they always so aggressive, even while we were giving them food? Why did they hate us so much? Elephants are intelligent creatures; surely they

must know by now thát we meant no harm? I could understand them wanting to escape. Maybe I too would be frantic
at being locked up . . . but this was something else. There
had to be a way to breach this bulwark of torment.

'Are we going to win?' David once asked over a steaming
mug, demoralized after yet another awful day. We were
drinking coffee by the gallon to keep alert.

'We have to,' I replied, shrugging with despondency.
'Somehow we just have to calm them down.'

The fact was I still didn't know how to do it. All I did
know was that the price of failure was unthinkable. But I
was starting to wonder whether we could ever break
through, whether we could ever settle them. The animosity
was so intense that perhaps the barrier between us was
impenetrable. Maybe too much damage had already been
done.

I just didn't know.

chapter seven

The psychic arrived at the *boma* after a particularly harrowing 'dawn patrol' with the herd again threatening to break through the fence. She came down from time to time and as I saw her coming I made a quick excuse to go and check fences on the other side, leaving her to David.

When I returned half an hour later, she had gone.

'What did she want?'

'Just to sprinkle some more of her good vibrations.'

David's face was contorted and I could see he was battling valiantly to control a guffaw. 'She also said she had communicated with the elephants and they had told her it was now safe for me to go in and walk with them.'

That set us off – perhaps it was the tension, but we broke up laughing so hard our stomachs hurt.

But when I stopped wheezing, I realized that as I was not convinced the psychic was helping matters it was best if she left us to our own methods.

I radioed Françoise and told her to tell the psychic politely that we had no further need of her services and to book a flight for her back to Johannesburg. As far as Françoise was concerned, that at least meant no more peanut-butter sandwiches on the menu.

However, in a bizarre way the psychic's prophecy did come true several days later. We did indeed have to go into the *boma* with the herd.

Nana and Frankie still regularly toppled trees towards the fence, but the ones close enough to do any damage had all been felled. However, there was a particularly tall acacia in a thicket some distance away that they started working on. Initially I didn't worry too much as it seemed too far from the electric barrier. But when it crashed down, it 'bounced' and some of the top branches snagged the wires, straining them to breaking point.

This caused an electrical short with lots of crackling which fortunately frightened the elephants off. Even more fortuitously, the wires didn't snap so there was still current. But the elephants would soon sense that this was a weak link and launch an assault. All they had to do was bump the fallen tree forward, the wires would give and there would be no stopping them.

We had to act quickly. We examined all options but it soon became crystal clear that there was only one solution: someone had to sneak into the *boma* with a bowsaw and hack the branches off the fence. But who would do such a crazy thing, and how?

David stepped forward. 'I'll go – as long as you keep them off me,' he said, eyeing the giants flapping their ears angrily on the other side.

I needed to think it through. David was volunteering for something I had never heard of being done before: getting into a sealed electrified enclosure with seven wild elephants and no quick escape route. It was insane, no matter how you looked at it.

I anguished for an hour or so. Could it be that by condoning this I was sending a young man to his death? What would I tell his parents, good friends of my family, if something went wrong?

Devising a plan would help me decide, so I concentrated on visualizing the scene. Then we would dry-run it until we had it right. David's life depended on that.

First we would miss a feed, then once the elephants were really hungry we would throw bales of alfalfa over the other side of the *boma* to keep the animals occupied as far away from David as possible.

Then I would place two rangers with radios at the energizers to control the current. This would be switched off at exactly the moment David was ready to climb in. As soon as he was in the *boma* the electricity had to be turned back on, otherwise the animals might sense the power cut and break out while we were busy. This, of course, would leave David trapped with 8,000 volts imprisoning him with the elephants.

Third, a ranger would be with me as my 'communicator' to relay instructions and operate my radio. I would have the rifle, ready to shoot but only if David's life was unquestionably threatened.

We rehearsed this several times until we were as prepared as we would ever be. David seemed calm – almost nonchalant – and I marvelled at his courage. He had been on the receiving end of the animals' intense aggression every day for the past week, and he was still prepared to go in.

I gave the signal and the rangers started heaving food over the fence to entice the herd away from us and hopefully keep them engrossed long enough for David to finish the job.

As Nana led her hungry charges to the food bonanza, I looked at David. 'You still want to do this?'

He shrugged. 'If I don't, we'll lose them.'

'OK,' I said, sweating at the mere thought of the enormous risk he was taking.

I nodded to the ranger next to me who picked up his radio and shouted to the energizer crew: 'Power off – go!'

David scaled the fence. Once he was in I threw over the bowsaw and gave the order: 'Power on – now!'

The switches went up. David was now caged inside the *boma*.

I loaded the rifle, steadied the barrel on the Land Rover's open door and zeroed in the sights on the animals on the far side.

David had his back to the herd and was sawing the offending branches with piston-pumping arms while I gave a running commentary from over the rifle sights. 'Everything's OK. No problem, no problem. It's working. You are doing fine; it's a piece of cake. Just a few more moments . . .'

In a blink everything changed. Frankie, who was slightly behind the rest of the herd, must have heard a noise as she suddenly looked up. Enraged that someone was in her territory, she broke into a charge . . . fast and deadly as a missile.

'David, get out! Now! Cut the power! Cut the power! Now! Now! She's coming!' I yelled.

But the message didn't get through to the rangers at the energizer. The drama of the charge had mesmerized the radioman next to me. He froze, completely stupefied by the dreadfully magnificent sight of an elephant in full charge.

David was trapped with Frankie hurtling at him like a rocket. He clambered wildly over the felled tree, grabbing at the fence as five tons of enraged elephant thundered up at impossible speed. He only had seconds to escape.

With my heart in my boots I swore and took aim. I knew it was too late – everthing had gone horrible wrong. I would put a bullet in Frankie's brain but she was speeding at over thirty miles an hour and, dead or alive, her momentum would smash into David and he would be pulverized. No creature alive can survive being hit by an elephant.

My trigger finger tightened – and in the microsecond that I was about to squeeze I heard the foulest language you could imagine.

It was David, right next to me, cursing the radioman who hadn't relayed the 'cut power' message. I jerked the rifle up as Frankie broke off and belted past us, trunk high, ears flared, turning tightly to avoid the wires.

Slowly I lowered the rifle and stared at David, dumb-struck. He had just scaled an eight-foot-high electrical fence. If he was shaking, it was with anger – not an overdose of electrons.

I know plenty of stories of people doing impossible things in dangerous situations, but 8,000 volts will smack you flat on your back no matter how much adrenalin is pumping. It's got enough juice to stop a multi-ton creature – you don't get bigger league than that.

Yet David had done it. Against infinitesimal odds, it seems he somehow missed touching all four of the prominent live wires in his frantic scramble for safety. How, we don't know. And neither does he.

But one thing is certain: if David had been hurled back-wards by the shock, Frankie would have been onto him, whether I killed her or not. She was too close and too fast. Nothing would have saved him.

As soon as everyone calmed down, David insisted on climbing back into the *boma* and finishing the job. I looked at him with total admiration; this young man had real cojones.

Frankie and the rest of the herd were again distracted by food at the far side, and David once more scaled the fence. But not before warning the radioman that if he messed up again, he would personally kill him.

'But you'll be dead,' said one ranger.

David led the booming laughter.

chapter eight

Leaving two rangers at the *boma*, David and I drove up to the main house for a much-needed break and a cold beer – not necessarily in that order. We were chatting on the front lawn when something suddenly seemed out of place. Something wasn't right.

It was my favourite fig tree. All its leaves were wilting. I strode across for a closer look and saw it was dying. Shocked, I called David over. There were no signs of disease, rot or any other external problems. It looked like it had simply given up.

'Magnificent trees like this don't just die,' I said, dismayed. 'What's happened?'

David prodded the trunk. 'I don't know. But remember – the psychic did exorcize an evil spirit from it,' he said with a wry grin.

I'm about as non-superstitious as you can get but even so, something shivered down my spine as we walked back to the house.

In the Zululand bush, the supernatural is as much a part of life as breathing. That's just the way Africa is. I remember years back, long before I acquired Thula Thula, I was rushing a Zulu to hospital after he had been bitten by a puff adder in a nearby village. The bite was potentially lethal but that did not concern him. What he was really worried about was that he believed it was not a coincidence. In his mind the snake was actually inhabited by a spirit sent to punish him for some transgression. Fortunately we got him to the hospital in time and he survived.

'So you reckon the tree's been killed by an evil spirit?' David interrupted my thoughts as we walked back to the house. He was chuckling, no doubt planning to milk this psychic stuff for all it was worth.

I laughed. 'This is Africa,' I said, and then heard Françoise scream.

She came running towards us.

'What's the matter?' I asked.

'Snake . . . big one! On the stove, in the kitchen.'

'What happened?'

She had been cooking pasta when a rat suddenly jumped out of the air-vents above the stove and landed on a pot next to her. A split second later a grey blur streaked down, whipped itself around the bar on top of the stove and sank its toxic fangs into the mesmerized rodent in one lightning hit. Françoise, who had never seen a snake that close before, dropped the spatula and bolted.

I ran to the kitchen to see the snake gliding fast towards me, heading for the lounge. It was a Mozambican spitting cobra, known locally as an *mfezi*. Despite what Françoise had said, it was average size – about four feet long. But *mfezis* have certainly earned their reputation of being second only to mambas as the most dangerous snakes in Africa. A bite is fatal if untreated, although spitting is their main form of defence and when they do so they unleash copious amounts of venom from virtually any position.

It was heading in Françoise's direction, so I rushed to get a broom to catch it. I have a strict rule that no snake is killed on Thula Thula unless the situation is life-threatening. If they're in the house, we capture and put them back into the bush. I have learned that with a cobra, this is most easily done by slowly easing a broom towards it as it rears up and then gently pushing it along the floor and under the snake until it leans over on top of the bristle-head. It's then lifted up, carried outside and allowed to slither off.

Although some neurons in my brain still jump whenever I see a snake – the same atavistic impulses that kept our ancestors in caves alive – I have no problem with them. They are vital for the environment and do immeasurably more good than harm by keeping vermin populations from exploding. Like almost all wild creatures, they will only attack if threatened; they're far happier running away.

I rushed back with a broom but I was too late. Max had already cornered the reptile, now reared to almost a third of its length with its long thin hood flared, exposing a yellow-pink underbelly scored with black bars. It was a compelling sight; loathsome yet stunning.

'Come here, Max! Leave him, boy.'

But the usually obedient Max didn't listen. Fixated on the *mfezi* he silently circled the upright serpent, which tried to twist round to face him.

'Maxie . . . leave him, boy,' I commanded. If the snake bit him, he could die. The neurotoxic and cytotoxic (cell-destroying) venom would reach his vital organs far quicker than in a human.

'Max!'

Then Max lunged, biting the *mfezi* behind its head. I heard the crunch as his jaws snapped shut like a bear trap. He bit again, and again.

He dropped the snake and came towards me, wagging his tail. The snake was chopped into three distinct pieces, its head still quivering from contracting nerves.

Max looked mighty pleased with himself. I was just relieved – until I saw his eyes. He was blinking furiously. The spitting cobra had lived up to its name and hit bang on target. *Mfezis* are extremely accurate up to about eight feet and actually spray instead of spit. This means a fine mist of highly toxic venom comes at you as a sheet, rather than as a single globule and it's vital to wear glasses and shut your mouth when threatened by them – especially when you're trying to move them off with a broom.

Françoise quickly got some milk. We bathed Max's eyes and I rushed him to the Land Rover. The nearest vet was twenty miles away in Empangeni, and if we didn't get there soon, Max could go blind. However, the fact we had managed to clean out most of the poison with milk so soon after the attack augured well.

The vet agreed that the milk had countered the poison, squeezed some paste into the pupils and said Max would be fine.

As we left, he jumped into the car, tail thumping like an overjoyed windscreen wiper.

'Who the bloody hell do you think you are?' I admonished. 'Rikki-Tikki-Tavi?'

Indeed, Max had been as quick as Kipling's *Jungle Book* mongoose. Throughout the fight he had never barked, extremely unusual for a dog. His utter silence had been his key asset. Most dogs prance in front of a snake yapping furiously, giving the reptile an easy target. Instead, Max had slowly padded around it without uttering a sound. The *mfezi* had trouble twisting to face him on the slippery tiled floor, enabling Max to get behind it.

I stroked his head. 'You're a natural bush dog, my boy.'

Later that night David and I returned to the elephants. Max, who adopted an almost bored expression whenever I checked his recovering eyes, came with us.

We inspected the *boma* and catnapped for a few hours in the Land Rover. Then at 4.45 a.m. I heard a slight rustle near the fence. I knew, with dread, it was Nana preparing for her pre-dawn breakout attempt, as she did every morning. I walked down, by now knowing exactly where she would be. Once again, Mandla was at her side, the rest of the herd queuing behind.

'Please don't do it, girl,' I said.

She stopped, tense as a spring as she watched me. I carried on speaking, urging her to stay, keeping my voice as low and persuasive as I could. I kept using her name.

Then she suddenly shifted her stance to face me head-on. The furious stare from her mucous-rimmed eyes faded for a moment. Instead there was something else flickering. Not necessarily benign, but not hostile either.

'This is your home now, Nana. It's a good home and I will always be here with you.'

With unhurried dignity, she turned away from the fence, the others breaking rank to let her through and then following closely behind.

After a few yards she stopped and let the others go ahead. She had never done that before – she had always been the first to disappear into the bush. She turned and again looked straight at me.

It was only for a few seconds, but it seemed to go on forever.

Then she was swallowed up by the darkness.

chapter nine

As the weeks progressed, the herd gradually started to settle down. So much so that we were now able to approach the fence at feeding time without being charged by enraged elephants. We also got some much-needed sleep.

Living rough in the wilderness is a salve for the soul. Ancient instincts awaken; forgotten skills are relearned, consciousness is sharpened and life thrums at a richer tempo.

Unlike being on a wilderness trail where each day is another trek to another place, David and I were not just transients and had to adjust in order to become accepted by the permanent residents on our wild patch. We had to blend into our environment as seamlessly as fish in a lake.

Initially the abundant wildlife regarded us as unwelcome colonizers. They wanted to know who we were, what we were, and what were we doing on their turf. Wherever we went, hundreds of eyes watched. I had that prickly sensation of being under constant surveillance and whenever I looked up, a mongoose, warthog, or tawny eagle would be peering from a distance . . . taking in everything, missing nothing we did.

But soon we too were creatures of the wild. The larger animals got used to us and sensing we posed no danger, started to move around us freely. The resident impala ram and his harem, normally as skittish as colts, grazed thirty or so paces away as if we were part of the scenery. Zebra and wildebeest came past regularly while kudu and nyala browsed nearby, completely at ease.

That didn't mean we were entirely welcome. A troop of baboons led by a posturing male complained bitterly as they sauntered past for their daily ablutions at the river. We had inadvertently pitched camp slap in the middle of their domain and their fearsome leader had no hesitation in venting his ire. Sitting on top of a Natal mahogany tree, he would show his dagger-shaped yellow teeth and snarl *HOOH, HOOH, HAAA* across the valley. *BOH*, *BOH*, his deep territorial call echoed down the riverbed. To him we would always be trespassers.

It was late spring and birds of all shapes and sizes, feathered in an explosion of African colours, chirped and sang the stories of their lives to all who would listen, while snakes – including the lethal black mamba – sought shade from the baking sun. My favourite was a beautiful rock python that lived in a group of boulders beside a gully. He was still a youngster, less than five feet long, but watching his olive and tan body rippling over the ground was as special as you could get.

I always kept a firm grip on Max's collar whenever this yard of elastic muscle glided past. Although he had long since learnt not to chase most wild animals, he still had a thing about snakes. Given half a chance he would have been onto the python in a blink.

The Land Rover's two-way radio aerial also made a great scaffold for a one-inch bark spider that imperiously took up residence. Despite her diminutive size, she was an absolute dynamo. Every evening she strung out her web using the aerial as a support, and every morning she gobbled it all up, saving each precious milligram of protein snared in the gossamer threads, only to rebuild it again at dusk. We named her Wilma and her three-yard-wide web was an engineering marvel, an absolutely formidable, super-sticky trap that seized any flying insect in a grip of silky steel, including four-inch longhorn beetles, which she would methodically suck the life out of.

Sometimes we needed to drive to the far end of the *boma* and as we started the vehicle she would hang on to her just-completed web in a flat panic at the engine's vibrations. In the end, we always took pity on her and walked instead.

At dusk, animals that lived in the sun went off to sleep wherever they felt safest. The landscape emptied, but not for long. It was soon repopulated under the light of the African stars by creatures of the night. Warthogs gave way to bush pigs with short, stiletto tusks; tawny and martial eagles were replaced by giant eagle owls that scouted the skies on silent wings, swooping down on vondos, plump oversized bush rats whose sluggish vulnerability is countered only by its prolific breeding capacity. Fiery-necked nightjars with bear-trap mouths customized for snatching insects in mid-flight soaked up the fading heat from the baked ground before soaring into the heavens. Bats, thousands upon thousands, scudded through the air and bushbabies, among the cutest creatures alive with their cuddly looking little bodies and huge eyes screeched raucous mating calls from the treetops.

Hyena, perhaps the most maligned and misunderstood of all Africa's animals for their unfair reputation of being savage scavengers, but one of my favourites, skulked in the alleys of the dark looking for dinner. *YOOUP YOOUP, YOOOOUP* they called, marking their territory with their manic cackles. Huge dog-like footprints the next day sometimes showed that they had come in for a closer look at us. We used the spotlight intermittently to track this seething theatre, only because leaving it on for too long lured swarms of bugs that attacked us in squadrons. It's bad bush practice to keep a light on continuously as light attracts insects,

insects attract frogs, and frogs attract snakes. Our only permanent illumination was the campfire.

One morning we woke to find leopard droppings near the Land Rover. The local male had marked his territory right where we were sleeping, delivering a firm feline message – this was also his space.

Living so close to the ground, so to speak, also gave me plenty of time to study the herd and I became fascinated by their individual quirks. Nana, huge and dominant, took her matriarchal duties seriously and like a fussy housewife utilized every inch of the *boma*'s confines to the maximum. She marked out the best spots for shade, the best shelter from the wind and – uncannily – knew feeding times to the minute. She also knew exactly when the waterhole and mud pond were due to be refilled by us.

Frankie was the herd's self-appointed guardian. She delighted in breaking away from the rest and storming past us at full speed, head held high and glaring fiercely just for the hell of it.

Mandla, Nana's baby boy, was a born clown whose antics kept us endlessly amused. Full of bravado he would regularly mock-charge us – just as long as his mum was close by.

Mabula and Marula, Frankie's thirteen-year-old son and eleven-year-old daughter were always quiet and well behaved, seldom straying far from their mother.

Nandi, Nana's teenage daughter and mirror image, was much more independent and would often wander around exploring on her own.

And then there was Mnumzane, the young bull and son of the previous matriarch who had been demoted from crown prince to pariah after his mother's demise. He was no longer part of the herd's inner circle and spent most of his time alone or on the periphery of the group. This was the eons-old elephant way; herds are fiercely feminized and once a male approaches puberty he is evicted. This is nature's way of scattering its seed otherwise all herds would be interbred. But sadly the trauma of young males being ostracized from their families can be heart-wrenching; similar to desperately homesick boys being sent to distant boarding schools. Usually in the wild they meet up with other young evicted males and form loosely knit *askari* bachelor herds under the guidance of a wise old bull.

Unfortunately we didn't have a father figure for Mnumzane, so he was simultaneously going through the agony of losing his mother and sister, as well as being evicted from the only family he knew and loved. Come feeding time, Nana and Frankie would roughly shoulder him away and he only got scraps after everyone else had had their fill.

We saw he was losing weight and David made a point of feeding him separately. His gratitude was wrenching to watch, and David, who has a natural affinity with all wildlife, started paying him special attention, slipping him extra alfalfa and fresh acacia branches every day.

Mnumzane's lowly status was confirmed one evening when we heard a series of prolonged high-pitched squeals. Denied the use of the Land Rover by Wilma's web-building activities, we sprinted to the other side of the *boma* to see that Nana and Frankie had the youngster cornered and were shoving him onto the electric fence.

'Look at that,' David panted as we ran up. 'They're using him as a battering ram, trying to force him through to make an opening.'

So they were. Mnumzane, caught between hot wires and a mountain of flesh and tusk, was screaming himself hoarse as electricity jolted through his young body. The more he screamed, the more they pushed.

Eventually just as we were about to intervene – although I'm not quite sure how – they released him. The poor fellow bolted and ran around the *boma* at full speed, loudly trumpeting his indignation.

He calmed down and found a quiet spot as far away from the rest of herd as he could. There he stood and sulked, miserable to his core.

This incident showed conclusively that Nana and Frankie understood exactly how an electric fence worked. They knew that if they could bulldoze Mnumzane through the live wires, they could break free without getting shocked.

Despite this, to my intense relief, by now the dreaded dawn patrol had stopped. Nana no longer lined up her brood at the northern boundary, threatening a mass break-out and despite the odds we seemed to have made some sort of progress in the few weeks they had been there. But neither of us expected what happened next.

The next morning soon after sunrise I glanced up to see Nana and baby Mandla at the fence right in front of our little camp. This had never happened before.

As I stood, she lifted her trunk and looked straight at me. Her ears were down and she was calm. Instinctively I decided to go to her.

I knew from hard experience that elephants prefer slow deliberate movements, so I ambled across, ostentatiously stopping to pluck a grass stem and pausing to inspect a tree stump – generally taking my time. I needed to let her get used to me coming forward.

Eventually I stopped about three yards from the fence and gazed up at the gigantic form directly in front of me. Then I took a slow step forward. Then another, until I was two paces from the fence.

She did not move and suddenly I felt sheathed in a sense of contentment. Despite standing just a pace from this previously foul-tempered wild animal who until now would have liked nothing better than to kill me, I had never felt safer.

I remained in a bubble of well-being, completely entranced by the magnificent creature towering over me. I noticed for the first time her thick wiry eyelashes, the thousands of wrinkles criss-crossing her skin and her broken tusk. Her soft eyes pulled me in. Then, almost in slow motion, I saw her gently reach out to me with her trunk. I watched, hypnotized, as if this was the most natural thing in the world.

David's voice echoed in the surreal background. 'Boss.'

Then louder, 'Boss! Boss, what the hell are you doing?'

The urgency in his call broke the spell. Suddenly I realized that if Nana got hold of me it would all be over. I would be yanked through the fence like a rag doll and stomped flat.

I was about to step back, but something made me hold my ground. There it was again, the strange feeling of mesmeric tranquillity.

Once more Nana reached out with her trunk. And then I got it. She wanted me to come closer and without thinking I moved towards the fence.

Time was motionless as Nana's trunk snaked through the fence, carefully avoiding the electric strands, and reached my body. She gently touched me. I was surprised at the wetness of her trunk tip and how musky her smell was. After a few moments I lifted my hand and felt the top of her colossal trunk, briefly touching the bristly hair fibres.

Too soon the instant was over. She slowly withdrew her trunk. She stood and looked at me for a few moments before slowly turning and returning to the herd that had gathered about twenty yards away, watching every move. Interestingly, as she got back Frankie stepped forward and greeted her, as if to welcome her return to the fold. If I didn't know better I would have said she was giving her a 'well done'. I walked back to the camp.

'What was that about?' asked David.

I was silent for a while, absolutely awestruck. Then the

words tumbled out, 'I don't know. But what I do know is, that it's time to let them out.'

'Let them out? From the *boma*?'

'Yes. Let's take a break and talk about it.'

We drove to the house for a mug of fresh coffee, animatedly discussing what had happened.

'Nana's now a very different elephant to the one that arrived here, that's for sure,' said David. 'In fact the whole herd is different. The aggro has gone like it's been switched off. Maybe we should phone KZN Wildlife and see what they say.'

'No . . . we should just let them out. Wildlife has already said we must keep them in for three months. They're not going to change their minds now.'

David nodded. 'You're right. Remember what we said one night after they came back from Umfolozi? That to get this herd on side we had to get the matriarch to trust at least one human? Well, that's now happened. She trusts you.'

'OK. Radio Ndonga and tell him to make sure the outer fence is fully powered. We'll let them out into the reserve early tomorrow.'

We drove back to the *boma* and the enormity of what we were about to do hit me. If I was wrong and the herd broke out, they would be killed. I started having second thoughts, but while doing the final fence patrol for the night, I noticed the elephants were more relaxed and calmer than I had ever seen them before. It was almost as if they anticipated something special was about to happen. Sensing that made me feel better.

At 5 a.m. a game guard radioed me from the energizer shed to say that power was 'off' in the *boma*. David lifted the gate's hefty horizontal eucalyptus poles off their hinges.

I called out to Nana, who was standing at the fence about fifty yards away, and deliberately walked in and out of the entrance a couple of times to show it was open. Then David and I went and stood on top of an anthill at a safe distance from the entrance to get a grandstand view.

For twenty minutes nothing happened. Eventually Nana ambled over to the gate and tested the space with her trunk for some invisible impediment. Satisfied, she moved forward, herd in tow, and then inexplicably stopped halfway through the exit. For some reason she would go no further.

Ten minutes later she was still standing there motionless. I turned to David, 'What's going on? Why doesn't she go out?'

'It must be the water in front of the gate,' he said. 'The trench we dug for the delivery truck is full of rain and she doesn't like it. I think she won't go through because it's too deep for Mandla.'

Then, for the first time, we witnessed a graphic demonstration of Nana's Herculean strength.

On either side of the gate stood two eight-foot-high, eight-inch-wide eucalyptus poles sunk thirty inches into concrete. Nana inspected these with her trunk, then put her head down and gave a push. The shafts buckled as the concrete foundations popped out of the ground like corks.

David and I stared at each other, stunned. 'My God,' I said, 'we couldn't even have done that with the tractor. And to think that yesterday I was letting her touch me!'

The way around the trench was now clear and Nana wasted no more time, hurrying the herd down a game path directly to the river. We watched the thick summer bush swallow them up.

'I hope we've done the right thing,' I said.

'We have. She was ready.'

I could only hope that he was right.

chapter ten

As soon as the herd disappeared, we struck camp. All this entailed was throwing sleeping bags and a fire-blackened kettle into the back of the Land Rover, but it was symbolic in the sense that we were moving on.

Max was still at the *boma* gate, watching the woodland that had seemingly gobbled up the elephants. I called him and he looked up askance, as if asking if I wanted him to pursue the animals. If I had said 'Fetch!' I have no doubt he would have bounded into the bush. Size meant nothing to him; he was absolutely without fear and had no concept that a single lift of Nana's foot would have converted him into a pancake.

After dropping David off at the lodge, I drove to the Ovambo guards' cottage to give an update.

I was about hundred yards away when Ndonga came sprinting up waving his arms. 'Quick, Mr Anthony. Turn off the motor and keep quiet,' he whispered. 'There's a leopard about forty yards ahead ... just to the right of us.'

I killed the engine and squinted into the bush, my eyes scouring every inch of the area where he was pointing ... and saw nothing.

'A leopard out in broad daylight? Can't be.'

Ndonga put a finger to his lips. 'I saw it just two minutes ago as you were driving up. Just keep still ... it'll come out again. Just watch that big bush over there. That's where it came down.'

The thicket was certainly big enough to hide a leopard. But leopards are primarily nocturnal and it would be highly unusual to see one wandering around at midday.

Then out of the corner of my eye I spotted one of the Ovambos come out from behind the house and nod at Ndonga. He was wiping his hands with a rag, which he quickly stuffed into his pocket when he saw me looking at him.

Ndonga, who had been crouching near the car, stood up.

'Well, I suppose you're right, boss. Your Land Rover would have frightened it off anyway. Pity. It's the first leopard I've seen on Thula.'

I nodded. We knew there were several leopards on the reserve from their tracks and the markings I'd seen recently by the Land Rover had confirmed it, but they had been vigorously hunted before we took over and as a result were so secretive that few had seen them. Thus Ndonga's account of one of these beautiful dappled cats bounding out of a tree in brassy sunlight so close to human habitation was absolutely amazing.

'So what's happening, Mr Anthony?' he asked.

'We've let the herd out. I want all of your guards to go on patrol and track them. Also, check the fences. Make sure the power stays up permanently. And double-check that there are no trees anywhere even remotely close by. I don't want the elephants shorting the wires again.'

'I've already done that. All trees near the fence have been chopped.'

The last time I had heard that was just before the herd had escaped from the *boma*. I didn't want to risk it again.

'You're sure?'

'Of course.'

'Well . . . OK. See you later.'

I drove off. The recent rains had brushed the bush in colours of green and gold and the fecund earth throbbed with life. Unfortunately, as beautiful as it looked, this rampant foliage would make the elephants more difficult to track. We needed to know all the time exactly where they were in case they attempted another breakout.

Biyela, our loyal gardener and everybody's friend, ran up to welcome us back as Max and I got out the car, glad to be home. As I walked through the door Françoise told me that Ngwenya, my security *induna* or foreman, wanted to see me.

He was sitting on a tree stump outside the verandah of the rangers' quarters about thirty yards from our house. This was unusual. He obviously didn't want to be seen approaching me. I walked over.

'*Sawubona*, Ngwenya.' I see you.

'*Yebo*, Mkhulu.'

We spoke for a bit about the unusually wet weather and the elephants. Then he got to the point.

'Mkhulu, we all know strange things are happening.'

'Such as what?'

'Such as the shooting of *nyamazane*' – game – 'on Thula Thula.'

I stiffened. I had been so absorbed in the elephants that the poaching problem had been put on a backburner.

'But now I am also hearing strange stories,' Ngwenya continued. 'And the strangest of all is that people are saying that Ndonga is the man who is doing the shooting. The man killing our animals.'

'What?' The blood drained from my face. 'What makes you say such a serious thing?'

Ngwenya shook his head, as if he too couldn't believe it. 'Ndonga shoots the buck, but the skinning is done by the other Ovambos and by Phineas, the gate guard. Then sometimes a truck with ice comes late at night with no lights and fetches it. Or sometimes Ndonga takes the meat to town.'

'How do you know this?'

'It is what the people here are saying. Also, I am told the other Ovambos are unhappy. They complain in the village that they are doing all the hard work and Ndonga gives them no money. He only gives them meat. Not even good meat – they get maybe the head and shins. That's all.'

'How long has this been going on?'

Ngwenya shrugged. 'Since the day you came. But I have only found this out now. That is why I have come to you.'

'Thanks, Ngwenya. Good work.'

'These are dangerous times.' He eased himself off the stump. 'The Ovambos must not know I have spoken to you. *Sale gahle*, Mkhulu.' Stay well.

'*Hamba gahle*, Ngwenya.' Go well.

I sat there, stunned as if I had been smacked on the head. This was a horrific accusation, not just because the poachers had killed so many animals, which was bad enough. But to add insult to injury, if Ngwenya's allegations were true, was that my own employees were guilty of poaching my animals with my own rifles. The Lee–Enfield .303s that the Ovambos had been issued with belonged to Thula Thula.

'Boss.'

I looked up. David was standing next to me.

'The electrician has arrived. He's at the gate. Should we take him down to the energizers?'

I nodded, remembering that we had booked the man to check the fence's electrics thoroughly now that the elephants had been freed. As we got into the Land Rover the radio crackled into life. It was Ndonga. I tensed with anger. My head guard may be innocent and I had to give him the benefit of the doubt, but Ngwenya's story rankled deep.

'We've found the elephants. They're right on the northern boundary.'

'Excellent,' I replied, fighting to keep the fury out of my voice. 'Keep an eye on them and wait for us. We'll be there in about fifteen minutes.'

With the electrician squashed between us straddling the Land Rover's gear stick and Max on David's lap we drove off. It made sense that the herd had emerged at the far border, the direction of their previous home, but nevertheless it was chilling news. Were they still determined to break out, I wondered?

As Ndonga had said, gangs of workers had indeed chopped down all trees within felling distance of the wires. Narrow vehicle tracks had been hacked out to make a rough road for anti-poaching patrols and maintenance checks along the boundary, so it was relatively simple to keep the animals in sight as we followed from a distance.

Nana was moving down the line, the tip of her trunk just below the top electric strand, sensing the pulse of the surging current. With her clan following, she had walked almost the entire twenty miles of the reserve's perimeter using her natural voltmeter to check if there was any weak link – any section without power in the fence.

By now it was nearly four o'clock. It had taken the animals most of the day to circumnavigate the reserve and I was relieved to see that despite checking for breaks in the power, Nana was not attempting to make direct contact with the fence. She wasn't going to take the pain and smash through like the previous matriarch had at the Mpumalanga reserve.

But just as the herd was completing its tour, we saw a large acacia standing proud right next to the wires that Ndonga's clearing gang had inexplicably missed. It was the only 'danger' tree along the entire border that had not been felled, and it stood out stark as a monument.

'Dammit,' groaned David. Both he and I knew what was going to happen next.

Sure enough Nana and Frankie stopped, saw the tree and loped over for a closer inspection.

'No, Nana no!' I shouted as they positioned themselves on either side of the acacia and started shouldering it, testing its resistance. There was no doubt they were going to shove it down and if we were going to prevent the inevitable breakout we needed to get closer. Fortunately a gate was nearby and we sped out of the reserve and onto an adjacent track putting us on the opposite side of the fence.

As we arrived, the tree was creaking wildly on its roots and Nana gave a mighty heave. With a rending 'crack' the trunk splintered down onto the barrier, collapsing the poles and snapping the current, causing an almighty short circuit. Forsaking caution I rushed up and snatched at the wires to see if they were still live. As I feared, the fence was dead. And with the herd almost on top of us, we had a real problem.

'No, Nana, don't do it!' I yelled with only a tangle of dead wires and flattened poles between us. My voice was raspy with desperation. 'Don't do it!'

Fortunately the frenetic clicking and snapping as the wires shorted had spooked her and she took a hasty step backwards. But for how long?

Thank God the electrician was there and as I pleaded with the agitated animals he and David got to work. With Nana, Frankie and the youngsters barely ten yards away, they calmly untangled the bird's nest of wires, chopped the tree free, reconnected the cable, straightened the poles and got the power going again.

While all this was happening, I continued speaking directly to Nana as I had in the *boma*, using her name often and repeating again and again that this was her home.

She looked at me and for at least ten minutes we held eye contact as I kept talking.

Suddenly, as if baffled by what all the fuss was about, she turned and backtracked into the bush. The others followed and we exhaled with relief.

It was only then that I realized I hadn't even considered picking up a rifle in case everything went amiss. My relationship with the herd had certainly changed for the better.

However, something else caught my attention during the commotion, something more sinister. It was the Ovambos. As the tree had come down, to a man they had bolted like startled rabbits. This was strange, I thought. These much-vaunted rangers were actually petrified of elephants, not quite what you would expect from experienced men of the bush.

Then it flashed. It was as if I was seeing clearly for the first time. A fog had miraculously lifted. Despite their braggadocio, these men were not game rangers at all. They never had been. They were soldiers who could shoot straight, but otherwise knew precious little about conservation. They were now out of their element. I had always wondered why the Ovambos, who were supposed to be top-drawer trackers, had led us the wrong way during the original breakout. Now I knew.

Any remaining niggles of doubt in my mind dissipated. It was suddenly as obvious as the sun beating down on us. The guards were indeed the poachers, just as Ngwenya had said. They were the ones who had been plaguing the reserve for the past year, decimating the buck population. The last thing they wanted was a herd of wild elephants on Thula Thula.

Having no experience with elephants, let alone this unpredictable herd, they realized that with angry jumbos around their poaching racket would be ruined. The reason was simple. Most poaching is done in the dark and one would have to be a brave – or monumentally foolish – man to trample around in the bush at night with this temperamental herd on the loose. It would be suicide. They desperately needed to engineer another escape so their lucrative sideline could continue.

Even though the evidence was completely circumstantial, the jigsaw pieces started fitting together. I suddenly remembered Bheki telling me a 'gun had spoken' at the *boma* on the night the elephants first escaped. Could someone have deliberately fired those shots to panic the herd and prompt a frenzied stampede?

This also explained why the fence wires had initially been strung on the wrong side of the *boma* poles. And of course there was no leopard at the cottage earlier this morning. I would bet the farm that they had been butchering illegally slaughtered animals and my unexpected arrival had almost caught them red-handed – literally. Ndonga had to distract me while they hurriedly hid the evidence. That's why the game guard had come out from the back of the house wiping off his hands: they had been covered with blood.

And what about the tree that had been left standing right at the fence? That was probably the most obvious clue of all. It was far too coincidental not to have been deliberate.

I had been set up. Totally fooled.

However, not only had we been grotesquely betrayed, but – more importantly – the elephants were now in danger.

'David,' I said, pulling him aside. 'I need to talk to you.'

chapter eleven

We climbed into the Land Rover and I fired the engine. I was fuming, not just at the Ovambos, but at myself for being so gullible. I had been taken in like a naive child.

'What's the problem?' asked David.

'The problem? The damn Ovambo game rangers. That's the problem.'

'Bloody idiots. They shouldn't have missed that tree. I mean, how dumb is that?'

'No,' I shook my head vigorously as I drove off. 'No, it's not that. It's the poaching. The Ovambos – they're our poachers. They're not rangers at all. They're the bloody poachers.'

There was a stunned silence.

'You're kidding me,' said David. 'Nah . . .?'

'It's them all right.' Red with anger, I listed all the evidence, from the wires on the wrong side of the *boma* poles to what Ngwenya had just told me.

David's face hardened as he took it all in. He, more than anyone else, had been at the frontline of the clashes with poachers.

He sat still, fists clenched. Then he said quietly, 'Turn around, boss. I need to have a chat with them about a few things.'

David's nickname in Zulu was *Escoro*, which means boxer, or fighter. Well-built, fit and unafraid, he had a reputation as someone you didn't mess with. He now had his sights set firmly on the Ovambos.

'Uh-uh.' I refused. 'I understand you're pissed off. I feel the same, but we have to do this cleverly. This is our biggest opportunity to smash this damn poaching ring once and for all. They can't know we're on to them.'

David looked at me, unconvinced.

'We've got to pretend everything's OK until we get all the evidence,' I continued. 'Otherwise we'll blow it. At the moment all we've got is hearsay and they will just deny everything.'

'OK,' he said with some effort. 'But when it's over we are going to have a little chat.'

'That's up to you. But until then we can't let the guards out of sight, even for a minute. We've got to get two of our best rangers up to their house permanently. Get Ngwenya to brief them so they know what's going on. I want them living and working with the Ovambos twenty-four hours a day and reporting their every move. That'll stop them doing any further shooting and buy us time.'

'Done, boss,' said David and a slow, wicked grin started to spread. 'Ndonga is also going to be seeing a lot more of me. I will be his new best friend, starting tonight.'

The next morning we were out early to see what the elephants were doing. After a couple of hours bouncing around in dense bush we found them grazing in the middle of the reserve, about as far from the fence as you could get. Mnumzane was a hundred yards or so from the main group, stripping leaves from a small acacia. We eased forward until we were close enough to see them clearly and I did a head count. Seven – all there, engulfed by long grass and succulent trees and stuffing their mouths like kids at a birthday party. With nearly double the rainfall, which meant double the food yield of their previous home, Thula Thula truly was a pachyderm paradise. I knew Nana, the most astute of matriarchs, would not fail to notice this rich bounty, especially after a dry Mpumalanga winter and the confines of the *boma*.

The tranquillity of the scene made it all worthwhile. After all the stress, drama, danger and frustration this hugely aggressive herd seemed at last serene in their new home. At least for the moment.

'They're exploring, and they like what they see,' said David. 'This must be better than anything they've known before.'

I nodded. Maybe, just maybe, our gamble in letting them out of the *boma* early had paid off.

We drove back up to the house where Françoise greeted us with a trencherman's breakfast of *boerewors* – spicy Afrikaner sausage – bacon, eggs, tomatoes and toast, and mug after mug of home-made coffee. Bijou, Françoise's little Maltese poodle, and Penny, the bull terrier, were with her and I always chortled at the contrast between her two dogs – both snow-white but one fluffy and soft, the other muscular and hard. Penny's loyalty was infinite. Thula Thula was her home and as self-appointed protector of the realm she guarded it with her life.

'Please tell Phineas I want to see him.'

Ngwenya shifted uncomfortably He knew what was coming.

'*Manje?*' Now, he asked.

'Yes, now.'

Ngwenya moved reluctantly to the door and then turned back to face me. 'We must be very careful Mkhulu. If the Ovambos hear we are talking to him they could kill him. These men have killed before. They are *tsotsis*, thugs of the worst kind and people in the village are very frightened of them.'

'That's why the village will help us when we go to the police,' I replied.

Phineas was the gate guard who had been used to skin the slaughtered animals. He was a simple, sickly young man, having long been afflicted by Aids, the scourge of modern Africa. On the streets the slang for Aids was 'slow puncture', a particularly apt description of how the disease gradually saps one's life and frail Phineas was no exception. We had moved him from the labour team to far less demanding gate duties to ease his day.

I was gambling that he would side with us and become a key witness. All I needed was the correct approach.

Phineas arrived and as is customary in rural Zululand, he came in without knocking. Crouching low, he moved across the room and then sat down without being asked. He averted his eyes and stared at the floor, which is considered good manners.

'*Yehbo*, Phineas,' I greeted him.

'*Sawubona*, Mkhulu,' he replied without looking up.

Instead of first politely discussing one's health or the weather, again customary in rural Zululand, I went straight for the jugular.

'Phineas, I hear that you have been tricked into skining animals that the Ovambos have stolen.'

The effect was instant. Phineas glanced around wildly, as if looking for an escape route. Then his sickly pallor turned even more ashen as his breath laboured out in wheezes, no doubt cursing his bad luck. If he had known what this meeting was about he would have headed for the hills and never returned. Now he was trapped.

'Come, Phineas,' I said, pressing the obvious advantage of surprise. 'Everybody knows what has happened and I don't want to hand you over to the police. Jail will be a bad place for you. I am offering you the chance to help us.'

His head slumped on his chest. Then, without warning, he started sobbing. Even though I knew that Aids had crippled his immune system, ravaging his physical and men-

100

tal health, I was taken aback at how quickly he broke and my heart went out to him. No doubt his conscience had also been preying brutally on his weakened state of mind.

'Ndonga promised me money,' he said, voice quavering. 'Then he did not pay me.'

'You told me the truth, thank you,' I said. 'But you will have to make a full confession to the police. If you do this, not only will you be protected from the Ovambos, but you will also keep your job.'

'I will do what you ask,' he said rubbing his eyes. 'I am sorry, Mkhulu.'

He then gave me full details of the poaching ring, exactly how many animals and what species they had shot as well as times and dates. I was astounded at the scale of the operation. These bastards had slaughtered at least a hundred animals – which translates into several tons of meat, and thousands of dollars of profit.

I now had my first witness. We spent the rest of the day piecing together information, interviewing other staff fingered by Phineas, collecting facts, and taking more statements until we felt we had a case. But I decided to stew on it all for a while and see what other stories emerged over the next few days.

In the meantime my rangers were busy moving into quarters next to the Ovambos while David was Ndonga's 'new best friend', constantly shadowing him and seriously curtailing any poaching activities. I also started calling Ndonga over the radio at all hours, day and night, asking where the Ovambos were, setting meetings in the bush and making surprise visits to their house.

The tension was starting to tell. Ndonga didn't suspect we knew anything but he was as jumpy as hell, never knowing what was coming next. Whenever the Ovambos went out in a group, my rangers would radio me and we would drive up to them from nowhere, exchanging pleasantries and just hanging out. The confusion on their faces was almost comic. The main thing was that they be given no opportunity to poach.

Oblivious to all this human intrigue, Nana and her family appeared to be settling in well and I decided to spend a morning watching them, just to see for myself.

After about an hour's drive I found them shading themselves under a sprawling giant fig right next to the river. It was still early, but already the mercury had rocketed to almost 100 degrees Fahrenheit. I stopped the Land Rover, crept forward and settled down under a leafy marula tree about fifty yards downwind. They stood motionless but for the gentle flapping of their ears, cooling themselves as best they could. Elephant ears are the size of a hefty woman's skirt and act as a natural air conditioner. Behind each massive flap of cartilage is a roadmap of veins that pumps gallons of blood just beneath the skin and gentle fanning cools the corpuscles, which in turn lowers the body temperature.

Mnumzane was about twenty yards nearer to me than the rest and sensed my presence. He moved closer and watched from a comfortable but wary distance, then continued grazing, glancing up every now and again. It seemed he preferred my company to that of the herd and made no effort to raise the alarm.

He was a superb specimen, well proportioned with strong tusks. He would soon grow into a great bull, lord of all he surveyed. But at the moment he was a confused and lost teenager, still aching from the death of his mother.

In the background Nana found a succulent young paperbark acacia tree and decided it was ideal for a family lunch. She pushed gently, testing the tree's strength, and then adjusted her angle; put her head down and with a push-relax-push motion worked up massive momentum. The tree rocked violently and as it swayed at the very end of its tether she gave a final shove and it came splintering down.

The rest of the herd ambled across to join in the feast. If there is one thing that elephants have, it's time, large dollops of endless time spent without having to commute to offices like less-privileged mortals. Even when a juicy bush banquet is on offer, they don't rush.

The sound of the tree crashing stilled the bush for a few moments and I noticed a nearby family of nyala prick up their ears. The bull scented the air, knowing instinctively what had happened. Once the elephants moved off, he and his harem would also be able to gorge on the felled acacia's juicy top leaves that they would never otherwise be able to reach. In fact, during dry winters when grazing is poor herds of antelope often shadow elephants for days waiting for the matriarch to bulldoze a tree down.

The noise also alarmed a *leguaan*, a large African monitor lizard that had been raiding birds' nests up in a red-flowered weeping *boerbeen* tree overhanging the river. Startled, the four-foot-long, black-grey reptile sprang off a high branch, twisting through the air and belly-flopping into the river.

At my feet Max heard the splash and thinking the reptile was a snake, was off like a shot into the reeds before I could grab him. Splashing about in crocodile territory was suicidal for even large animals, let alone a dog, and when he came out shaking his dripping torso like a sprinkler, I tersely reprimanded him. Try as I may, I was unable to wean him off his snake fetish.

None of this perturbed the elephants. Nana, Nandi and Mandla stood on one side of the fallen tree with Frankie, Marula and Mabula on the other, methodically converting leaves and bark into edible mulch with the most powerful molars in the animal kingdom. Although they were now one family, each group was the remnant of a much larger herd

103

that had been cruelly whittled by sales and execution. They still sometimes instinctively bunched in their original two groups.

A draught eddied through the saplings and cosseted my back. The wind was edging to the south. When I had arrived I was downwind, but with the subtle shift I now had to move fast.

As I stood I saw the tip of Nana's trunk suddenly angle and swivel towards me, snatching a trace of scent. She then stood back and, lifting her trunk to verify the odour, turned to face in my direction.

Collecting my binoculars and water bottle I climbed into the Land Rover with Max just as she started advancing towards me, the rest of the herd falling in behind her. There was plenty of time to drive off, but I was intrigued by the fact that she was actually heading my way. Normally she would have hurriedly herded her family in the opposite direction.

I manoeuvred the Land Rover into a good getaway position, steeled my nerves and waited. At the last moment, just yards away from me, she changed direction ever so slightly and walked past the vehicle, followed by her family who each turned to stare as they passed. Frankie, who was bringing up the rear, splayed her ears and gave an aggressive shake of her head towards me.

Then suddenly, she swung off the back of the line, triumpeted harshly, and started coming at me, fast as a truck, her ears flared and trunk raised high. I knew instinctively it was a mock charge, and the worst thing to do would be to drive off as this could encourage her, perhaps spark a real charge. I braced myself as she pulled up spectacularly just yards away in a whirlwind of flapping ears, dust and rage. After tossing her head in anger once or twice, she stomped off back to the herd with her tail angrily erect.

I stared after her, transfixed. Even though I had seen it many times a charging elephant is one of the most awesome physical spectacles in the world. I'll have to be careful with Frankie, I thought, once I had regained my ability to think. She was still too ill-tempered, too eager to vent her fury. Even though Nana was the matriarch, Frankie was far more dangerous.

I followed them for a bit, thorns squeaking and stabbing the Land Rover's paintwork until the bush became too wild and I turned off on an old overgrown track and set course for home.

I had just gulped down a pint of ice-cold water when the phone rang. The wildlife dealer was on the line.

'Really, Lawrence, I can't for the life of me understand why you're wasting your time with this herd,' he said. 'I can let you have a much better one within a week and your problems will be over. You know, you could easily get yourself killed by this lot. They need more space, to be completely away from humans. Surely you owe that to them.'

'You may be right,' I said, fumbling for a pen and some paper. 'By the way, I never got the name of your company – or even your phone number. What is it?'

I wrote down the details and immediately dialled the Elephant Managers and Owners Association in Johannesburg, asking for Marion Garaï.

'Marion, do you know who these people are?'

'Oh God, Lawrence. Please don't tell me you're dealing with them.'

'Why?'

'This lot was trying to get your herd first but I beat them to it. They are registered wildlife dealers, perfectly legitimate, and I had heard they had already pre-sold your animals to a Chinese zoo – that's why I was in such a hurry to get them to you. They're pretty upset with me and are now trying to get the animals back to fulfil their contract. If you sell them to him, your elephants' lives will be a misery. There're few animal rights laws in China, so anything could happen. And even worse, the zoo only wants the babies so the two adults will probably be shot. Please . . . please don't deal with them.'

'Well, you can relax,' I said, relieved finally to hear the truth. 'My elephants are going nowhere.'

I phoned the dealer and told him politely never to contact me again.

He was flummoxed. 'You can have all this money plus a new herd and you prefer to keep the problem, which is only going to get worse. Don't come crying in three months' time because it will be too late for us. And for you.'

'I'm not selling.'

'OK, OK.'

He then hesitated for a bit and I could tell he was mentally wrestling with something. 'Listen . . . don't tell my boss I told you this, but the previous matriarch, the one they shot, wasn't so bad. I reckon she was just trying to get the herd to better water and grazing, that's why she kept busting the fences. She was just doing her job.'

I put the phone down as that revelation slowly sunk in. The old matriarch had been doing her duty to her family – and she had paid for it with her life. They had even shot her baby daughter. My anger flared; no wonder this herd was traumatized.

I never heard from the dealer again.

106

chapter twelve

During the next few days fresh information about the poachers kept popping up, all of it helpful.

The Ovambos, unable to hunt due to our constant surveillance, had taken to slipping out into the village at night and getting rat-faced drunk at the local shebeen, a traditional, usually illegal, tavern. The more they drank the more they talked, and we made sure we always had an informer there. With alcohol-fired machismo, they bragged openly about their exploits. Slowly we were piecing together our case.

'OK, what do we do now?' David asked.

'We go to the police and give them the statements. I have set it up with a lieutenant who's expecting us.'

The next day we drove into Empangeni, met with two senior policemen and recounted the full story, handing over all the affidavits.

'This is an open and shut case,' said one after reading Phineas's statement. 'They're as guilty as hell. We'll be out there later to make the arrests.'

That was exactly what I wanted to hear and at 5 p.m. on the dot two police vans arrived. David and I led them through the reserve to the Ovambos' cottage. It was strangely silent, with no one to be seen. Leaving the cars quietly, we split into two groups, heading for the front and back of the building.

We were too late. As we burst into their rooms, all we found were rifles strewn on the floor and cupboard doors flapping open. All their personal possessions were gone. No doubt they saw us coming and instantly hotfooted it. They were now running for dear life through the bush and without knowing which direction they had taken, there was no way we would catch them before dark.

The police said they would put a general alert out for the fleeing guards, which was all we could do for the moment. 'They are probably halfway to Namibia by now,' one of the police said ruefully.

Back at the house I recounted the drama to Françoise and we strolled outside, watching the blood-red sun ease itself down beyond the sweeping hills. The reserve looked tranquil. Perhaps I was imagining it, but with the guards gone the whole mood had changed – as if some particularly malignant force had been purged.

chapter thirteen

Thula Thula, at last, was finding its equilibrium.

The elephants weren't trying to be serial escapers and the poaching problem was largely solved. I knew we would never entirely stamp out poaching. In Africa a few tribesmen shooting the odd impala or duiker for the pot is going to happen whatever you do, and spending night after night out in the bush from dusk till dawn on guard against a few poorly armed youngsters soon loses its romance. It's when the operations go commercial, as what had happened to us, that problems skyrocket.

On another front, my discussions with the *amakhosi* and the tribes about converting their surrounding cattle land to a game reserve were continuing well and progress was being made, albeit in tiny fractions, as the idea started taking hold. Trying to persuade thousands of Zulus, for whom cattle are an iconic form of wealth, that they should switch the use of their land to wildlife was an ambitious undertaking and fraught with many complications, cultural and otherwise. But there was no doubt it was the right thing to do. Patience and persistence were the keys.

So now for the first time I could concentrate on our core mission – running an African game reserve.

It is a tough, rewarding life. Each day starts at dawn and not only are there are no weekends, but if you are not careful you can also quickly lose track of the days of the week. Fences have to be checked and fixed daily, roads and tracks must be repaired and wrested back from bush encroachment or you lose them forever. The never-ending invasion of alien plants needs constant attention – some plants are invaders from other countries, varieties that don't have natural enemies in Africa and are not palatable to wildlife, so their growth is rampant. Then there are game counts and veldt assessments, dam inspections and repairs, fire breaks to maintain, anti-poaching patrols, maintaining good relations with neighbouring tribes, and a hundred other things to do. But it is a good, clean life with just enough danger and adventure to keep you on your toes and enjoying it.

The elephant herd was settling in nicely and staying away from the fences. I spent as much time as I could near them. Despite only being out of the *boma* for three weeks, they were already stuffing themselves on a myriad of delicacies and putting on weight noticeably.

Obviously I always kept a comfortable distance and was as unobtrusive as possible, watching and learning about their behaviour, where their favourite watering holes were, what they were eating and where. But sometimes things didn't always go to plan. Once I got a fright when I thought the herd was some distance away. I got out of the Land Rover to make a call on my brand-new cellphone.

Something made me look over my shoulder. To my horror, about twenty yards behind watching me was Frankie. And behind her was the rest of the herd.

The Landy was only a short distance away and with an alacrity that impressed even me, I yanked open the door and leapt inside. However, in my haste I had dropped my fancy new phone, and the elephants were now milling around it. I had no option but to wait until they moved off before I could retrieve it.

Then it rang; the ringtone piercing the wilderness like a

whistle blast. The elephants stopped, and then almost in unison, moved over to the source of the alien noise. Frankie was there first, snaking her trunk over the piece of plastic, trying to figure out what it was. The others joined in and I watched this bizarre spectacle of seven elephants swinging their trunks over a chirruping cellphone in the middle of the bush.

Finally Frankie decided she had had enough. She lifted her mighty foot above the phone and thudded it down. The ringing stopped.

The herd moved off, ambling along in their own sweet time. When they were finally out of sight I got out of the Landy to fetch the phone. It was embedded an inch into the ground and I had to prise it free. The clear plastic section of the casing was shattered.

As an experiment I punched in a number – and it rang. It was working just fine.

I later phoned Nokia and told them about the incident, congratulating them on the ruggedness of the phone. After a long silence the manager thanked me and hung up. I reckon even they didn't believe their products could withstand being stomped on by a wild elephant.

However, it wasn't just the elephants that were adjusting. With the removal of the Ovambo guards, scores of other animals suddenly appeared on the landscape, as if by magic. Wherever I went I saw kudu, nyala, herds of wildebeest and impala and a host of smaller game scurrying about seemingly without a care in the world. Previously hunters had taken a shot at any creature that moved, and then the poachers had muscled in, blinding antelope with megawatt spotlights and shooting indiscriminately from vehicles both at night and during the day. No wonder the animals had been so skittish whenever a Land Rover drove past. Until now the only time I had really had occasion to appreciate the wildlife on Thula Thula was when David and I were camping outside the *boma*. A car engine would set the entire reserve in panic mode – with good reason, as I now realized.

No longer. Almost overnight, a radical transformation had occurred. Hyena became more brazen in the evenings and we even got occasional glimpses of leopard, lynx and serval, the beautiful tawny black-spotted cats of the night, whose pelts are unfortunately still highly prized. The more the creatures lost their fear, the more of them we encountered and with mounting jubilation I discovered that despite mass poaching, we still had healthy populations of almost all of Zululand's indigenous animals thriving on our doorstep. The whole reserve was now truly energized, and us with it.

I found this totally astonishing. How could the simple removal of the guards have such an instant effect on the game? How could they know they were now safe; that the major poaching threat had been removed? Obviously this would not be regarded as evidence in a court of law, but to me, in the natural order of things, it was proof that the animals themselves now knew it was over.

Years later I was in the Sudan on a conservation project when I heard an incredible story on good authority that sounded similar to my own. During the twenty-year war between northern and southern Sudan elephants were being slaughtered both for ivory and meat and so large numbers migrated to Kenya for safety. Within days of the final ceasefire being signed, the elephants left their adopted residence en masse and trekked the hundreds of miles back home to Sudan. How they knew that their home range was now safe is just another indication of the incredible abilities of these amazing creatures.

Immersed in the bush each day with no pressing problems reignited another of my loves; birdwatching. With its diverse habitats Thula Thula has over 350 identified species of bird and is an absolute haven for 'twitchers', those unusual people obsessed with spending every free moment watching birds.

On one glorious Zululand morning David and I were following the herd on foot through thick riverine bush, our footsteps on the leaf litter the only sound, when we came across a troop of monkeys grouped on top of a tall, flat acacia robusta. They were chattering and screaming insults at a magnificent martial eagle circling just low enough to demand their attention, but high enough for them to show some bravado.

Or so they thought. Emboldened by the distance, the little creatures with their animated black faces were recklessly exposing themselves at the edge of branches instead of hiding within the foliage.

As we watched, another martial appeared, coming in low and fast on huge silent wings. Flying barely ten feet off the ground and skirting tree trunks with deft twists and turns, her fiercely hooked beak and snowy undercarriage were just a blur as she glided under the tree canopy, hidden from the raucous monkeys. With a wingspan of more than seven feet, a martial in flight is always a stunning sight. But up as close as this it was pure wizardry – as she came over us we could feel the wind from her wings.

With an imperceptible twitch of her tail feathers she suddenly pulled into an almost vertical climb heading straight up for the troop like a Stealth jetfighter. Before the monkeys could even guess what was happening she had plucked one off a branch, and was soaring through the sky to meet her mate with the still squirming primate hooked in her gnarled talons.

The tawny eagle is also a masterful predator and, often hunting in tandem like the martials, it is a particular threat to newborn fawns in the breeding season. One day, Nana and the herd were browsing off on our left when for some reason I glanced skywards and picked out two of these majestic raptors, just specks in the azure sky, swooping vertically in perfect synchrony and eventually blasting into the tree canopy at impossible speed. They are going much too fast, I thought, as they plummeted through the tangled green foliage – they can't possibly stop in time.

But a tawny can plummet down from the sky, strike its prey, and then land in the space of just a few yards. As we rounded the corner we found them both with their claws sunk into a nyala fawn, flapping their giant wings in unison as they coordinated their take-off to lift the deadweight. The impact of the high-velocity attack had instantly killed the fawn, but the mother was determined to fight back with all her worth. She grabbed her baby's foot in her mouth and with legs locked stiff as metal shafts, she anchored herself in an awful tug-of-war to prevent the birds from flying off. The eagles, startled by our sudden appearance, dropped their booty and glided back into the heavens.

No matter how heart-wrenching the situation, we never interfered with nature. Brutal as the food chain is, that's the balance of life in the wild. Terrible as the tragedy was for the nyala mother, the eagles also had to feed their young.

But it's not all blood and gore; there are also the brilliant colours and exquisite song in Zululand birds. Plum-coloured starlings, turquoise European rollers that winter with us, the gorgeous bush-shrike, blood-red narina trojans and count-less others boasting plumages so flamboyant, the visual feast was unbelievable. Catching sight of a gwala gwala in flight, the only time it flashes its vivid scarlet wing feathers, can send the soul soaring.

It did mine. Poaching, elephant charges . . . well, that was all yesterday, I thought happily.

I didn't know how wrong I was.

chapter fourteen

One morning Françoise joined me on the quad bike, a four-wheeled all-terrain motorbike, while I tracked the herd.

As we zoomed off on a dusty track, I marvelled at the profound transformation she had made in adapting to a life in the bush. Unlike me, her sophisticated upbringing in the buzzing metropolis and boulevard cafes of Paris were light years removed from the African outbacks of my youth.

A good illustration of this was the first time she held a banquet at Thula Thula for some Parisian friends and laid a table out on the front lawn. It was groaning with Camembert and Brie cheese, exotic fruit, freshly baked rolls, salamis, pâtés and decorated in the most splendid wreaths of scarlet, white and mauve bougainvillea you could imagine.

That I considered these, her favourite flowers, to be rampant alien invaders cut no ice with her at all. 'Zey are exotic and beautiful, and must be protected,' she had instructed Biyela the gardener. Biyela having fastidiously verified the translation with Ngwenya, thereafter defended the colourful bushes with typical Zulu tenacity, threatening me with whatever garden implement he was carrying whenever I appeared too close.

She was still laying out the table helped by a friend when a passing troop of monkeys swooped from the trees. Instead of merely chasing the mischievous animals away, Françoise and her companion fled into the house and resorted to shouting Gallic insults from behind a large plate-glass window.

Undeterred by the colourful language and unable to believe their luck, the troop settled in and leisurely devoured the best French cuisine in Zululand. Fortunately they didn't have a taste for champagne, or else a few magnums of the good stuff would have gone down their gullets as well.

By the time Ngwenya and I had shooed them away it was too late. The monkeys had scattered into the trees grasping hunks of squelchy cheese and handfuls of pâté – not to mention every morsel of fruit and bread that had been laid out. The fact that I was almost paralysed with laughter didn't help the situation much either.

But that was more than a year ago. Now she was much more comfortable in the bush and with her arms tight around my waist we rode through as shallow section of the Nseleni River to a high lookout point to see if we could find the elephants.

The hill had a panoramic view and we spotted them briefly in thick bush bordering the river below, close to where we had just come through. We must have missed them by fifty yards or so and it worried me that I hadn't detected them – especially with Françoise riding pillion. I couldn't shake that niggling unease as normally I'm able to sense when the elephants are around.

'There they are again,' I pointed, and we watched as the elephants loped into view about a mile away, moving in single file across the deep-green flood plain disappearing back into the riverbed.

'They're moving off. Let's give them a bit of time to cross the river and go after them.'

About ten minutes later we rode back down the hill onto the flood plain and I slowly eased the bike down the cutting into the lazily flowing river, driving through with feet held high to avoid a drenching. Once on the other side, I gunned the motor to scramble up the steep incline and we shot to the top of the riverbank.

Absolute disaster! I suddenly became aware of huge grey shapes morphing all around us. Incredibly we had ridden bang into the middle of the herd! The elephants had stopped to graze right at the exit of the river crossing – something I had not anticipated as I had thought they were on the move.

Shock shuddered through my body. I suddenly felt minuscule, puny, unprotected on a tiny bike surrounded by edgy five-ton mammals. And even worse, I had Françoise with me. My throat tightened as my mind raced; how do I get out of this? With a river and steep bank behind and a herd of agitated elephants in front, the options were limited.

What was even more disconcerting was that we had also cut off Marula and Mabula, who were slightly behind us, from their mother Frankie. They panicked and started squealing loudly. And if there was one single thing that could aggravate our already dire predicament even more, it was getting between an aggressive female elephant and her frightened young.

We were in trouble. Deep trouble.

Nana who was a few yards away on our right took two menacing steps forward with her trunk held high, and then thankfully stopped and backed off. That was terrifying enough on its own, but the real problem was coming from behind her: Frankie.

I frantically tried to turn the bike and make a bolt for it, but the riverbank was too steep, the bike's turning circle too wide. We were hopelessly trapped.

Trying to sound as unconcerned as possible, I said to Françoise, surprised that my voice was still steady, 'I think we have a problem.' I was absolutely horrified that I had placed her in such mortal danger.

By now Frankie was furiously reversing out of a thicket, trying to swivel and charge us. I drew my 9-mm pistol and handed it to Françoise to protect herself if anything happened to me. Basically, it was a peashooter as far as an elephant was concerned, but as a last resort, a shot may distract Frankie.

I then stood up on the bike to face Frankie who was now coming directly at us – fast, furious and deadly. Clive Walker, the famous African game ranger, describes the experience superbly in his book *Signs of the Wild*. 'An elephant charge is accompanied by the sound of screaming demons. Except perhaps for the prospect of imminent hanging, there is nothing that serves to concentrate the mind more wonderfully.'

That summed it up exactly. On Frankie thundered. I pleaded for this to be a mock charge, desperately looking for signs that she just wanted to scare us away from her young. The key indication of this was if her ears flapped out. But no – with mounting horror I watched her fold her ears back and roll up her trunk to take full impact when she hit. A rolled trunk meant she was going all the way. This was for real, and with that awful realization my sensations heightened surreally, like in a slow-motion car crash. I heard someone hammering in the far-off village as if it was next door, while high above me I watched an eagle soaring and marvelled at its graceful flight, as if I had nothing better to do. I had never seen a sky so blue.

On she hurtled, her huge frame blotting out all else. Lifting my hands as high above my head as I could I started yelling at her, then began screaming at the monstrous sight in a last-ditch attempt to pierce her mist of rage.

Then just as I thought we were goners, her ears suddenly cracked out and she broke off and unrolled her trunk. But the massive momentum hurled her right up to the bike where she towered directly above us, glaring angrily through tiny eyes. I involuntarily sat down on the bike and looked up at the crinkled underside of Frankie's throat in petrified wonder. She shook her huge head in frustration, showering us in the thick red dust from a recent sand bath and then backed off a few paces.

Marula and Mabula scampered past her. After making another two or three terrifyingly threatening gestures at us Frankie turned and followed her son and daughter into the bush, away from us.

I eased stiffly down off the saddle and turned to Françoise. Her eyes were tightly closed and I gently whispered that it was over. It was OK. The two of us sat still, too stunned to do or say anything.

Eventually I found the energy to start the bike and pulled off in the opposite direction to the herd. We drove through the bush which seemed so still after the charge, as if the birds and trees themselves knew what had happened.

Eventually we saw a truck carrying some visiting friends, waved them down and got off the quad bike. As they came across, Françoise started vividly describing what had just happened, gesticulating energetically. The only problem was she still had the cocked 9-mm pistol in her hand, finger on the trigger and each time she emphasized some dramatic point she waved the gun around. Our friends scattered for cover until I managed to retrieve the gun and cleared the breech.

Back home I told the astonished staff what had happened. 'I can't believe you're still alive,' said David, whistling through his teeth. 'She must have made a conscious decision not to kill you. Why do you think she did that?'

A good question. Elephants rarely break off once they're at full steam and I still couldn't believe that Frankie had actually halted at the last minute. Why had she changed gears, dropping down from a lethal real attack to a mock charge? It was virtually unheard of.

The next day I got on the bike and drove back to the river crossing where we had so nearly lost our lives to try to figure it out. I needed some answers. But try as I might, the crucial moments of the charge were a total blank, as if my mind couldn't grapple with the horror.

So I retraced our route, driving through the same river crossing several times, mentally scrolling over the incident again and again. Slowly the details started fleshing out. I remembered I had been standing on the bike and screaming as she charged. But what was I yelling? My mind was still a void.

Then in an instant it came flooding back. I was screaming, 'Stop, stop, it's me, it's me!'

That was all. In retrospect it sounds rather ludicrous, but that's exactly what happened. To shout 'It's me' at a charging elephant, the most aggressive female in a herd protecting her panicked babies is about as lame as it gets. Yet it stopped her, and I knew then that she had somehow recognized me from the *boma*. I still believe she had spared our lives because she had witnessed her matriarch's interaction with me the day before I let them out.

chapter fifteen

'The power's down again,' said David with a grimace, 'this time on the western boundary.'

We were having endless problems with the fence. Our electrified border was temperamental and unreliable, given to more mood swings and irrational behaviour than a menopausal rhino. Everything affected it. Too much rain drowned the current. Too little rain affected conductivity. Lightning struck it with regular monotony, sparking out the voltage. Hyena, bushpig and warthog constantly dug holes beneath it, shorting the circuit. These were just some of the obvious problems; sometimes I swear it went down just because it damn well felt like it. It certainly didn't make our task of keeping a herd of angry elephants – one of which had just charged me – inside the reserve any easier.

We had also just discovered that both Nana and Frankie had been impregnated by the dominant bull sometime before leaving the previous reserve. As elephants have such bulk, it's often difficult to tell early on when they are carrying, but it had by now become obvious that our two adult females were gestating.

Consequently, rule number one on the reserve was that the power always had to be on or we risked losing the elephant. Not that they were trying to escape any more, but all it took was for Nana to be walking near the boundary and sense that there was no power – and who knows what would happen? That meant there were mandatory dawn and dusk inspections along the entire twenty-mile perimeter, and often others during the day as well. We never went to bed with the fence not fully operational.

The problem this time was not only that the power was down, the Land Rover also wouldn't start and it was getting dark.

'No problem,' said David. 'I'll take the tractor.'

I looked across at Gunda Gunda, the onomatopoeic Zulu name for our faithful twenty-year-old beast. She was reliable all right and would do the job but she had no headlights and a twenty-mile bush drive in the dark without night vision can be a hairy ordeal.

The African wilderness is merciless and to survive you need every genetic advantage you can muster. Consequently almost all animals have excellent night vision enhanced by a reflective membrane behind the iris, which catches even distant starlight and magnifies it. This membrane is why their eyes reflect so brightly in the dark when a light is shined at them. The big cats apparently have the best night vision but all species rely on acute eyesight either to hunt or to escape the predators of the night.

Well, not all species. There's a notable exception; the planet's most dominant creature is completely night blind. And that's us – *Homo sapiens*.

Try walking in thick bush on a moonless or cloudy night without a flashlight and see what I mean. It's so black you can't see anything . . . and I mean anything. Unless you can navigate by the stars (provided there is no cloud cover) you'll be lost, maybe even panic-stricken, within minutes.

I once crashed on the quad-bike at night about four miles from the camp. I lost my flashlight in the accident and had to walk home in the dark. I still remember that journey with trepidation today. I was completely blind and walked through the bush with both hands in front of me so at least

I knew if I was going to hit something. I could have fallen into a hyena den and wouldn't have known until I woke up – or more likely, didn't.

It took hours to get back and I was a bruised, nervous, thorn-scratched wreck when I did. What concerned me most as I blindly stumbled along was that every other living creature around was watching my antics as clear as day. To any predator I would have appeared as a wounded or disabled animal. Twice, when the bush seemed to suddenly come alive, I frantically fired shots into the air with my pistol. I was lucky to get home.

So how did our ancestors survive the eons without keenly developed night vision? I know plenty of scientists and not one of them has ever been able to explain satisfactorily to me how puny, tasty, night-blind *Homo sapiens* endured so spectacularly when everything around us had to have excellent night vision if they were to make it through a summer, never mind evolve.

Yet despite my reservations, David jumped up on Gunda Gunda and set off into the dusk. It was only when he was gone that I realized he had forgotten his radio.

I went back to the house, made some phone calls and then walked out and sat on the lawn overlooking the reserve trying to spot David's flashlight blinking on the far boundary when I heard a low moan crescendo into a rasping roar that made my blood chill. Max also froze staring out into the dark, alert.

'It can't be,' I thought, and then I heard it again, oscillating eerily across the wilderness. This time there was no mistake. It was the call of a male lion marking his territory. As we had no resident lions on the reserve, this meant an itinerant animal had broken in.

But even worse, the call was suddenly reciprocated, a curdling growl that bounced off the cliffs. That meant there were at least two lions roaming on the reserve. And of all

123

places, the roars were echoing from the western boundary – exactly where David was driving along without headlights. They must have come in through the fence while the power was down.

Out in the dark every creature on Thula would have heard the ominous call, for it was death itself calling, beckoning out for you.

Nana too would have heard it. I imagined her standing frozen, ears flared, trunk up, smelling the air to work out where the call came from and thinking of the youngsters in the herd. Her tactics and habits would now change, as would everything else on the reserve.

I bent down and patted Max, reassuring him.

It sometimes happened that lions broke out of the nearby Umfolozi game reserve and went walkabout, raiding cattle and generally striking fear far and wide in the villages. When lions are on the loose they totally control the country-side. They're difficult to corner and find cattle or other livestock exceptionally easy prey. If they become too much of a problem, they are usually hunted down and killed by rangers.

The breakouts are a result of pressure exerted, often forcibly, on young males by the dominant lion to quit the pride. An alpha male will not tolerate competition and once male cubs mature, they are chased off. However, with all territories in the reserve already taken by other resident prides, the youngsters are often forced outside the protected areas and into the human domain.

These young males, usually brothers, are absolutely for-midable and will stay out until they are older and stronger, all the while gaining hunting and fighting skills. They then go back into the reserve and challenge a patriarch for his territory and his harem. And at two against one, they're often successful.

I love lions, one of Africa's most charismatic and iconic

creatures, but I wished this pair had chosen somewhere else to do their 'gap year'. We weren't ready for them at Thula Thula just yet.

However, my prime concern was for David. While he was on the tractor with its noise and greasy fumes he was relatively safe. But he was looking for an electrical fault, and to find it he would have to get off the vehicle and walk along the fence, sometimes for long distances. I knew he was carrying a small torch but no rifle, and walking in the bush at night unarmed with lions in the immediate vicinity is crazy stuff. If we had heard the lions earlier he certainly wouldn't have gone out and I was hoping against hope that he had also heard the calls. But Gunda Gunda is pretty noisy and I couldn't bank on that.

I called Bheki who was at the rangers' house – he had also heard the big cats – and told him David was out alone. Bheki shook his head and clicked his tongue. I could see he was also worried.

'We have to go to him,' I said. 'Please get my rifle and bring plenty of bullets.'

I wasn't looking forward to the march in the dark but there was a rough outside dirt track running parallel to the fence for much of the way where there was little danger as the big cats were inside the reserve. If we were lucky we would find David and the hole the lions had dug.

Then we heard it again: that spine-chilling roar. It was close, perhaps a mile or two away. By now I was acutely alarmed – the lions must have scented the tractor, but would they also smell the human driver? And just how hungry were they? They may not have fed for several days.

The answering roar came back – this time even closer.

'Bheki, we must move faster,' I urged.

The Zulu grunted. He was as concerned as I was. David was extremely popular on Thula Thula.

Gripping our rifles tight, we broke into a jog – well, as

fast as you can go in the darkness. Even with flashlights it is always difficult out in the bush at night. Neither of us noticed our numerous trips and falls over rocks and bush roots. There was one aim only: to get to David before the lions did.

About two miles later we saw a dim flickering light and to our intense joy it was David at a gap in the fence with Gunda Gunda chugging away close by.

I was about to yell a warning, but he beat me to it.

'Lion! Big ones!' he shouted, then pointed to the hole. 'They came in there. I left the tractor running to keep them away. Their spoor is all over the place.'

Relief washed over me. This guy was indestructible. 'Leave the tractor here for the night and walk back with us on the outside path.'

We closed the hole where the lions had dug under the fence pushing up the wires and shorting the electrical strands, which got the power up effectively trapping the lion in the reserve, and walked home. Tomorrow would be an interesting day.

Telephone etiquette in the bush allows calls only after dawn. The sun was barely up before I had the Parks Board section ranger on the line.

'Have you lost a couple of lions?' I asked.

'Ja,' he replied. 'Two got out day before yesterday and have been causing chaos around a couple of villages. They're on the move, going your way actually. Have you seen them?'

'They're both on Thula,' I replied. 'Do you want to come and get them?'

'We're on our way. Try and keep tabs on them until we get there.'

All the reserve staff were told to be extra cautious and the work teams were sent home. None of our employees had experience with lions so we weren't taking any chances.

While we were waiting for them to arrive I went out to

find the herd. I picked up their tracks and shortly afterwards found fresh elephant dung within yards of fresh lion scat. They had crossed paths with the big cats but there was no real risk as an elephant herd is far too formidable for lions, however hungry they were. Provided of course the youngsters didn't wander off.

I couldn't find them and went back to the house. Standing on the front lawn staring out into the bush, I remembered a harrowing incident last year when a hunting lioness charged Craig Reed, the senior ranger at Umfolozi. He was out on horseback with his five-months pregnant wife, Andrea, when the giant cat suddenly charged out of a reed bed at them. Craig's horse was spooked and bolted, but the lioness had already targeted Andrea and gave chase. An expert rider, she galloped through the bush at full speed. Scenting the danger, the horse needed no encouragement and was in full flight when Andrea's foot suddenly slipped out the stirrup and she started sliding out of the saddle.

As she fell she somehow managed to grab hold of the stirrup and was dragged through the bush as the horse galloped on with the lioness in hot pursuit. She watched horrified as the lioness got closer and closer until it was at her feet, and then, resigned to her fate, she let go. Amazingly, the lioness jumped right over her sprawling body, and got her claws into the horse.

By now Craig had managed to turn his horse and frantically rode up firing shots into the air, scaring the lioness off. Thankfully Andrea was OK, although badly bruised and shaken, and in true frontierswoman tradition, gave birth to a fine baby boy four months later.

The moral of the story is always to treat these magnificent creatures with absolute respect. I pondered this over a hurried breakfast and then met up with Bheki and his men to follow the spoor from the hole where the big cats had come in. But Thula Thula's hard clay soil makes tracking extremely difficult when it's dry and after a few hours the trail had disappeared altogether. There also weren't any vultures circling above, which meant the lions hadn't made a kill last night. That would have made our lives much easier.

The Parks Board arrived and we searched the reserve for two days, alternately picking up and losing the trail until a fence check revealed a big hole under the wire. They were gone. We later heard that they had returned to Umfolozi.

A few weeks later I was in Umfolozi on a night drive, when I asked the driver to pull over for a 'pit stop', having drunk several cups of coffee. It was pitch-black and as I opened the door he said casually, 'Better check first,' and flashed a spotlight through the open door.

There lying in the long grass, just ten yards from where I was getting out, were two big male lions. I swear they were the same youngsters that had been on our reserve – it was close to our boundary and I simply had that uncanny feeling. We had just seen the resident male, a giant beast sporting an impressive golden mane, with his harem less than a mile away.

No doubt these two had returned from their walkabout at Thula Thula, hard and lean, to challenge him for the spoils.

chapter sixteen

The southern white rhino is very big. Surprisingly big – especially if you are on foot and one steps out of the bush in front of you. It's the second-largest land mammal on earth and can easily weigh three tons. Prized by poachers for its horn, of which the one just in front of me had a particularly fine pair.

We had just had three delivered to the reserve and this female, still doped from the sedative, had groggily wandered away from the other two. This posed a big problem. The elephants were close by and unknowingly she was ambling directly towards them. We had to cut her off – and trying to dissuade a mountain of muscle and horn still hungover from travel tranquillizers from going in her chosen direction was not something I relished.

'David,' I called into the radio. 'I've found her. Can you bring the Landy across? We're at the south end of the airstrip.'

'Roger, boss,' came the instant reply. 'Thula Thula international airport it is!'

I watched this beautiful creature not fifteen yards away walking unsteadily on short dumpy legs which could usually propel her into an unbelievably fast charge in no time. Clad in a prehistoric suit of armour impervious to almost anything except a bullet, she tottered along, completely unaware of my presence. A magnificent 40-inch horn like a sabre at the tip of her elongated head added gravitas to an already imposing form. This was the stuff poachers dream about.

Max stood by me transfixed by the beast. Bush-hardened as he was, he was not used to rhino this close and apart from his twitching nose taking in the scent, he didn't move.

I kept a wary eye on the herd browsing upwind when I heard a soft sound behind me and turned to see Mnumzane coming up the airstrip downwind, testing the air.

Damn it! Of all the bad luck . . . we were too late; he must have caught either my or the rhino's scent and started to slowly walk in our direction.

'David,' I whispered into the radio, 'Mnumzane's right here.'

'So am I, boss,' he replied as the Landy bounced out of the bush onto the airstrip. Giving Mnumzane a wide birth, he pulled up next to me and jumped out leaving the motor idling.

'Somehow we have to keep Mnumzane and the herd away from her,' I said pointing to the dazed rhino. 'They're too close. I really don't like this at all.'

'I brought the horse feed you wanted. That should delay him for a while,' he replied.

'Yeah, but the smell might also bring the other elephants over. We're going to have to shield the rhino with the Land Rover, put ourselves between her and any elephant that gets too inquisitive. But first let's try and get Mnumzane out of the way.'

David jumped into the back of Landy and sliced the first of the large sacks of horse pellets with his Leatherman knife. He placed the open bag at the tailgate and crouched down next to it. 'I hope they like this stuff.'

'We'll soon find out,' I said, getting behind the wheel and driving slowly towards Mnumzane.

David was making light of it, but this was a deadly serious business. Elephants will usually only bother rhinos if they don't get out of their way – which rhinos invariably do. However, our latest addition was still shaking off the effects of sedatives injected to pacify her during the journey to Thula Thula, and thus would not be able to take in her surroundings. If she stumbled into Mnumzane or the herd . . . well, anything could happen.

What we planned to do was divert Mnumzane's attention from the groggy creature by giving him a taste of the protein-rich pellets and then enticing him as far away as possible by laying a food trail. It was dangerous work as David would be completely exposed on the open back of the pickup as he poured the feed out to excited elephants following just yards behind. Mnumzane was only a teenager, but he still weighed about three and a half tons and we had to be very careful.

I cut across in front of the youngster then reversed back to where he stood confused and a little petulant about the noisy intrusion into his space. David chucked out some feed and I drove off a short distance. To my dismay, he ignored the offering and resumed his meander up the airstrip towards the rhino.

'Reverse again!' shouted David, holding the bag ready to pour. 'But this time get much closer.'

'OK . . . but be bloody careful.'

I gingerly edged the vehicle backwards . . . 'Closer, closer!' David called, keeping a wary watch on the young bull.

Suddenly, not liking what was going on, Mnumzane lifted his head aggressively and turned sharply towards us, ears spread wide.

'Just a little bit more . . .' said David ignoring the elephant's blatant warning, and just as I thought we were too close he quickly tipped the bag and I slammed the vehicle into first, easing off with David laying a long trail of feed away from the rhino.

Mnumzane watched us go; relaxing his flared ears and

unfurling his trunk to smell the pile of pellets on the ground. He snuffled some into his mouth and a few seconds later he was piling in like a glutton. The ploy had worked.

'That will keep him busy and we've plenty more chow if the others come across,' said David hopping off the back and getting into the passenger seat, shoving Max between us.

At the mention of the other elephants, I looked up to where they were grazing about forty yards away. As I did so, Nana's trunk suddenly snaked up. Even though she was upwind, elephants have such a superb sense of smell that they can pick up minute eddies swirling ever so slightly against the prevailing current.

'Here we go,' said David. 'She's smelt something. Either the rhino or the food, and now she's inquisitive. Just pray that she doesn't come this way.'

But of course she did. With the herd following, she started moving towards us, checking the air continuously, sniffing for the source of the scent.

'Damn it!' We now had the herd coming in on one side of the poor rhino and Mnumzane on the other. Even worse, they weren't advancing in single file which would have been much more manageable. Nana was in the centre with Frankie, her daughter Marula and firstborn son Mabula on the left, while Nana's young son Mandla and stately daughter Nandi spread out on the right.

Straight in front of them, still secreted in the bush was the woozy rhino, which to my dismay had begun settling down for a rest, making herself even more vulnerable.

'OK,' said David, 'let's do it again, draw them away with the feed.'

He leapt onto the back of the Land Rover and this time cut open two bags and got ready to pour a trail while I reversed in.

The reaction of the herd was interesting. They picked

up the scent and cautiously came towards us while David scooped pellets out as fast as possible. Mabula and Marula stopped and started sniffing at the strange fare but the rest, led by Nana and Frankie, continued on, slowly following the trail left behind the Land Rover.

Then – of all things – the Land Rover stalled and I couldn't restart it. Thankfully the cabin rear window had long since lost its glass and with Nana almost on top of him David somehow squeezed his large body through the tiny gap and dived onto Max in the passenger seat in a tangle of limbs.

Then the elephants were on us. We were surrounded.

David turned and stared at the miniature window that he had somehow scrunched through. 'Don't think I could do that again,' he laughed. 'Amazing what a shot of adrenalin can do.'

Fortunately it was the feed the elephants were after and the two adults yanked the remaining bags off the back and tried standing on them to smash them open. Frankie, frustrated in her attempts to open one bag, grabbed it by the corner with her trunk and flicked it high into the air – thankfully in the opposite direction from the now-sleeping rhino. It sailed above our heads for at least thirty yards and landed with a thud, scattering its contents. Given that the bag weighed 120 pounds and she had only grasped it with the tip of her trunk, the height and distance of the throw was truly awesome.

The elephants loped off after the broken bag and while they were busy gorging themselves we were able to sneak out to fix the Land Rover. It was a disconnected fuel line and soon we restarted it. Now knowing that they loved horse feed I radioed for more and we were able to lay juicy trails of food leading the herd far away from our new arrivals.

We weren't so lucky with Mnumzane. He had unfinished

business with the rhino, and soon lost interest in the scraps of feed on the ground, walking back towards where she lay.

There was nothing left to do but get between them and keep him away as best we could. My heart jumped at the thought, for even at his age he could easily toss our vehicle over if he wanted to. Bull elephants don't like to be forced to do something against their will.

I drove past Mnumzane up to the drowsy rhino and blocked his path, leaving the motor running. He could easily walk around us of course, so the plan was to keep moving in front of him, obstructing him from the rhino and hope he got the message without feeling he had been interfered with. And particularly without provoking a charge.

On he came until he was about ten paces away and then stopped and watched us guardedly, assessing the situation with elephantine intelligence. As we predicted he started making a wide circle around the vehicle. Now came the tricky part because not only would he be much closer, but he would realize he was being thwarted.

'Hold on,' I said quietly as I gently moved the Landy forward to block him.

Again he stopped, this time less than five yards away and then he changed tack. I reversed and as we started moving his ears flared out and he swung to face us head-on. He had taken up the challenge and the tension in the Landy ratcheted up as he took an aggressive step towards us, head held high.

'Shit!' said David quietly.

'No! Mnumzane, no!' I called out the open window, ensuring that my voice conveyed intention rather than anger, or worse still fear. 'No!'

Again he stepped forward, ears belligerently splayed, tail up. This was no game.

'No, Mnumzane! No!' I called again, as I reversed in a tight semicircle to keep him away. 'No!'

Out of the corner of my eye I saw the rhino wake up, stumble to her feet and start moving off, giving us precious space in which to manoeuvre. Relieved, I swung the Landy around until we faced the temperamental elephant head-on with about ten yards separating us.

As we confronted each other he began swinging his front foot, a sure sign that he was going to charge. Without thinking I dropped the clutch and briefly lurched the Landy at him, and then again, challenging him directly.

'Whoa!' said David, gripping the dashboard. 'Here he comes!'

Then as we braced for the inevitable charge, he suddenly broke and ran off at a gait, trunk held high. I had to press home our advantage and immediately followed him, goading him away until he reached thick bush and disappeared.

'Flippin' hell,' said David, expelling breath with a whoosh. 'That was a close one. I wouldn't try that with an adult bull.'

He was absolutely right. Mnumzane's youth was on our side, but it had worked and the rhino was safe. We posted a ranger with the rhino with instructions to call if any elephants reappeared and I went off to find Mnumzane and make my peace with him.

chapter seventeen

Frankie's charge at Françoise and me, terrifying as it was, had in its own strange way strengthened the bond that I had been building with the herd. The fact that the matriarch Nana had not joined in was an impressive breakthrough. She had launched a few aggressive steps towards us, which is only to be expected of a wild elephant, but then she almost instantly halted. To me, the fact that she had not overreacted was significant.

Frankie, who had a sinister reputation already, had broken a full-blooded charge as soon as she recognized me – something virtually unheard of in the elephant world.

However, what happened a few months later, was even more surprising.

Françoise and I were fast asleep when Bijou's persistent growling woke us. Bijou – jewel in French – is Françoise's tiny Maltese poodle, the obligatory accoutrement of almost an entire nation of French women. Bijou enjoyed a privileged life beyond anything Max or Penny could ever hope to aspire to. She had the choice food, even real steak, and slept on the bed between us where for a time her major accomplishment was nearly destroying our sex life.

She was not a watchdog, so when she started growling I realized something serious was going on.

I jumped out of bed, grabbed my shotgun and then heard what the problem was – a heavy scraping on the roof accompanied by soft thuds. The other dogs were also alert. Penny's hair stood stiff as wire on her back and she was crouching protectively next to Françoise. Max was sitting at the door, ears cocked but calm, watching me quizzically for instructions.

I pulled on some trousers and then tentatively opened the top half of the stable door leading to the garden, shotgun at the ready.

Whoa! A giant figure suddenly loomed up and I got the fright of my life, hastily stepping back and tripping over Max, then staggering backwards until I slammed into the opposite wall, sprawling in an undignified mess on the floor. I somehow managed to keep the cocked shotgun from hammering into the wall and discharging a shot.

For there, standing in the doorway, casually pulling the grass from our thatched roof was Nana.

Woken by the commotion, Françoise was sitting up in bed holding Bijou tightly – staring at the apparition in the doorway. Like her, I couldn't believe my eyes. Of all the spooky things that I could have imagined outside my front door at some ungodly hour, a full-grown elephant was definitely not one of them.

Recovering my composure I got up and walked toward the door and – not really knowing what to do – began talking softly to her.

'Hey, Nana, you scared the hell out of me. What are you doing here, you beautiful girl?'

I will always remember her response. She stretched out her trunk and I did likewise with my hand as if it was the most natural thing in the world. For a few magnetic moments we connected. I stood a little closer, taking care to stay at the edge of her reach so she couldn't grab me, and she moved the tip of her trunk over my T-shirt and then touched me on the head and face. I held my ground, completely entranced by the exhilarating combination of danger and affection. Considering that she couldn't see what she was doing as her eyes were above door level, she was surprisingly gentle.

She then lowered her head and moved forward, almost as if she was trying to come inside, and with that Bijou barked. The spell was broken.

I doubt whether many people have had a ten-foot, five-ton wild elephant trying to squeeze into their room via a narrow door, but take it from me, it is not a soothing experience.

Bijou and Penny went ballistic, sprinting around the room barking like banshees. Surprised, Nana backed off a few paces and flared her ears.

Alarmed that the dogs were going to be stomped flat, Françoise grabbed Penny and stuffed her into the bottom of a built-in clothes cupboard. She then rushed after Bijou who, assuming the unlikely role as protector of the realm, was now for reasons known only to her having a go at Max, shrieking at him in high-pitched Maltese. I'm convinced that Nana was just too awesome for the tiny poodle to grasp and thus she assumed all the confusion was to be blamed on a bemused Max, who sat patiently ignoring her.

Françoise caught her and as she was putting the semi-hysterical pooch into the cupboard, Penny pushed open her door and came back into the fray. She wasn't going to let anything – not even an elephant – get between her and Françoise.

Françoise managed to scramble Penny into her arms again and as she pushed her back in the cupboard, Bijou bolted out. It was an absolute circus. Eventually we locked all three dogs in the bathroom, and I was able to concentrate on Nana.

With all the commotion she had moved off about ten paces and it was only then I saw that the entire herd was with her. I looked at my watch: 2 a.m.

'This is amazing,' I said to Françoise who had joined me at the door. 'This is completely bloody amazing.'

'What are they doing here?'

'I have no idea. But we might as well enjoy it while it lasts.'

Enjoy it we did. There was an air of contentment as the animals strolled around the lawn in the moonlight, casting giant shadows across the garden like ghosts of the prehistoric world.

As they moved off to the front of the house I dashed across the lawn to the rangers' quarters to wake David.

He shot up in his bed. 'Poachers again?'

'No. The elephants are here. Come quickly.'

'What do you mean . . . here?'

'Here at the house. They're on the front lawn.'

'Our front lawn? Our elephants . . . ?'

'Come . . . get dressed.'

I rushed back to Françoise.

'You'd better wash before you come near me,' she said, pointing at me with feigned revulsion on her face. I looked at her, perplexed, then put my hand on my chest to feel a gooey, sticky mess.

'Your head,' she said, wrinkling her nose. 'It's also all over your head.'

I strode over to the mirror and saw exactly what she meant. I was covered in pachyderm slime. I must have had a half a pint of mucous from Nana's trunk spread all over me.

'I'll wash later. David is joining us on the verandah. Let's go and watch.'

I let Max out of the bathroom and the three of us sneaked across the lawn to the rangers' house, keeping a sharp eye out for any stray jumbos and then went out onto the front verandah. Here Françoise had a grandstand view of the herd destroying her cherished garden; they pushed over trees, tore

139

apart her favourite bushes and ate every flower they could find. I must say she seemed less entranced by the visit than I was.

David came out and joined us. 'This is unbelievable. They're all here,' he said, eyes straining against the gloom, 'except Mnumzane.'

'No, he's here too. I saw him earlier.'

David found him standing alone in the dark about twenty yards away. 'Poor guy. They tolerate him, but only just. He's got no adult relatives so he's always a Johnny-come-lately. I really hope he turns out OK.'

'He's a big boy,' I replied. 'He'll be fine.'

Nana looked up from the garden she was demolishing and with a bunch of prized shrubs in her mouth ambled over to us. Max, who had moved a few paces onto the lawn, silently retreated to the relative safety of the verandah and then followed Françoise when I suggested she go inside in case Nana got too close.

It was something I just couldn't get used to; the daunting vision of this gargantuan form looming ominously closer, apparently fixated on demonstrating her affection by standing right next to me. It was like having an infatuated Tyrannosaurus rex showering attention on you. What was even more mind-blowing was that not that long ago she would happily have killed me.

We decided to play it safe and David and I moved back inside the double door and watched her imposing bulk approach. She stopped at the low verandah wall and for the second time that dark morning stretched out her trunk to me. She couldn't reach me, so I decided to hang back and watch and wait.

However, I underestimated her persistence – and her strength. Frustrated at my reluctance to come to her, she decided to come to me, trying to squash her vast frame between the two brick pillars that straddled the verandah entrance. This obviously didn't work, and we watched open-mouthed as she then gently placed her forehead on the left pillar and gave an exploratory shove.

That certainly got my attention. I remembered what she had done to the gate poles at the *boma* and had no doubt she would bring the whole verandah roof down if she wanted to. I hastily stepped forward and she stopped shoving and lifted her trunk. Once again she snaked it over the top of my body. It was a good thing I hadn't changed for I received another liberal basting of slime, while the sound of her deep rumbling stomach reverberated through the house, drowning out the thumping of my heart.

Satisfied, she eventually ambled away and joined the rest of the clan as they finished off the few remaining exotic plants in Françoise's now obliterated garden.

Then suddenly an eight-week-old kitten we had slipped past us and completely oblivious of the herd walked out onto the lawn. We only noticed after it was too late and watched in horror – there was nothing we could do to get her back as she was now among the herd. The elephants got very interested in this tiny thing and all sauntered over for a close inspection. Still the tiny cat didn't react – I think these alien creatures around it were simply too big for it to comprehend, just as they had been for Bijou. Soon it was surrounded and as the elephants put their trunks out, waving the tips around this tiny curiosity, it would swipe at them with its paw, playing with them.

Eventually the elephants got tired of it and walked off, leaving the kitten alone on the middle of the lawn.

Except Frankie. She initially walked away, and then when she was about twenty yards off, she suddenly turned and ran at it. It was a sight I don't think I will ever see again – a five-ton elephant charging a five-ounce cat.

The kitten finally realized something was wrong and skittered back to us just in time.

141

We stayed up watching until 5 a.m. when, at the first hint of light, Nana moved off with the herd in tow. They were soon eaten up by the dense bush.

I stared after them. A sense of emptiness seeped into my universe. A part of me was leaving with them.

chapter eighteen

Later that morning I woke with a glorious glow of satisfaction. The herd's visit to our home had graphically demonstrated that we had made substantial progress. To think that not so long ago I was begging for their lives while the Parks Board issued elephant rifles to their rangers with 'shoot on sight' instructions. Now I was trying to keep them out of our living room.

It seemed the rehabilitation of the herd was all over bar the shouting and we had reason to celebrate our achievements. But whoever came up with the maxim 'pride comes before a fall' certainly knew what he was talking about.

I was enjoying a leisurely late breakfast, still replaying Nana's extraordinary nocturnal display of affection in my mind when I was bumped back to earth by a frantic call from the rangers.

'Mkhulu! *Mbomvu!* We are in danger; the elephants are trying to kill us.'

It was Bheki breathlessly shouting out the emergency *Mbomvu* – Code Red, the bush equivalent of Mayday.

I grabbed the radio.

'Mkhulu standing by. What's your position?'

'We are at the fence near the river where it leaves the reserve. The elephants are chasing us. We are running. Mkhulu, it is bad!'

I could hear the panic rising in the normally stoic ranger's voice. They were many miles away on the other side of the reserve and there was no chance we could get to them in time. The herd had certainly moved along quickly to be so far away from our house. A few hours earlier they had been trampling Françoise's garden flat.

'How close are they?' I shouted into the radio.

'They are here. She is trying to kill us! The big ones want to kill us!'

Bheki is a hugely experienced ranger and the horror in his voice startled me. He also is one of the toughest men I know.

'Get out, Bheki!' I yelled into the radio. 'Take your men through the fence, cut it or find a place and go under.'

'Ngwenya is out already. We are trying to go under.'

Then I heard two shots over the radio.

'Shit! Bheki what's happening? Who's shooting?'

'It's Ngwenya. He's shooting . . .' The radio went off in mid sentence.

'Go! Just get out!' I shouted, desperately trying to make contact, but Bheki's radio stayed dead.

David who had been listening ran off and brought the Land Rover over, driving across Françoise's mutilated garden to our front door. I climbed in and he pulled off cursing the Landy's infamously wide turning circle as he spun the wheels through the soft sand of demolished flower beds and sped for the gate.

'Bheki, Bheki come in, come in.'

But there was no reply. The radio remained ominously silent for the forty minutes it took us to hurry across the reserve, bouncing across the ridged tracks at breakneck speed, not knowing what we would find, and not daring to imagine the worst.

Then about a hundred yards from the fence I saw the herd milling about restlessly. On the other side, barely visible in the thick bush huddled Bheki and his men. I did a

144

quick head-count, first of the rangers, and then the elephant and exhaled deeply in absolute relief. They were all there.

Frankie noticed us first and angrily lifted her foot, stamping the ground until it trembled, shaking her mighty head. She was extremely agitated by whatever had happened and was letting us know it.

We pulled over and called out to the rangers who gingerly emerged from the thicket, all eyes on the herd now starting to move off.

'Are you OK?' I asked. 'What happened?'

'*Ayish* . . . Mkhulu, these elephant are crazy,' Ngwenya said with a sweep of his arm at the departing herd. 'We found them here on the fence and they wanted to kill us. They charged us and we ran and ran but they chased us. Then just as we thought we were finished, we found the stream that goes under the fence and we crawled out. The electricity was biting us but we had to go on. My radio is finished. It was in the water.'

I took out a pair of pliers, snipped the fence and lifted the electric wires with a stick so they could crawl back into the reserve.

'You were lucky,' I said, as I rejoined the severed fence. 'Now you have seen up close how dangerous these elephants are. Tell the others, tell everyone working here to keep their eyes open and stay far away from them.'

I knew this episode would quickly spread through the village – with hugely colourful embellishments – which I hoped would further discourage potential poachers.

But that was not my main concern. Instead, what really alarmed me was the fact the herd had no obvious reason to charge the rangers. Either the animals had been inadvertently provoked by Bheki and his men, or they were just hell-bent on ridding their new territory of all strange human beings. Perhaps the guards with their rifles reminded them of poachers from earlier encounters in their troubled lives.

However, the more I thought about it, I began to believe the real reason was probably more innocuous. The rangers had probably been casually chatting among themselves and paying scant attention to their surroundings when, before they knew it, they had stumbled into the elephants' space. Suddenly they were in deep trouble. Or at least that's what I hoped had happened. We would never know, but what was certain was this was still an extremely dangerous herd and there was lots of work to be done before we could relax. If indeed we ever could.

On the upside, my rangers now knew exactly how alert they had to be in the bush and I was sure they wouldn't make the same mistake twice. And to their eternal credit, they hadn't shot directly at the animals but kept their heads and got out of the reserve.

They all climbed on the back of the Landy and we drove back to the house, whereupon they called all the other staff together and animatedly recounted their perilous experience as only Zulus, who are born raconteurs, can do, with everyone laughing loudly as they argued about who ran away the fastest.

My sons Dylan, twenty-one, and Jason, twenty-three, from my first marriage were arriving later that day to spend some time on Thula Thula and I was looking forward to seeing them. Jason is a city boy who enjoys the bush. Dylan on the other hand is nuts about the wild and spends every spare moment he can out in the sticks.

We had a treat in store for them as David and I had chanced upon an active hyena den a few weeks earlier and planned to stake it out that night. Soon after the boys arrived we packed some supplies and drove out to the den, but to our dismay found that it had recently been abandoned. The clan had moved on.

Dylan couldn't hide his disappointment and had walked off looking for their spoor. Soon we heard his low whistle.

'Dylan's calling us,' I said. 'He's found something.'

We pushed through the undergrowth and eventually found him crouched in a clearing. 'Rock python,' he whispered excitedly and spread his arms wide. 'Huge.'

Thula Thula and its surroundings are prime python territory, so much so that the snake has become the totem of the local Biyela tribe who believe that the spirits of their ancestors sometimes return in the form of this magnificent constrictor. Whenever a python is seen in the village, instead of killing it as they would do with any other snake, the people gather to watch and sometimes tie a goat to a stake as an offering. Rock pythons are Africa's largest snakes and can be extremely aggressive when disturbed. And these are big reptiles we're talking about; ten or twelve feet long is not unusual.

But what Dylan had found astounded me. It was the biggest python I have ever seen, its golden brown body with tan and olive blotches stretched at full length in the bush.

However, that's not what Dylan was looking at. Instead he was pointing elsewhere, and as we moved across I saw another snake – even bigger. This was a once-in-a-lifetime sighting and of course no one had a camera. It's axiomatic that if you want to see something really special in the bush, you leave your camera behind. Both snakes were resting, immobile after a day's basking in the sun and we were able to walk up reasonably close without alarming them. Dylan paced them out. The first was fifteen feet long, the second a super trophy size seventeen feet.

'That puts paid to my snake reference book,' said David. 'It says that pythons only grow to fourteen or fifteen feet.'

We gazed at these incredible specimens, each as thick as a muscular man's arm, until it got dark, then continued our vigil by torchlight, leaving only when the batteries started running low – not surprisingly none of us wanted to be anywhere near these monsters in the dark.

The next day when we returned they were gone.

I have not seen a snake of that magnitude since. And probably never will. But it was heartening to know they were out there, safe, protected and breeding.

chapter nineteen

Each day I made a trip into the bush to spend time with the herd, not only to check on their habits and movements, but because it was so invigorating being out there with them. Most importantly I wanted to continue investigating some strange aspects of their communication that intrigued me. I had opened the door to a brave new world and wanted to take advantage of every minute in the bush alone with them.

I was on foot searching for elephants on a hot afternoon, when for a split second it felt as if the herd was right there, as if I had been daydreaming and walked into them. I quickly gathered myself and looked around, but surprisingly they were nowhere in sight.

A little later it happened again. It was the lightest touch and then it was gone. Again I looked around but there was still no sign of them. Something inexplicable was going on. I was surprised that in all the time I had spent with elephants I had never noticed anything like this before.

So I waited, going back to doing exactly what I had been doing before – just being part of the bush, and not expecting anything to happen. Suddenly, I got it again, a strong sense of anticipation that the herd was close by, and with that Nana emerged out of a nearby thicket followed by the others. I was gobsmacked. I had somehow picked up that they were there well before seeing them.

In time I found that this experience also manifested itself

in reverse. Sometimes while searching for them I would eventually realize that they were not in the area at all, that they were somewhere else. Not because I couldn't find them, but because the bush felt completely empty of their presence.

After a couple of weeks of practice I started getting the hang of it and, eventually, under the right circumstances, it became easier and easier to find them. Somehow I had become aware that elephants project their presence into an area around them, and that they have control over this, because when they didn't want to be found I could be almost on top of them and pick up nothing at all. A little more experimentation and research and it became clear what was happening. Much like a lion's roar at an audible level, the herd's deep rumblings, well below human hearing, were permeating the bush for miles around them, and I was somehow picking this up even though I couldn't hear it at all. They were letting everything and everyone know where they were in their own elephantine way, in their own language.

One morning while driving gingerly along a boulder-strewn track I sensed that elephants were around and then heard a distinct trumpeting. I stopped and a few minutes later it echoed again, this time considerably closer. Suddenly a breathless Mnumzane lumbered out of the woodland, stopping right in front of the Land Rover, cutting me off and staring intently at me through the windscreen. He had never come that close before.

He was absolutely calm and I sat in the vehicle, my heart beating loudly. Twenty minutes later I was much more relaxed and he was still there, browsing all around the Landy and showing no inclination to leave.

Then the radio squawked into life and he tensed at the guttural invasion of the elemental serenity. It was the office, requesting that I return to base. But as I started pulling off Mnumzane quickly moved in front of the vehicle, and without malice, deliberately blocked the way. Puzzled, I switched the Land Rover off and he nonchalantly returned to his grazing. However, as soon as I keyed the ignition he again moved into my path, relaxing only when I switched off.

It was clear that he didn't want me to leave. I rolled opened the window.

'Hello, big boy. What's up today?'

He slowly, almost hesitantly, came around to the window, standing a yard or so away, looking down at me with his wise brown eyes. He rolled his head leisurely and seemed completely content, emanating easy companionship I felt as though I was in the presence of an old friend. This was what intrigued me: the emotions that I experienced when I was with them. For it seemed to be their emotions, not mine.

They determined the emotional tone of any encounter. This is exactly what Nana had done to me in the *boma* when she decided it was time to leave. And this is what Mnumzane was doing at this very moment – passing on the sensation of being with an old friend. I recalled too the hostility in the *boma* when they first arrived. The antipathy reached out across the wires and you could feel it all around the enclosure, whether they were in sight or not.

My attention returned to Mnumzane and then it dawned that he had chosen me for company over his own kind. That was why he had trumpeted out telling me to wait as I drove past, which is why he wouldn't let me leave.

I felt absolutely humbled, the hairs on my arm stiff with goosebumps as this colossus towered above me so obviously wanting to be friends. I decided to make the most of the experience – or rather privilege – and stayed put.

He continued feeding and the nearby trees took a hammering as he moved from one to the next, snapping branches like twigs and stripping the leaves, creating a clear browse line. Every now and again he would lift his massive head

151

and unfurl his trunk at me, sniffing to make sure I was still there.

Eventually, after about another thirty minutes he turned and stepped aside to let the vehicle through.

'Thank you, Mnumzane. See you tomorrow, my friend.'

His tilted his head for a moment and then with that peculiar graceful swaying gait melted into the bush.

I drove off. When the radio barked with David asking where I was, I didn't answer. I was too awed to speak.

As I spent more time with Nana and her charges, they too started coming closer and closer until they were happy grazing near the Land Rover. I was watching them on one occasion when Nana suddenly stopped feeding and walked up to the vehicle.

I didn't move. I could sense that she was being friendly so didn't feel threatened, but I was totally unprepared for what happened next. Infinitely slowly – or so it felt – she stretched her trunk through the window to greet me. It was shockingly intimate, and although she had touched me before both in the *boma* and when she came up to the house, I believe this was the elephantine equivalent of an affectionate pat. She was letting me know that she was just fine with me being out there with them on their turf. Despite the obviously danger-ous circumstances, I had never felt more comfortable, nor more at ease.

Even Frankie was becoming more accommodating and would stand quite close to the vehicle with Mabula and Marula. The battleaxe had a soft side and once even started reaching out with her trunk, but lost her nerve and withdrew as soon as I put my hand up.

Despite the feel-good factor, I never forgot that these were wild elephants and whenever they came close I manoeuvred the Land Rover continuously to ensure I was never cut off or put in a situation where I felt trapped or uncomfortable.

These encounters gradually became more and more spontaneous and as the months went by I started getting individual greetings from the rest of the herd. They didn't go as far as putting their trunks in the car as Nana did, but they would come right up and lift them as if waving. What they were doing, of course, was smelling me. I seemed to have been accepted as an honorary member of the group.

But in the process the Land Rover was taking a hell of a beating. Elephants are extremely tactile, always touching, pushing and brushing against each other, and when these hefty jumbos bumped the vehicle, which they did all the time, they left crater-sized dents. The Landy eventually looked as though it had been in a particularly eventful NASCAR race. It attracted a lot of attention on my rare town trips and was quickly named 'the elephant car'.

The herd also loved to play with anything that protruded on the vehicle. My side-view mirrors were long gone, yanked off as if they were made of paper. Both radio aerials went the same way and I had to have screw-ons fitted, which I could remove before venturing out to meet the herd. The windscreen wipers were stripped off so often that I gave up replacing them, just driving with my head out of the window if it rained. And of course anything left in the back was carted off into the bush, including a spare wheel that we never recovered.

For some reason they found the texture of metal fascinating and would spend hours feeling it. They loved the heat pinging off the engine, especially if the weather was cold, and would rest their trunks on the hood for long periods. In summer when the hood was searing hot they would lay their trunks down on it and then quickly yank them off, only – inexplicably – to scorch themselves again a few minutes later.

Nana and Frankie, who had both been impregnated before arriving at Thula Thula, were coming to the end of their term and I kept a special eye on them. Elephants have a gestation period of twenty-two months, which meant that, amazingly, they had gone through two dartings and captures, and had been on the run while pregnant without adverse effect.

Every week or two they came up to the house, so we eventually strung an electric wire around Françoise's garden otherwise they would have trampled it flat and gobbled up the shrubbery. But even that didn't deter them from visiting; they would stand patiently at the wire until I came down and said hello.

One week I went to Durban on business and on my return was surprised to see all seven elephants outside the house, waiting expectantly as if part of a reception committee. I put it down to coincidence. But it happened again after the next trip, and the next. It soon became obvious that somehow they knew exactly when I was away and when I was coming back.

Then it got ... well, spooky. I was at the airport in Johannesburg and missed my flight home. Back at Thula Thula, 400 miles away, the herd was on their way up to the house when, as I was later told, they suddenly halted, turned around and retreated into the bush. We later worked out that this happened at exactly the same time as I missed my flight.

The next day they were back at the house as I arrived.

I soon accepted that there was something extremely unusual about all this; something that transcended the limited realm of my understanding. What has been scientifically proven is elephants' incredible communication ability. As I had learned, elephants transmit infrasound vibrations through unique stomach rumblings that can be received over vast distances. These ultra-low frequencies, which cannot be detected by the human ear, oscillate at similar wavelengths to those transmitted by whales; vibrations that some believe quaver across the globe.

But even if those wavelengths only vibrate for hundreds of square miles, which is now generally accepted in the scientific community, it still means elephants are potentially in contact with each other across the African continent. One herd speaks with a neighbouring herd, which in turn connects with another until you have conduits covering their entire habitat, just as you or I would have a long-distance telephone call.

When scientist Katy Payne, of the Elephant Listening Project at Cornell University, discovered these elephant sound waves it was a startling breakthrough, one which would change our entire concept of elephant behaviour. There is a concrete link between advanced congenital intelligence and long-distance communication. For example, a frog's communication skills consist solely of primal mating croaks as its pond constitutes its entire universe. It has no need to expand further.

But elephants are communicating across vast distances, which shows that these giants of the wilderness are far more developed than we ever believed. They possess a vastly greater intellect than previously thought.

If you doubt this, consider the following: would elephants have evolved such incredible communication abilities just to transmit a series of meaningless rumbles and grunts? Of course not. Evolution is ruthless; anything not essential to survival withers on the gene-pool vine. Thus it is only reasonable to postulate that elephants are using these advanced long-distance frequencies for a specific purpose – to communicate coherently, one to another and herd to herd.

So are they are telling each other about what is happening to their world and what we as humans are doing to them? Given their intelligence there is no doubt in my mind that this is exactly what is happening.

chapter twenty

Even though the Ovambos were long gone, poaching continued sporadically and while we tried our best to stamp it out, losing the odd impala on a game reserve whilst galling, was tantamount to shoplifting from a department store. But suddenly the situation changed. The Buchanana police station commander called me in and said he had information that rhino and ivory poachers were in the area. As any game ranger knows, these thugs were in a different league altogether: highly organized, heavily armed professionals who wouldn't hesitate to kill anyone who got in their way. They knew what they were doing, as we soon found out.

We didn't even hear the shot. It was fired from a .458 calibre rifle on the far side of the reserve, quiet and lethal. We only discovered the victim days later when out on patrol I noticed scores of white-backed vultures circling down in an aerial funnel.

Something had died. Something big and we needed to get there fast to find out what it was. However, the corpse was in dense thornveld, far off any track, and by the time we had hiked there we were scratched, tired and greasy with sweat.

Hyenas had already made gaping red inroads into the carcass, opening up the armour-plated skin for the vultures which swarmed over the rank grey cadaver. There must have been a hundred of them squawking, flapping and fighting to tear at the carrion.

Those that had fought themselves into prime positions were stretching their elongated necks deep into the festering intestines, gorging themselves. Moving about on the edge of the melee were two black-backed jackals darting in and out between the huge birds and snatching at the meat. Judging by the state of decomposition the mound of putrefying flesh seemed about three days old.

It was a southern white rhino female, her gore-congealed snout grotesquely crumpled as both horns had been cleanly severed – probably with a chainsaw. Even though she had only been with us for less than a year, I knew her well, always stopping at a safe distance and 'chatting' to her whenever I saw her. She was the one we had distracted Mnumzane from with the horse feed, the day rhinos were first introduced on Thula Thula. My distress was compounded by the evidence that she was pregnant, the remains of the foetus scattered amongst the disgorged entrails.

This was the work of expert poachers. They must have been hiding inside the reserve for days watching the rhino's movements and ours and meticulously planning the murder of this magnificent animal. Nature had lost a prime breeding female and we would feel the loss keenly. We only had four rhinos so it was not only a financial setback, it was even more of a blow to our pride. We had been out-manoeuvred and that really hurt.

But we knew the poachers were still out there somewhere and would come back. Everyone was itching to have a go at them. We wanted justice – not just for the poor rhino, whose horns would be smuggled to the Orient to satisfy the nonsensical belief that it harboured aphrodisiacal qualities, but for all the animals they had slaughtered.

It was early evening a week later when we heard a muted rifle crack and saw spotlights periodically blinking far out in the reserve. This was the mistake we had been waiting for. Within minutes we were armed and ready for hot pursuit. We now only tracked on foot as the headlights and diesel-growl of a Land Rover were a dead giveaway, providing poachers with plenty of time to melt into the bush. It's a hard slog; done almost at a jog following the brief flashes of torches that the poachers flicked on and off to get their bearings.

Conversely, this meant we couldn't risk giving away our position using flashlights ourselves. However, our trump card was that we knew the shortcuts and could find our way through the bush far better than them. It was pitch-black and the biggest danger, of course, was stumbling blindly into the elephants, or another rhino. I didn't even want to think about that.

A shootout with poachers is called a 'contact', copying military jargon, and it can be as hairy as a war zone. Everybody is armed, it's dark and both sides are overdosing on adrenalin. Our guards usually work in teams of two: one toting a .303 rifle and the other a pump-action shotgun loaded with heavy SG ball-bearing shot. I prefer a shotgun, as it's more accurate at close quarters. At night it's always close quarters.

However, this time I had my son Dylan and four men – including Bheki and Ngwenya – with me and silently we approached, eyes straining to pick up the glimmer of a torch. We were almost at the boundary and closing in fast when I felt something brush against my leg. I nearly jumped out of my skin. Somehow suppressing a yell I looked down and there in the dark was Max, his tail wagging madly. He had somehow got out and followed our trail; it was another adventure he was determined to participate in.

I obviously didn't want him with us but it was too late, so I ordered him to heel and he dutifully fell in behind me.

He was small enough not to be a target, I justified to myself, and may even be able to help.

Then we heard a suppressed cough, and a torch flickered briefly up and down the fence, searching for the hole they had earlier cut. We had them. They were coming along the fence in our direction.

I nodded at Bheki who touched two of the others, whispering to one to circle around to the fence behind the poachers and the other to go up to the fence in front of them to cut off their escape routes. Bheki, Dylan and I moved over and took cover behind some termite mounds. The trap was set.

Then I heard the soft scratch of Bheki's safety catch being clicked off. We all did the same and waited. Tension was building, and the adrenalin-driven anticipation that every soldier in every war has felt in the seconds before battle, pervaded my senses.

The poachers moved silently alongside the fence, flashing their torches on and off as they looked for their exit until they were only thirty yards or so away.

Bheki reached over, touched my arm and nodded. We both leapt up, switching on our spotlights and shouting at them to lay down their weapons.

The megawatt beam illuminated at least eight men all carrying rifles. These were the professionals all right.

Then all hell broke loose as the startled poachers opened fire, most shooting wildly from the hip in their haste.

Bheki and I flicked off our lights as we dived for cover. I landed in some thorny scrub at the base of the termite mound, trigger finger twitching but I dared not shoot as they would see the muzzle-flash and target me. Impossibly I felt a wet lick on my face. Max, concerned as to why I was on the ground was checking on me. I grabbed him and held him down.

Ngwenya and the other ranger on the fence line had also

opened fire and the gunmen knew they were well and truly cut off.

It was now a stand-off, both sides waiting for the other to fire first to give away their positions. They were trapped at the electric fence and although they outnumbered us almost two to one, they couldn't know that yet as they had been blinded by the brief burst of flashlight.

I sensed Bheki a few yards to my right, an excellent man to have with you in a firefight: tough, loyal and ruthless. We had been in this situation before and I knew he was waiting for the exact moment as I was. The waiting would soon get to them and they would decide to run for it, firing wildly to deter pursuit. Then we could target them.

The black silence was stiflingly claustrophobic. Unbearable – but I knew it would be even more so for them.

Suddenly a fusillade of lead cracked and twanged above our heads and we instantly fired back. There were so many muzzle-flashes that you couldn't tell who was who.

Then silence again.

I was sure we had got at least a couple of them. Shotguns at that close range are extremely effective, but there were no groans of the injured or the rasping breath of someone trying to choke intense pain.

Then one of the poachers called out: 'Hey, *amafowethu*, why are you shooting your guns at your Zulu brothers? Why are you doing the white man's work?'

Silence.

'*Amafowethu* – my brothers. We do not want to kill you. Let us go and no one will get hurt.'

Silence.

'We have a big buck here. There is plenty of *inyama* for all. We will share it with you. Real bush meat – not the stuff women eat.'

Silence.

'Come and join us!' another called. 'We will feast like kings tonight.'

Bheki inched slightly towards me, whispering so low I could scarcely hear him.

'They're trying to distract us while they climb the fence. I hear the wire moving.'

Then suddenly he roared the ancient Zulu war cry, '*Uzodla iklwa lethu*' – you will eat our spears – and as he opened fire someone screamed and pandemonium erupted, guns barking like a cacophony of wild dogs.

I worked my pump-action shotgun furiously, spraying a maelstrom of SG in the direction I presumed the men would be scattering. Dylan did the same.

As suddenly as it started, the firing stopped and we reloaded. We waited for five minutes, an eternity in that deathly silence, but nothing stirred.

Then I heard a low groan – at least one man had been hit. Shotgun at the ready, I moved to the edge of the mound, stuck out my arm and flicked the spotlight switch.

In fact we had wounded three of them; one sprawled at the foot of the fence, shot through the legs by a .303 and two others badly punctured with shotgun pellets. The rest had got away, but judging by the gouts of blood dripping from where they had scrambled through the fence, there had been some serious casualties.

Thankfully, the six of us were unscathed.

Bheki shouted at the injured men, brightly illuminated in the spotlight beams, telling them that if they so much as looked at their guns he would kill them. We adjusted the beams to their eyes to blind them while he walked over and snapped on handcuffs.

Then Ngwenya came across and looked into their faces. 'These men are not from the village. They are not even Zulus,' he spat on the ground. 'They're Shangaans, bushmeat traders and ivory poachers from far away. Tonight they will have learned not to come back again.'

One of the rangers radioed for a vehicle while the rest of us patched the wounded thugs up as best we could. Max sniffed around for a bit, and then just sat and watched as if this was all in a day's work. The injured men watched him fearfully – Max can look pretty ferocious.

Soon afterwards a Land Rover arrived and we drove the injured to the Buchanana police station where an ambulance was called. I handed in the poachers' weapons to the police, a .375 and a .458 – both calibres capable of killing an elephant. There were no bullets. They had shot at us with everything they had, emptied their magazines before trying to make a run for it. Our men still had fifty rounds left. That was the difference – they had run out of ammo and we hadn't.

I was hoping also to track down the dead rhino's horns, but the police said they believed these had been shipped out of the country on a Taiwanese trawler moored in Richards Bay harbour on the same night that the animal was killed.

Fighting poachers is all about bush rumours and reputation. The poachers will always go where pickings are easiest and the syndicates, many of them employed by the same buyers, all speak to each other. The news of our victory tonight would spread like wildfire and we would be left alone for a while.

We were coming of age. We had taken on a team of hardened professionals and won.

After a peaceful few weeks in which I was able to spend wonderful sessions with the herd we got the terrible news that Phineas, the gate guard and our prime testifier against the Ovambo guards, had died. Flu and bronchitis had swept through the village and Phineas's Aids-wracked immune system simply couldn't fight the virus. As sad as this was, I also had to reflect on the fact that we had lost our key witness.

A few days later I got more bad news. The Ovambos, who had been tracked down to Durban, had abandoned their jobs in the city and for all intents and purposes disappeared from the face of the earth.

I reported all this to the prosecutor who looked over the file and said matter-of-factly, 'I'm sorry Mr Anthony but we no longer have a case.' He closed the file and shrugged.

As always with running a game reserve, one problem disappears and another crops up. Our next challenge came with an unexpected visit from our accountant. He had bad news: our money was running out fast. We had not opened the reserve to guests as we were still settling the elephant herd, and so we had been operating on capital with no income coming in.

'You need to increase your bottom line,' he said. 'Unless you do something to start making money and quickly, there's going to be a problem.'

It wasn't just cash flow. Thanks to a series of interest rate hikes, our budgets had been thrown into disarray. I scrutinized the numbers from all angles, trying to crunch them this way and that but to no avail. It seemed as though we had to throw in the towel. The thought of putting Thula Thula on the market made me feel ill.

Then Françoise spoke. 'Let's build the little luxury lodge we've always wanted. We need to attract more guests if we want to generate income – and we can't do that without building some accommodation for tourists.'

'No. That means borrowing money at these extortionate rates,' said the accountant. 'That means even more risk.'

He scratched his head, punched a whole lot of figures into his calculator and then looked up at us.

'You know, Françoise may be onto something. Building a

small "boutique" guest lodge may sound crazy in the current financial climate, but it actually makes sense. You need to start creating more revenue. And getting guests is one way to do it.'

I stared at the figures gloomily. 'Well, I think the elephants are now settled enough for us to bring back visitors. But we don't have lions yet, and tourists will want to see big cats.'

Françoise looked at me, eyes shimmering with enthusiasm. 'You know what? I will cook to replace the lions. God knows Zululand needs a place with quality food.'

She came from a family of superb cooks and had been studying on and off under top French chefs in Paris. Suddenly it all clicked into place.

'You're right,' I said, feeling as though a weight had been yanked off my shoulders. 'A small luxury lodge with a gourmet restaurant would give us an edge. It may just work.'

I gave her a hug. 'Let's do it.'

The thrill of it seized the moment and I went off and came back with a bottle of champagne that we had kept for a special occasion.

'I am afraid I can't stay,' said the accountant nervously looking at his watch. 'I must get home.'

Without a word I followed him out to his car, shot a hole in his tyre with my 9-mm pistol, and said to him, 'We will make up a bed for you. We don't have a lot of visitors and unfortunately you have an unexpected puncture. Tonight we are celebrating.'

The poor man sat down and resigned to his fate and took the beer I offered him.

'The champagne's for Françoise.'

She deserved it. Françoise took over the project and before we knew it a beautiful lodge about two miles from our house started to materialize, rustic yet opulent and set in a grove of mature tambotie, maula and acacia trees on the banks of the Nseleni River. The new Thula Thula was being born. By the end of the year, two years after moving there, our boutique lodge was up and running.

There are two types of game reserve lodges in Africa: those owned by big corporations; and those owned by conservationists who need the lodge so they can earn income to continue their conservation work. We were certainly amongst the latter. But in any event, Françoise proved to be spectacularly right and our lodge, staffed entirely with local Zulus, was soon getting regular bookings. With plenty of hard work and a bit of luck we could be all right.

chapter twenty-one

David looked worried. 'Notice how quiet everything is?'

We were sitting on the lawn watching the tree-studded hills of Thula Thula shimmering like a mirage in the early morning thermals. I took a swig of coffee. 'No. Why?'

'It's the elephants,' he said. 'They've gone to ground . . . we can't find them anywhere. If we hadn't checked the fences, I would've sworn they've broken out.'

'Nah. They're happy here. Those breakout days are gone.'

He shrugged. 'Maybe. But where are they? We're not even seeing signs of them on game drives.'

I pondered this for a while. The herd was now so calm that we had been able to take reserve guests up reasonably close, providing excited nature lovers with excellent photo opportunities.

Then an image of Nana suddenly flashed through my mind, mirroring the last time I had seen her when she had stretched out her trunk into the Landy. Her belly was as swollen as a barrel . . . of course, she must have gone deep into the bush to give birth. As we didn't know the date of conception, we weren't sure exactly when she was due.

I loaded up the Land Rover with a day's supplies and set off, searching as far into the most impenetrable parts of Thula Thula's wilderness as I could get. But there were no fresh signs of them whatsoever. I looked in all the lush feeding areas and their favourite hidey holes, but again not a trace of them. The largest land mammals had seemingly vanished into thin air.

Well, not quite. Finally, in the early afternoon I noticed some fresh tracks in an area we call Zulu Graves, a 200-year-old burial ground dating back to the days of King Shaka, founder of the Zulu nation.

'Coooome, Nana!' I called out, singing the words in the timbre they were now used to. 'Coooome, my *babbas* . . .' They always seemed to respond to the Zulu word for 'babies'. In this case, I didn't realize how prophetic my call was.

Suddenly the bush started moving, alive with the unmistakable sound of elephants, and the mixture of thrill, fear and affinity I experienced every time I was in their presence coursed through my veins. I called out again, high on anticipation.

'Coooome, *babbas*?'

Then I saw her. She was standing well off the rough dirt road, watching me but reluctant to advance further. 'That's strange,' I thought, 'she normally comes.'

She dithered for some time, neither coming forward nor retreating into the bush, almost as if she was uncertain of what to do next. Then I saw why. Standing next to her was a perfectly formed miniature elephant, about two-and-a-half feet high – perhaps a few days old. As I had suspected, she had just given birth. I was looking at the first elephant to be born in our area for over a hundred years.

Not wanting to intrude I stood there with my heart pounding, wishing I had brought a camera. Then she took a few steps forward, then a few more, and finally started walking slowly towards me with the baby tottering alongside on tiny unsteady feet, its little trunk bobbing like a piece of elastic.

She was still about thirty yards away when suddenly Frankie appeared, ears flared. It was a stark signal for me to back off. I jumped into the Land Rover, reversed to create a safe zone, then switched off and watched.

Gradually the rest of the herd emerged from the bush, eyeing me warily while milling around Nana and the baby.

I watched enthralled as the tactile creatures continually touched and caressed the little one. Even Mnumzane was partially involved, standing at the periphery as close as he was allowed, watching the goings on.

Then Nana, who had been facing me, started walking up the road. I quickly got in, slammed the vehicle into reverse and edged further back, acutely aware of the granite bush maxim that you don't go anywhere near an elephant and her baby. But she kept coming and I figured they wanted to use the road, so I reversed off at right angles into the long grass to allow them to pass well in front of me.

To my absolute surprise Nana left the road and followed me, with Frankie and the others just a few yards behind. I was no longer in her way so there was no need for this. They could have just strolled past – this was a conscious decision to come after me and my heart started thumping overtime. I quickly shoved Max off the front seat onto the floor and threw my jacket over him. 'Stay, boy,' I said as he settled down. 'We have visitors.'

Squinting hard into the sun, I tried to detect any hint of hostility . . . any edginess that I was intruding in matters maternal. There was none, not even from fierce-tempered and still-very pregnant Frankie. All around, the bush breathed peace. It was as if a group decision had been made to come to me.

Nana ambled up to my window and stood towering above the Land Rover, dominating the skyline. Below her was her baby. Incredibly she had brought her newborn to me.

I held my breath as her trunk reached into the Land Rover and touched me on the chest; the sandpapery hide somehow as sensitive as silk, then it swivelled back, dropped and touched the little one, a pachyderm introduction. I sat still, stunned by the privilege she was bestowing on me.

'You clever girl,' I said, my voice scratchy. 'What a magnificent baby.'

Her massive skull, just a few yards from mine, seemed to swell even larger with pride.

'I don't know what you call him. But he was born during the first spring showers, so I will call him Mvula.'

Mvula is the Zulu word for rain, synonymous with life for those who live with the land. She seemed to agree and the name stuck.

Then she slowly moved off, leading the herd back the way they had come. Within minutes they'd evaporated into the bush.

Two weeks later they disappeared again and I made another trek to Zulu Graves. They were there, at exactly the same place and time as before. This time it was Frankie with a perfect new baby. I went through the same backing-off procedure to ensure I didn't invade their space and eventually she too came to me, herd in tow. However, she didn't stop like Nana had, just doing a cursory walk past to show off her infant.

'Well done, my beautiful girl,' I said as she slowly came level with the window, maternal pride in full bloom. 'We will call him Ilanga – the sun.'

I shook my head in wonderment. A little over a year ago she had almost killed Françoise and me on the quad bike. Now she was proudly parading her baby. It blew my mind just thinking about it. We had travelled a long road together.

That evening they all came up to the house. Frankie's little one had walked nearly four miles through thick bush and she was only a week old. This time Frankie stood in front of the others right at the wire facing me.

'Hello, girl. Your baby is so beautiful! She really is!'

169

Frankie stood caressing her calf, visibly glowing with pride. All the while she was looking directly at me. This was the closest we had come to linking directly with each other. We both knew something precious had passed between us.

These almost inconceivable experiences had a sequel several years later when my first grandson was born and the herd came up to the house. I took baby Ethan in my arms and went as near to the patiently waiting elephants as his worried mother would allow. They were only a few yards away. Their trunks went straight up and they all edged closer, intensely focused on the little bundle in my arms, smelling the air to get the scent and rumbling their stomachs excitedly.

I was repaying the compliment to them, introducing them, trusting them with my baby as they had with theirs.

A few days after Ilanga's birth a message arrived from the principal chief in the area saying he wanted to see me and I drove out to his kraal – homestead – in the country. As was customary, I called out my name and waited at the rustic gate next to the cattle enclosure to be invited in.

Nkosi Nkanyiso Biyela was the essential cog in the Royal Zulu project to involve tribes in conservation, and he and I had become good friends. Descended from Zulu royalty, he conducted himself as an aristocrat and with his beard, handsome wide features and regal pose, looked remarkably like King Goodwill Zwelethini, the reigning monarch of the 10-million-strong Zulu people, to whom he was related.

I was then shown to the *isishayamteto*, the large thatched hut reserved for important matters. Some freshly brewed Zulu beer was placed on the floor and after tasting it himself, his aide brought the beer to me for a sip straight from the traditional calabash. This drinking bowl was then passed to the other two aides who did likewise. Zulu beer is a wholesome, low-alcohol drink brewed from maize meal and sorghum. While the yeasty ripeness smells like cheesy feet and is guaranteed to turn up a tourist's nose, it's a taste I acquired years ago and this was a particularly good brew. I asked the *Nkosi* to pass my compliments to his wife, the brewmaster.

'Thank you for coming,' he smiled, accentuating the wrinkles on his good-humoured face. 'I want you to attend the tribal court and speak about our game-reserve project. My people must hear directly from you on the matter.'

We left the hut and walked across to the courtroom where the *Nkosi* held council and tried cases once a week.

There were perhaps a hundred people squashed inside the hall, many in traditional clothes with others standing outside. I was shown to a chair in the front row while the chief went to the podium.

He introduced me and I stood to speak.

The project was sensitive, principally because it involved both actual and potential cattle land. I had already spent the better part of two years holding meetings and workshops throughout the area, explaining the workings of conservation and outlining the benefits that eco-tourism would bring to communities in this desperately deprived area.

It was a tough task. Over the last month I had been taking tribal leaders into the Umfolozi reserve and was shocked to discover that most of them had never seen a zebra or giraffe – or much of the other indigenous wildlife so iconic of the continent. This was Africa, their birthright. They lived on the borders of an internationally acclaimed game reserve, yet as a direct result of apartheid they had never been inside. Historically they considered game reserves to be 'white concepts, mere excuses to seize their land', and as they had never been included by the previous government, even with the abolishment of apartheid this was not going to change overnight. They had absolutely no idea what conservation was about, or even why the reserve was there. Worst of all, a large chunk of it was traditional tribal territory that had been unilaterally annexed and this resentment had festered over the generations. It was historically their land and it had been wrested from them with no consultation whatsoever. No wonder that they were at best ambivalent about what they perceived to be the 'white man's' concept of conservation.

Looking at the sea of faces before me in the room, hardy sons and daughters of the soil, I talked about the huge potential the Royal Zulu promised in improving their lives. I spoke of job opportunities, skills training, wealth creation, and education – all which would spring from the project. I appealed to them to all support the project, not only for themselves, but for the sake of their children – and, most importantly, for the sake of the earth, the mother of us all.

But old habits die hard; old resentments burn long. As soon as I finished speaking, cattle owners who coveted the land for their herds sprang to their feet, giving impassioned speeches about the Zulu heritage of keeping cattle. However, there was plenty of land for all. It was all about tradition, and the conservative cattle owners did not like the idea of change. In rural Zululand cattle are a primary form of currency and they didn't want the status quo to alter, whatever the reasons or benefits.

'How will you pay your *lobola*, your dowry, if there are no cattle? We will have no wives!' one thundered to sustained applause.

'And what about sacrificing cows to the ancestors? Are we now going to use bush pigs?' shouted another to derisive laughter.

The discussion went on in the same vein for the next couple of hours until the *Nkosi* finally put up his hand to end it. Despite obvious opposition, I was not displeased with the outcome of the meeting. I had achieved an important goal. Everybody now knew I had been invited by the *Nkosi* and that he would not have brought me if he was against the project.

But if I was aware of that, so were the cattle owners. The significance of the *Nkosi*'s summons would not be lost on them and I sensed bitter clashes ahead.

I then decided to stay and watch the *Nkosi*, renowned for his biblical Solomon-style wisdom, preside over a trial of one of his subjects who had stabbed another during an argument.

Both parties gave their version of events and when they were finished the *Nkosi* delivered his verdict. The stabber was sentenced to a substantial fine, albeit in keeping with his modest income, as well as eight lashes. Judging by the murmurs of the crowd, this was considered a fair outcome.

Then everything went into overdrive. Chairs were scattered, as the court orderlies stepped forward, grabbed the poor man, stripped off his shirt and forced him onto his stomach in the middle of the room. They sat, one on each arm to ensure he couldn't move, as out of a side door emerged a huge man carrying a sjambok, a wicked six-foot-long whip made of twined hippo hide. Without any ceremony he ran up to the prostrate criminal and brought the whip whistling down on his bare back with as much force as he could muster. The violence of the strike shocked me and I waited for the man to scream. He stayed silent.

Eight lashes later and the skin on the man's back was a pulped bloody mess and he was pulled to his feet and led groggily out of the door. Yet still he did not utter a sound.

'He didn't cry out once,' I said to the aide next to me. 'I'm impressed.'

'He must not,' he replied. 'A criminal gets an extra two lashes every time he squeals.'

Tough justice indeed, but it was justice quickly dispensed in keeping with Zulu traditions and one thing was certain: the knifeman wasn't going to stab anyone else in a hurry.

A few months later I was privy to another incident of brutal justice, which gave a jolting reminder that just below the thin skin of civilization lay much of what is wrong with this exotically beautiful country.

I was driving in the deep rural areas surrounding Thula Thula when I noticed a vocal group of men from a neighbouring tribe walking down the road dragging something. At first I thought it was an animal, perhaps an impala they had shot, but to my surprise it was a man who had been so severely assaulted that he couldn't stand. As I pulled up they dropped the semi-conscious body onto the ground like a rag doll.

'*Sawubona*, Mkhulu,' said one who recognized me.

'What's happening?' I asked, getting out of the Land Rover, shotgun in hand, horrified at the bloodied condition of their prisoner.

'This man has raped and murdered a woman. We are taking him down to the river to kill him,' one replied casually, almost in a 'why don't you join us' tone.

'Are you certain it's the right man?' I asked, trying to defuse the situation. As I spoke the crumpled victim moaned and tried to crawl away, only to be viciously kicked back by one of the group.

'It is him,' they replied. 'His house has already been burned.'

'Why don't you take him to the police? He will be severely punished by the magistrate.'

'Ha!' spat one caustically. 'The magistrate . . . he will do nothing.'

Tiring of the conversation they grabbed the beaten man and started dragging him along.

'But surely there must be another way. Is there nothing I can do?' I said, blocking their way.

As I stood before them, their mood changed in an instant. The leader of the group's eyes hardened.

'This is not your business Mkhulu. Leave us,' he said, ignoring the fact that I was carrying a shotgun. The tone of his voice was final. If I pushed more I would be transgressing the shadow line into a tribal matter, with possibly violent repercussions. I stepped aside.

As I drove off, I thought of going to the police but the nearest station was thirty miles away on a barely drivable road. I wasn't even sure they would have a vehicle to respond with. As for a search, they would never find the body and the perpetrators would have long since disappeared into the surrounding huts and hills.

Such is Africa, the flawed, beautiful, magnificent, beguiling, mystical, unique, life-changing continent . . . its seductive charm and charisma, its ancient wisdom so often stained by unfathomable spasms of blood.

That night after returning from the meeting I got further bad news. David told me he was resigning to go to England. He had met an attractive young British guest at the lodge, whom I noticed had kept extending her stay.

'It's just "khaki fever", David,' I teased, referring to the well-known attraction some female guests have for uniformed rangers. 'When you get to England, whatever you do don't take off your uniform or it will all be over.'

Nevertheless he left and it was a massive blow to us. He was an integral part of Thula Thula and had been my right-hand man and friend for so long it was like losing a son. He loved the bush so much – I just couldn't imagine him in rainy England.

The lodge had just opened and David had been a tremendous help to Françoise in getting it up and running, but she took it with her customary good humour. 'I know guests sometimes steal a towel or soap,' she said, 'but this one stole our ranger.'

Sadly we had to move on and she advertised in various wildlife publications for a new reserve manager. The first applicant phoned from Cape Town.

'I'd like to come up for the interview but the flight's expensive,' said the caller. 'So if I come all that way and spend all that money, I must get the job.'

This was not the conventional method of impressing potential employers; in fact, it bordered on impertinence. I was about to tell him to take a running jump when I paused for a moment . . . perhaps Brendan Whittington Jones, a name more suited to a firm of august lawyers than a game ranger, could afford a touch of 'unusualness'. He certainly had impressive credentials on paper. But how could I decide on his merits – or, as his phone call suggested, otherwise – without first seeing him? This really intrigued me. All my life, I have been attracted by unusual approaches.

'Do you play sport?' I asked, the question coming out of nowhere.

'Yes. Field hockey.'

I mulled this over for a second or two.

'You can start as soon as you get here.'

Field hockey is a gentleman's game. My father was an international player and for whatever reason he always said it was a sport which attracted the right sort of people. I decided to follow his advice, though probably not the way he intended it.

Brendan arrived a few days later with a battered suitcase containing his sum total of worldly goods. He was an athletically built young man with a shock of strawberry-blond hair, a slow smile and a deliciously sardonic sense of humour. He would need it to sustain him at Thula Thula.

He had a degree in zoology and wildlife management with a major in entomology and loved insects with an almost mystic passion. Through him I learned that everything in the

176

wild happened 'down there' on the ground and in water. In the mulchy stew of undergrowth and seething-yet-still ponds and rivers, the often invisible bug world is the font of any wild eco-system.

However, he also loved animals and his bright attitude and innate sense of fairness quickly won over Françoise and the staff.

It wasn't long before he had adopted an epileptic young warthog which he called Napoleon. The grandly named hog had been abandoned as an infant by his mother and we had found him wandering aimlessly on the reserve, lost and alone and easy prey for any passing leopard or hyena. The poor creature we found out later, sometimes had seizures, which is probably why it had been dumped by his mother. However, Napoleon soon regarded Brendan as his surrogate mother and even joined him in his bed at night. Max also took to Brendan immediately and tried to emulate Napoleon by slipping out of our room one night and getting into the new ranger's bed.

Going into Brendan's room the next morning was an experience. Once you had cut through the fog of sweaty bush clothes, Max's jowly head emerged from the blankets, followed by the quizzical Napoleon, then a little later bleary-eyed Brendan.

Françoise, who took to Brendan immediately, was aghast at this somewhat eccentric ménage à trois.

'How will you ever find zee wife if you sleep with zee dog and zee pig?' she asked, shaking her head.

Soon after Brendan had settled in I received a surprise call from David. He had just landed in Johannesburg.

'It didn't go well in England, boss. I've just got back to Johannesburg. I'm stuck in a traffic jam and I hate it. Can I have my job back?'

'But I've just employed someone else.'

'I don't care. You don't have to pay me, I'm coming

anyway. I'll be there tonight,' he said, putting down the phone before I could reply.

He certainly meant it. The summer rains had fallen in torrents over Zululand and the Ntambanana River had burst its banks, cutting off Thula Thula from Empangeni. The roads were quagmires and virtually impassable.

David's father drove him as far as he could, just past the Heatonville village where the Ntambanana was in full spate and completely swamping the concrete bridge. No problem for David; he somehow forged the raging river in the dark on foot and then hiked a sodden twelve miles until he reached Thula Thula.

He arrived sopping wet and covered in mud but ecstatically happy to be back in the bush. Brendan took one look at this drenched, muscular apparition and then shook his head, laughing.

'OK. I'm handling the scientific side and will concentrate on the environmental studies – which you really need to get done. He could have his old job back.'

They complimented each other extremely well and in time they became the closest of friends, so much so that the staff nicknamed them 'Bravid the clone ranger'.

chapter twenty-two

Late winter, with its mantle of copper, chocolate and straw, had cloaked the land. The bush had shed its dense summer foliage and game viewing had soared magnificently for the increasing number of guests who were discovering Thula Thula.

'We must put in burns this year,' I said to David and Brendan, 'we have to open up some of the thicker areas.'

All game reserves burn sections of the land in late winter, primarily because the act-of-God fires that have raged through the countryside since time immemorial are nowadays always extinguished as soon as they take hold. A wilderness needs fire for a variety of reasons, not least to regenerate itself. Dead growth is burnt off and the land is reborn as green shoots take root among the fertile ashes.

We always burned our lands late in winter as all smaller life forms were hibernating and thus safe underground. Burns are done in selected blocks usually defined by roads and rivers which act as natural firebreaks. They are called controlled burns, which is a misnomer for I've yet to see a fire that could safely be labelled 'controlled'. Fires have an inconvenient habit of jumping breaks and wind shifts can switch their direction in an eye-blink. Thus even 'controlled' burns often end up with a lot of people chasing one crisis after another.

Malicious fires – arson, in other words – are even worse

because by the time you reach them they are already at inferno stage.

David and Brendan nodded at my instruction. 'When do you want to burn?' asked Brendan, eyeing the skies. It was vital to pick the weather just right, with a mild wind blowing in the direction you want your fire to run.

'Let's select the areas, and if the wind is right do it the day after tomorrow.'

Within hours, the decision was wrested from our hands.

'Fire!' shouted David into the radio with binoculars fixed on the highest hill on the reserve. 'Fire behind Johnny's Lookout! Code Red! Code Red!'

Even with the naked eye I could see the first wisps of smoke streaking crazily into the sky.

Every able-bodied man on the reserve responds immediately to a Code Red: rangers, guards and work teams instantly stop what they are doing and rush to the main house as fast as they can. Those close by sprint; those far off leap into the nearest truck.

Within minutes we had about fifteen men assembled and David and Brendan gave a quick briefing and organized them into teams. They clambered onto the vehicles grabbing as many bottles of drinking water as they could carry. They knew from experience it was going to be a hard, thirsty day.

David was in the first truck and braked briefly to pick me up. 'This was started on purpose,' he said as I got in. 'Three men were seen running away. I've sent Bheki and Ngwenya to the other side of the reserve to check for poachers in case it's a diversion.'

Arson was a new poaching tactic – or at least new on Thula Thula. One group had cottoned on to the idea that starting a fire on the far side of the reserve would suck up all our manpower and thus they could hunt on the other side at will. It had worked, but only once, as we soon wised up. Bheki and Ngwenya were experienced veterans and would be more than a match for any thugs they came up against.

It was a mild day and as we already had plenty of firebreaks set up in preparation for the controlled back-burns to arrest the fire, I wasn't overly concerned and expected we should wrap this one up quickly. Our teams split up with Brendan's group driving a half a mile or so in front of the blaze, ready to set the first back-burn where fires are lit across the front of the approaching fire in order to destroy anything inflammable in its path. It's called back-burning as the fire is set to burn backwards into the wind, towards the main fire coming at it.

'OK, everybody is in place,' barked David into the radio. 'Go!'

Brendan's team immediately lit clumps of grass and started dragging the back-burn along the edge of the road, spreading it out wide in front of the fast-advancing flames.

We couldn't have timed it worse. Ten minutes later the wind switched and a squall came screaming out of nowhere, sweeping the back-burn away from us to join the main fire already flaring rapidly across the veldt. Instead of one fire to fight, we now had two. From a routine drill, we now were in big trouble.

Four hot, sooty hours later our water was finished, our back-burns were failing, and the flaming monster was ripping through the bush completely out of control. Watching it effortlessly jump block after block I realized with horror that we were now fighting for the life of Thula Thula itself.

All animals understand fire well. Their survival synapses instinctively know that fire is a friend as well as a foe as it re-energizes the bush. Provided they are not trapped, which can cause blind panic, they watch developments carefully and will either cross a river or backtrack behind the blaze and wait on the previously scorched patches where they know they're safe.

181

This time the fire was a formidable foe with the intense heat popping burning clods of grass high into the sky. The Zulus call them *izinyoni*, bird nests, and these sizzling ashes caught in the super-heated vortexes were the dreaded harbingers of the main fire, sparking as they blew ahead and settled in tinder grass, starting new burns every few minutes.

Then incredibly the blaze jumped the river as nimbly as a galloping Derby contender. I stared from my vantage point with mounting despair. We weren't going to make it. This was too big even for professional firemen. With the howling gale rendering the back-burns totally useless, my men armed only with buckets, hand-pumps and fire-beaters had precious little chance of winning the day.

The inferno then leapt across another break and the chaotic gusts swirling around the hill ripped into it, driving massive black-orange flames up the slope below me.

I froze, despite the intense heat. There was a crew directly in the blaze's path that would be frazzled in seconds if we didn't get them out. I hurriedly sent two rangers into the thick smoke to shout to the men to run for their lives.

Twenty minutes later as the ten-foot wall of flames roared ever closer the two rangers returned – but without the crew they went to find.

'What happened?' I shouted as they came out of the bush, gagging from the smoke.

'They're not there. We couldn't see them!' one yelled back.

My mind raced. Not only was the reserve under threat, but we were on the brink of losing people as well. There was no way the men at the bottom of the hill could survive two crackling walls of fire clashing together on top of them.

There was nothing we could do. Brendan had the only water tanker with him. And he was miles away trying to light the rearguard of back-burns, our last flimsy glimmer of hope in stemming the runaway flank that threatened to torch the rest of the reserve, including the lodge and our homes.

Without a word David sprang into the Land Rover, flicked the headlights on and drove as fast as he could into the smoke and flames. All I could hear was the vehicle's horn blaring as he drove to let the trapped men know where he was. No one could see anything in the billowing soot.

Ten minutes later he broke back through the smoke. There, sitting on the back of the vehicle, was the missing fire crew. Biyela, our gardener, was calmly smoking a cigarette.

As he jumped off the truck I shouted to him: 'Did you get a light for your *bhema* in there?'

He looked at his cigarette. '*Hau!*' he laughed with delight.

We desperately piled onto the Land Rover and David sped off, just yards in front of the flames. There was only one road out of the area, and as long as David kept his foot to the floor, perhaps we could make it.

As we raced for our lives I scoured the bush below us looking for any sign of the elephants. The fire could not have come at a worse time for Nana and Frankie with their two new babies. I was terrified they would be trapped and as the situation worsened I could think of little else.

The road took us parallel to the advancing fire which was now a mile wide, flaring and roaring and leaping on our right, drowning us in toxic fumes and swirling tendrils of smouldering ash.

'The elephants came through here!' shouted David above the crackling bellow of the flames. He pointed to the ground. 'Those tracks are as fresh as hell.'

I motioned for David to stop and quickly got out and felt the dung between thumb and forefinger. It was slimy and wet, sure evidence that they were nearby.

'They stopped here!' I shouted back. 'Probably to rest the babies, but more so I think to let Nana assess the situation. I think she is trying to get to Croc Pools.'

I looked back at the barricade of flame and felt my stomach tighten. Trees were being incinerated whole without pause. Nothing in its path could possibly survive.

'God, please make it, Nana,' I said under my breath as I got back into the vehicle.

David gunned the engine and we bounced down the track as fast as we could. Suddenly he swerved wildly as a female nyala bolted out of the bush right in front of us. The poor creature, panicked out of her mind and blinded by a deluge of smoke and ash, ran straight into a tree and careered off into another. With a sickening crack that we could hear above the inferno, her leg snapped. Petrified and unable to get up, she lay there staring with stricken eyes as we drove past.

I grabbed the rifle off the seat next to me and David, seeing what had to be done braked hard in a cloud of dust, jerking the men at the back off-balance and then reversed.

'Boss!' he shouted as I got out. 'Quickly! Quickly or we're not going to make it ourselves.'

I lifted the Lee–Enfield, leaned on the open door, and two rapid shots later the poor creature was out of its pain and we were again hurtling through the bush in a race with the devil; to crest the hill and then turn onto another track that would at least take us out of the path of the raging monster. We didn't even have time to load up the dead buck.

David made the top with the flames minutes behind and the men in the back cheered wildly. But I feared their jubilation was premature. The awful reality was that we were still trapped. There was no road out; the towers of flames were rampant on both sides, about to engulf us within minutes and for the first time I felt panic slithering into my thoughts.

'Where to?' yelled David. 'Hurry or else we've had it!'

Then in a flash I realized what we had to do. Nana had shown the way.

Me and Françoise with our little princess, Bijou, at the Lodge.

Max, my Staffordshire bull terrier when he was young.

A helicopter returns after hours of fruitless searching for the runaway herd. The elephants had escaped from Thula Thula shortly after arriving from a different reserve.

Me with Baby Thula outside the room she lived in following her rescue.

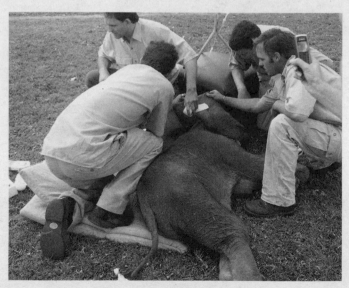

Baby Thula being put on a drip shortly after her rescue.

Mnumzane and friend
moving past the lodge.

Nkosi [Chief] Pniwayinkosi Chakide
Biyela in full traditional regalia.

The very first game drive with foreign guests in 2000.

The herd bathing in the Gwala Gwala Dam.

Me with Vusi, Bheki (rear) and Ngwenya under a beautiful Zululand sky.

Rangers on a bushwalk – a favourite with visitors.

Frankie, with then-baby Ilanga, leading a young Mabula and Marula.

Nana being overly friendly and nearly pushing me over with her trunk.
Her new baby, Mnumzane's son, is at her side.

My beautiful big boy Mnumzane arriving for a bush chat.
Look at the size of him: I am 6 ft 3 ins and only come up to his tusks!

Mabula standing in front of me
pondering his next move.

Mvula (left) and Mandla growing up.

'Croc Pools!' I shouted back. 'If Nana thinks it's safe enough for the herd it'll be safe enough for us.'

Somehow amid the acrid blinding smoke David found the turn-off and ten bumpy minutes later we rounded the corner at the pools just as Nana was shepherding the last of her charges into deeper water. She and Frankie were standing at the edge of the dam in the shallows with babies Mvula and Ilanga, making sure the others were safe.

Nana looked up at us, and only then did I understand why they were there. It was not just because of the water; the veldt around every game reserve dam is always over-grazed and consequently there was little fuel for the fire to consume in a thirty yard radius.

'Clever, clever girl,' I thought. In our haste even we hadn't thought of Croc Pools, let alone the natural safety barrier.

We drove to the opposite side, manoeuvred the Land Rover into a bare spot as close to the Pools as we could, splashed water over it to cool it down and then waded knee-deep into the pool. The coolness and relief was exquisite.

There is a good reason why this particular stretch is called Croc Pools and I looked around hurriedly. There in the reed beds to our left were two huge crocodiles lying still in the shallows, watching through hooded reptilian eyes. Fortunately because of the drama of the fire their major concern was survival, the last thing on their minds was lunch. We would be fine where we were. For good measure, though, I reached down and grabbed Max's collar tightly. He was filthy with ash so I quickly washed him, which would also protect him against the approaching fireball.

And there we were, a herd of elephants, two huge croco-diles, a dog and a bedraggled sweaty group of men united by the most basic instinct of all – survival.

As Hades itself approached we watched yellow-billed kites soaring and swooping down on seared insects fleeing the flames, while flocks of glossy starlings darted in and out of the smoke doing the same. Two large monitor lizards came hurtling out of the bush and splashed headlong into the water next to us. Then a herd of zebra came galloping out of the fumes and stopped. The stallion sniffed the air before changing direction and speeding off with his family. They knew exactly where they were going – they would outpace the fire.

The thick smoke poured from the burning bush over us, obliterating the sun and we stood together in the surreal murk of midday twilight, broken only by the flaming orange and red of the biggest inferno I have ever seen.

Then it was on us, the heat sizzling and hissing across the water. Yet in that intense theatre I became aware of something transcending the din and fury and chaos. I felt Nana's stomach rumblings roll across the water, a dominating, calming presence. There she stood, towering over the dam, shielding the babies with her body and spraying water over herself. I found myself doing the same, scooping water over my head as if I had joined the herd.

And then the sizzling abyss swept past and the sun broke bleakly through the murk and mayhem. We stared out at the blackened apocalyptic landscape, gulping air into smoke-seared lungs. We had made it, thanks to Nana. She had saved us all. How she drew us to Croc Pools was something I was to gain more insight into later.

Suddenly the radio came alive. 'David, David, David! Come in! Where the hell are you guys? I've got big problems here, I need men fast.'

It was Brendan.

'We're on our way!' yelled David as we scrambled for the Land Rover. 'Hold on for fifteen minutes. We'll be there.'

'The fire's jumped our boundary,' shouted a soot-blackened Brendan as we arrived. 'It's gone over into the next farm trapping a troop of baboons. They came out of the bush screaming, burning alive. It was terrible. At least six or seven are dead.'

He wiped a grimy paw over his bloodshot eyes. 'It's those bloody chromolaena weeds. They burn so hot nothing can stop them and the farm next to us had hundreds of acres of that alien rubbish growing thick and wild on their land between us and their sugar cane. The fire's right in the middle of the cane now. No doubt they'll blame us for it.' *Chromolaena odorata* is particularly bad in a fire as it has a high oil content and as each bush takes light it burns in a bright fireball destroying trees and bushes close by.

The ever-shifting gusts at last switched favourably and using that to our advantage Brendan got a last gasp back-burn going and I watched, throat in mouth, as his little fires gobbled up the bush in front of the flaring wall, starving the advancing blaze.

Now we were able to respond to the incessant calls for help on the other side of the reserve where all the remaining staff had gathered in a last-ditch Alamo-style stand to protect the lodge and houses.

Exhausted to our bones, there we confronted another wall of fire, and it was then I saw the most amazing sight. Driving along a remote road going straight towards the oncoming fire was a car with a family inside. They were completely lost. The driver pulled up and obviously unaware of the terrible danger they were in started jabbering away in Italian.

'You are the luckiest man alive,' I said laughing at the incongruity of the situation. 'I will give you a tracker to take you out.'

As they left, the inferno thundered over the hill and then just as it seemed the thatched lodge and our homes were about to be atomized, a phalanx of 4x4s loaded with firefighting equipment came revving though the smoke down the road. Every nearby farmer had heeded our emergency calls and now a wall of water confronted the wall of flames. The cavalry had truly arrived.

Thirty minutes later the seemingly unstoppable holocaust had collapsed. It was now just a mopping-up operation. But in its wake, it had destroyed more than a third of the reserve.

Fortunately the change of wind, which so nearly wiped us out, also brought the first pre-spring showers. That night a torrent of fresh rain sluiced clean the charred black earth.

The next morning, elephant, rhino, zebra, impala and other animals were out on the burned areas, eating fresh ash as they always do after a fire, absorbing the salts and minerals their bodies craved.

Two weeks later the areas that had been so apocalyptically torched were emerald green. Thanks – unwittingly – to the poachers, the bush clearing was done perfectly and we now had thousands of new acres of virgin savannah.

None of us, however, forgot that we had almost lost Thula Thula.

Or that we had an elephant to thank for our lives.

chapter twenty-three

Most of my interactions with the herd had been from a Land Rover. This was deliberate as I wanted them to get used to vehicles.

It worked; our guests had great safaris and photo-opportunities as Nana and her family acted as wild elephants do, oblivious of the Land Rovers, provided of course the rangers kept a reasonable distance and respected their privacy.

But now I wanted to do it on foot, not only as I planned to introduce walking safaris, but I wanted the herd to get generally acclimatized to humans in the bush, or else labourers and rangers would always be at risk.

Taking Max with me I set out to find them for my first experiment. The herd was in an open area, grazing and browsing on the plentiful summer offerings. Nearby there were big trees for me to climb, a somewhat crucial consideration if something went wrong and I had to run for it.

Perfect! I pulled over next to a spreading marula and got out, leaving the Landy's door open for hasty access if necessary. It's vastly different communicating with elephants out in the open on foot compared with doing so from vehicles. If you step away from a vehicle with elephants close by, you wake up quickly.

Purposely going upwind so they could get my scent, I zigzagged toward the herd, ambling along as if on a Sunday stroll, Max by my side. Everything was going well until I was about thirty yards away and Frankie's trunk swivelled near the ground as she got my scent. I immediately stopped as she peered myopically at Max and me, but after a short while she ignored us and continued feasting. So far so good, and I continued my erratic approach in their general direction.

Just five paces closer and Frankie suddenly lifted her head sharply and aggressively spread her ears.

Whoa! I stopped but this time she continued glaring at me until I backed off for five or six paces. That seemed to make her happy and she went back to grazing.

I repeated the process several times over the next hour, a few paces in and then out and always got the same reaction. Studiously ignored, then angrily confronted. That's interesting, I thought, she has created a boundary: outside I am welcome, inside she gets tetchy.

After checking the distance and making sure I could reach the Land Rover at a run if things went awry, I pushed through the imaginary boundary and walked closer in.

That did it! She swung around, took three aggressive steps towards me with trunk held high and I backed off – pronto.

I then drove to the other side of the spread-out herd, got out and repeated the process with Nana. The same thing happened, except that Nana would let me get much closer than Frankie did, and her reactions were petulant rather than aggressive.

Over the next weeks, through trial and error I learned that the herd set a very real albeit invisible boundary inside of which nothing – well, no human anyway – could enter. I also found that individual elephants did the same thing when straying from the herd. The boundaries were flexible but generally the adult's 'space' had a much smaller perimeter than the youngsters'. However, it was trial and error, and you had to be able to gauge it by judging the elephant's demeanour and every elephant's space was different and could be different on different days.

By repeating the exercise in the neighbouring Umfolozi reserve I discovered that generally a bull would tolerate closer intrusions than females. The reason was simple – big bulls are extremely confident of their ability to defend themselves and allow you to get closer. The smaller the elephant, the less confident they are and the wider the space they demanded. A mother and newborn baby away from a herd had the widest.

I had long noticed a similar phenomenon with other animals. A 'fright–flight' distance it is called, but with elephants it was more like an 'attention–attack' boundary.

So far so good, but to have walking safaris on Thula Thula I needed a completely settled herd otherwise the risk was not worth it. More research was needed so I did my experiment again, but this time with Vusi, a well-built, fleet-footed young ranger who bravely volunteered to be the guinea pig. All he had to do was repeat my earlier procedure of slowly walking around the herd as I watched their reactions. I dropped him off, estimated the herd's safety boundary, told him where it was, and then told him to walk.

Big mistake. Thankfully Vusi hadn't gone too far when Frankie bristled on full alert and the startled ranger legged it back to the Landy quicker than Carl Lewis.

A bit more experimenting with the brave young man and it became clear that as far as the herd was concerned, the boundary with a stranger was much, much wider.

OK, so how could I get the elephants to draw the boundary in? Not only for me, but for anyone walking on the reserve. I started hanging around the edges of the safety periphery, minding my own business until they got used to me being on foot, and then I slowly tried to move a bit closer. The key to this was patience; it took endless hours of just being there. I also found that ignoring them or facing away attracted less attention.

Although tedious, this was an extremely tense procedure and I was constantly ready to dash off at a hair-trigger's notice.

Eventually I started to despair. I was making zero progress, even Mnumzane would not come closer while he was with the herd – until one day Nana ambled over in my direction to access a small tree she fancied and shrank the no-go boundary by half without even looking up at me. A little later Frankie and the others joined her.

Then it dawned. As far as the herd was concerned, the boundary was not set in stone. They will reset it – but only when they are good and ready. It has to be their decision. You can't do it. Only they can.

From this I also gleaned another important rule in associating with wild elephants and that is never to approach them directly, but rather put yourself in their vicinity and if they want to, they will come closer to you. If not, forget it: they take their imperial status most seriously.

During this time one elephant charged me repeatedly. Young Mandla, now a healthy two-and-a-half-year-old standing almost four foot. He would put his ears out and run at me for about five or six yards and then bolt back to the safety of his mum – Nana – who kept an eye on things but always ignored his 'heroic' antics. It became a great game between us and every day I would call out and talk to him as he put on his show and we would have fun, with him getting braver and braver and closer and closer. I had to be very careful with this as he was big enough to seriously hurt me but there was never anything but fun in his game.

Then one day Nana and Mvula were a little way from the herd grazing when she slowly started walking in my direction. Good God! Has she decided to come across to me? She had approached me before in my vehicle, which she knew, and at the *boma* and the house, but on those occasions I was safe. This time, unless I bolted before she got any closer, I would be stuck out in the open without any escape route whatsoever. This was an entirely different ballgame.

She lumbered on in such a friendly way that I steeled myself and decided to stay and see what happened, gambling that the rest of the elephants would stay away.

Closer and closer she came with Mvula scampering at her heels. I glanced nervously down at Max who was watching keenly, dead still. He looked back up at me and suddenly wagged his tail. He hadn't sensed anything dangerous. I hoped his judgement was on track for this was a very big elephant coming at us.

Suddenly some atavistic survival trigger, vehemently at odds with my decision to stand fast, jerked and the compulsion to flee this gargantuan alien shape exploded within me. I could scarcely breathe. It was all I could do to hold my ground. To this day I don't know how I managed not to bolt. But stay I did and then she was there, her huge form towering above me, obliterating the sky.

I think she sensed my trepidation for she purposefully stopped about five yards away and simply started grazing again, oozing tranquillity. When you are standing five yards away from a wild five-ton elephant you are acutely aware of every little thing that goes on around you, especially the elephant's emotional state.

I somehow retained enough presence of mind to reflect on the incongruity of standing out on an open plain with a matriarch and her baby – the most treacherous of all situations – but there was such an innocence about our impromptu 'get together' that it helped me maintain both my dignity and my ground.

Five minutes later she was still there and I realized we

were actually hanging out together. She was slowly moving around grazing, and I relaxed enough to notice that she had the most graceful table manners. Her trunk would search out and deftly encircle a chosen clod of grass, which she would pluck and delicately tap on her knee to dislodge soil from the roots and gently place in the side of her mouth leaving just the roots protruding. A gentle clamp of the molars and the roots would drift away while she savoured the morsel. I noticed too that she was very fussy about what she ate and the scent of each plant would be carefully sampled before being devoured.

Her browsing was no less fascinating. She would adroitly remove the leaves from a young acacia, place them in her mouth and then snap off a branch. As soon as she had finished chewing the leaves, the stem would go in one side of her mouth like a kebab and a little while later be ejected on the other, stripped white of all bark, the only part she was after.

All the while Mvula would peek at Max and me from behind his mother's tree-trunk legs, occasionally stepping out to get a better look. Max sat silently, occasionally moving a few yards to smell where Nana had been standing, but otherwise just motionless.

I was intensely focussed on this magnificent creature standing so close to me. All the while Nana kept glancing across or staring at me. Every now and then she would turn her massive body slightly towards me, or move her ears almost imperceptibly in my direction. Her occasional deep rumblings vibrated through my body.

So this was how she communicated ... with her eyes, trunk, stomach rumblings, subtle body movements, and of course her attitude. And then suddenly I got it. She was trying to get through to me – and like an idiot I hadn't been responding at all!

I looked pointedly at her and said 'Thank you', acknowledging her, testing her reaction. The alien words echoed across the silent veldt. The effect was immediate. She glanced across and held my gaze, drawing me in for several deep seconds, before returning contentedly to her grazing. It was almost as if she was saying, 'Didn't you see me, what took you so long?'

The final piece of the puzzle clicked perfectly into place. While I had been standing there like a robot, she had been prompting me to accept her presence and give some sign that I recognised her. Yet I had been as stiff and rigid as a plank. When I finally acknowledged her, just with a simple 'thank you', she instantly responded.

I had learned something of this before in dealing with some animals, but that 'Eureka' moment with Nana really drove it home to me. I had at last grasped that the essence of communicating with any animal, from a pet dog to a wild elephant, is not so much the reach as the acknowledgement. It's the acknowledgement that does it. In the animal kingdom communication is a two-way flow, just as it is everywhere else. If you are not signalling to them that their communication has arrived with you then there can be no communication. It's as simple as that.

Eye movements are perhaps the most important. A flick of the eye, a look, or the tiniest glance may seem like nothing to humans, but in the animal world it's a very big deal indeed. Attitude, facial expressions (believe me elephants can smile beautifully) and body language can also be significant.

And how do you acknowledge them. Well I found that just a look, can be enough. Staring, whilst sometimes appropriate if you have a close relationship with the animal, can be interpreted as a challenge by strangers. Just using words in the tone you would naturally use to convey your feelings can achieve a lot.

There are other factors of course. Granting respect is as

important as it is with humans. Animals have an uncanny ability to pick up on your state of mind, especially if you are antagonistic or hostile. All it takes to make progress is an open-minded attitude, and with a bit of patience and persistence it eventually clicks into place. The best part is you will recognize it when it happens. Believe me anyone can do it, and as many people already know, it is so worthwhile. There are no deep secrets, no special abilities, and definitely no psychic powers necessary.

The wrong way to go about this is to say: Well, researchers have 'proved' that animals only understand fifty words or something similarly absurd. Or that communication with other species is an illusion. Communication is not the preserve of humans; it is the one thing that is truly universal.

I looked up to see Frankie leading the bunch across. There was no way I was going to risk that sort of interaction with the entire herd. I immediately took my leave, thanking Nana and telling her I would see her again soon, humbled by the experience.

It was a superb day, a gentle breeze taking the edge off the sun and I decided to walk back to the house with Max. I gave Vusi the Landy to drive back and we backtracked along the elephant spoor. The Nseleni River gushed and swirled angrily against the rock face far below our path and I was amazed at how close to the cliff the herd had been walking as even the babies' footprints were sometimes just a couple of yards away from the steep precipice. Elephants are seldom orderly when they are on the move. There is plenty of activity as they jostle, play and push one another as they amble along to wherever they are going. Yet they were obviously quite comfortable and surefooted enough to edge along this huge vertical drop. I recalled Cobus Raath, the vet who had delivered the herd, telling me that an elephant can go where a monkey with a briefcase can't. He was right.

About 500 yards further along Max suddenly stopped and came onto full alert, glancing at me and staring. Eye movements are a major means of communication in the animal kingdom and I knew he had sensed something so I paused and followed his line of vision to the only place in the area which could seclude anything at all, a small bush standing proud in the short grass. A few minutes later I was certain there was nothing there and called him, but he refused to move. This had never happened before; in fact Max was one of the most obedient dogs I know. I called quietly and then called again, and he just looked at me briefly and continued staring. I glanced around again but nothing seemed out of the ordinary. He must be imagining things.

'Come, boy, there's nothing out there,' I said and was about to go and get him, when suddenly I heard a cough right next to us. A very distinctive cough – leopard! I seldom carry a rifle, the traditional accessory of every ranger on a bush walk. This time wishing I did, I grabbed for my pistol.

Quite impossibly there was a leopard hiding under that single tiny bush barely ten yards away. Even though I heard it and knew full well it was there, it was so inconspicuous that I still couldn't see it. I grabbed Max's collar and held him tight, and fired a shot into ground. I dislike firing a weapon in the reserve but the big cat was waiting in ambush too close by to do anything else.

In a lightning blur of dappled gold, a large male leopard came out of the shrub and bolted. If it had come at us from that distance it would have been a nightmare, but going the other way he was poetry in motion, one of nature's most stunningly beautiful creations.

However, apart from that little adventure, I was extremely happy with the day's events.

After Nana had deliberately let me 'hang out' with her and Mvula, everything changed. It was now easy being around them and even Vusi my guinea-pig ranger could walk to within a reasonable distance without reaction. A little later I got four rangers to stroll past the herd a few times as if on a game walk and – *voilà* – we had done it. Even Frankie didn't raise an eyebrow.

Nana had obviously taken her decision and communicated it to the rest of the herd. And from that I learned another important lesson. Previously traumatized wild elephants appeared to regain a degree of faith in new humans once the matriarch has established trust with just one new human. But it must be the matriarch. My close relationship with Mnumzane hadn't altered the herd's attitude towards me one iota, despite the fact that they obviously communicate all the time.

Now, thanks to Nana, guests could walk in the wild near these magnificent creatures, an experience to be savoured for a lifetime. Yet barely two years ago Frankie had tried to kill Peter Hartley the manager of the Umfolozi reserve while he was tracking them during the breakout.

That put it all in perspective. We were moving along well.

However, it wasn't just us 'tracking' them. One evening when the lodge was full and a candlelit dinner was being served on the verandah to animated guests gushing about the day's bush experiences, Nana suddenly appeared on the lawn right in front of the lodge, herd in tow.

'Wow, she is a bit close,' I thought, watching her movements carefully. And with that the cry went up.

'Elephant, elephant!' shouted two first-timers who, immediately shushed by more seasoned bush lovers, continued pointing excitedly, while others grabbed for cameras as the whole herd came into view between the lodge and the waterhole. It was a great game-viewing experience but the problem, as I quickly realized, was that they were not going to the waterhole, they were coming up towards the lodge.

Elephants operate on the steadfast principle that all other life forms must give way to them and as far as they were concerned foreign tourists at a sit-down dinner round a swimming pool were no different from a troop of baboons at a waterhole.

Nana came towards us without breaking step. I waited until I knew that she was definitely not going to stop or alter course, and whispered loudly to the guests. 'Let's go! Go, go!'

This prompted a rush for the cover of the lodge.

But there are always some people who know better. They're always men, usually in a group, and without fail choose to pick the most ludicrous occasions to 'prove' their manhood. As the guests hurried off to safety, one particular 'big city' group stayed exactly where they were, lounging exaggeratedly over the dining chairs and feigning indifference as the herd drew nearer.

Frankie looked up and flicked her ears at the unmoving group, who, unable to recognize the customary warning, stayed put. Not getting the appropriate response, she then took a few quick steps towards them, ears flared like a cape and trunk held high.

'Bloody hell!' shouted one. 'She's charging!' Chaos erupted and chairs flew everywhere as the 'macho' men blindly ran into each other in a most unedifying every-man-for-himself stampede.

Satisfied that she had got the respect she deserved from this errant group of primates, Frankie dropped her ears and fell back in behind Nana as they all ambled across the lawn up onto the lodge's tiled game-viewing patio. They stood huge and imposingly out of place, surveying their alien surroundings.

The coast was clear, and attracted by the strange paraphernalia of the fully decorated dining table they moved over to explore. The investigation of the delicate fare with their heavy trunks led me to believe that whoever coined the phrase 'a bull in a china shop' had never actually seen an elephant in a china shop. Glasses and plates were swept aside by careless trunks and smashed all over the place. Similarly candles and holders were tossed on the floor and then the tablecloth was violently yanked from below the remaining crockery and cutlery, completing the debacle.

Discovering that some of the mess was in fact edible, they delicately picked up and ate every bread roll and salad remnants off the floor, walking over glass shards as if they were paper. The table was roughly shoved aside, cracking open as it did so, and I watched in amazement as first one chair then another went airborne. Tiring of the dinner they focused on the now obvious purpose of their visit – the swimming pool.

'That's what they're here for,' I thought. 'They know about the pool. They've been here before, probably late at night.'

The swimming pool was their new waterhole. All Nana was doing was simply clearing the guests away as she would do to any other animals so they could drink in peace.

She dropped her huge trunk into the pool and sucked gallons of the sparkling clear water up her elongated prehensile nose. Throwing her head back she delivered it messily to her gaping wrinkled mouth and gave the rumbling go-ahead to the others.

And they had an absolute ball. Mvula, Ilanga and Mandla to the delight of the now peeking guests cavorted around slipping on the tiles while the larger animals drank their fill and bathed themselves in huge squirts and sprays.

All was sort of going well until suddenly Nana picked up my scent. She slowly swung around and lumbered towards where I was standing next to a thatch pole just inside the lodge patio. I held my ground as she lifted the tip of her dripping-wet trunk across to my chest. The show of affection was understandably misinterpreted by several of the

200

hidden guests, who, by now certain of my impending death, bolted silently for the safety of the bathroom.

'Clever girl! You found the cleanest water on the reserve – and managed to scare the hell out of everyone in the process,' I added, with just a touch of discipline in my voice.

I took a step forward and raised my hand to the body of her trunk and caressed her. 'But you really are frightening the hell out of the guests and you really do need to leave now.'

Nana decided otherwise, and five minutes later she was still standing there peacefully, while in the background Frankie stared and flicked her ears at any guest who so much as moved from their hiding places.

Nana really needed to go; the lodge certainly wasn't the place for her and her family to visit, so I took my leave of her and backed off three or four paces under the thatch, clapping my hands lightly and encouraging her to move off.

Well, she didn't like that at all. Moving forward she leaned her head on the support pole in front of me, and gave a heave. With that the lodge's whole roof shifted and controlling my urge to shout I quickly moved forward again and resumed stroking her trunk speaking soothingly to her. Incredibly, she leaned forward again, this time with more force, and judging by the melancholic groaning of the timber supports it seemed that the whole structure was on the verge of collapsing.

I instinctively did the only thing I could and putting both hands high on her trunk pushed back on her with all my strength pleading with her not to destroy our livelihood.

And there we stayed, her leaning on the pole and me pushing back on her for an eternal thirty seconds before she stepped back, shook her head at me and walked away, taking a huge dump on the patio to show her disgust.

It was a game of course. Nana could have collapsed the

pole easily and my puny effort at pushing her off was but a feather in the wind. She was just making a point.

The rest of the herd followed as she walked down onto the lawn and eventually moseyed off back into the bush.

'Now I know you are completely mad!' shouted an astounded and angry Françoise coming out from behind the bar and ignoring the emerging guests. 'What the hell are you doing? Do you want to die? Oh-la-la, you are crazy *non*, pushing an elephant!' And with several loud shouts of '*Merde*' she stormed off to the kitchen to try to resurrect the dinner.

The next morning we put up a single electric strand around the lodge grounds at adult elephant head height. To keep Nana happy, we also set up a water pipe from an underground well to a new drinking trough just outside the wire.

The arrangement works well and even if the wire is down, they never try to come back to the lodge.

chapter twenty-four

A week later I got the sad news that my good friend *Nkosi* Nkanyiso Biyela had died. He was no longer a young man and had been unwell for some time. Despite expert medical attention from my own doctor, he succumbed. It was not unexpected. A fortnight earlier we were sitting outside together and despite the sub-tropical heat he shivered uncontrollably even with a blanket around his shoulders.

The tribe was in deep mourning and wailing echoed across the hills. Nobody came to work at Thula and we knew we would be operating with skeleton staff until well after the traditional funeral proceedings reserved for royalty, which would last weeks. All Zulu chiefs are kings for life, though colonialism degraded the title.

Nkosi Biyela was a man of his times, a powerful traditional leader with a foot in both worlds. He had grasped both the value of tested tradition as well as the necessity of modernity. Using tact and wisdom, he had begun the absolutely thankless task of merging the proven 'old' with the prophetic 'new'.

He was succeeded by his son Phiwayinkosi Biyela from his first wife, whom I only knew slightly. I attended the colourful induction ceremony bearing gifts.

The family members promised to arrange a meeting with him, which never materialized despite frequent requests.

The new *Nkosi*'s authority was soon tested. Shortly after

he took power a simmering tribal dispute boiled over into violence and from the reserve we could hear sporadic gunfire crackling about a mile away near the village of Buchanana. I placed guards on the boundaries to make sure nothing could possibly affect Thula Thula.

After a day of trying I eventually managed to get the local police on the phone.

'What's going on?' I asked the captain, an amiable Afrikaner who had just taken over the station.

He sighed wearily. 'Faction fight.'

Just what I had expected. Faction fights – as tangled and eternal as Appalachian feuds – are internecine tribal disputes. They are as messy and bloody and old and brutal as the ancient land itself. They can continue forever, from generation to generation, as a brother seethes over a sibling's murder or a son remembers a dead father.

As is often the case, this feud was over land. Buchanana village, my immediate neighbour, was created in the late 1960s when Zulu tribes surrounding the town of Richards Bay were evicted to make way for the harbour development, the biggest in Africa. These unfortunates were simply dumped onto traditional Biyela land without *Nkosi* Biyela's permission, such was the arrogance of the apartheid government of the day.

The displaced people's leader's name at the time was Maxwell Mthembu and they eventually became known as the Maxwell people. Faction fights between the Maxwells and the Biyelas predictably erupted and went on for years until Maxwell, whose clan was on the run against the numerically superior Biyelas, finally acquiesced and paid allegiance to *Nkosi* Nkanyiso Biyela. In turn, Maxwell was appointed a Biyela *induna*, a headman, and his people continued to live where they were on Biyela land and were integrated into the Biyela clan.

Thus *Nkosi* Biyela got his tribe's traditional land back with minimum bloodshed. But tribal loyalties are rooted far deeper than treaties of convenience forged in a fireside chat. The people of Buchanana were still very much 'Maxwells'.

Now with the death of Nkanyiso Biyela, the Maxwells revoked their pledge to be loyal to the Biyela clan. That alone was serious business, but the Maxwells also wanted to keep the land that historically belonged to the Biyelas. The Biyela clan was incensed. Groups from both sides took up arms.

The initial clash was short and sharp. Then the skirmishes went underground, taking the form of isolated attacks and ambushes at night. This was all happening right on my doorstep. My problem was that nearly all of our employees were Maxwells and came from Buchanana. So while Nkanyiso Biyela was my good friend and my relationship with the Biyelas sound, I also knew the Maxwell leader Wilson Mthembu, who had taken over when Maxwell died in the early 1990s. Mthembu had a tiger by the tail and I knew there was no way his people could win the war, but to openly support the Biyelas with the Maxwells as my immediate neighbours would be juggling with live coals. This was a lose–lose situation and I decided to try remaining neutral. I sat it out with fingers crossed, hoping that the new *Nkosi* Biyela could sort it all out soon.

To a Westerner, even someone as close to it all as me, Zulu tribal politics is mind-bogglingly complicated. I soon discovered to my dismay that instead of being an impartial observer, I was overnight a central issue in this imbroglio. Still lurking in the background of all this unrest was that powerful cattle-owning cabal who hankered deeply for the Royal Zulu land and wanted to torpedo the game-reserve project. I knew who they were from the hostile questioning I'd faced at tribal meetings while promoting the project, but

I knew nothing of their background. Whenever I asked, my informers would just shrug and say 'they're the cattle owners'.

Just as the Maxwells saw the death of Nkanyiso Biyela as a convenient moment to declare independence, the cattle cabal saw the death of the highly esteemed *Nkosi* and the hostilities with the Maxwells as an opportunity to wreck my relationship with the late Nkanyiso Biyela's family – and especially with his son, the new chief.

Zulu society is prone to rumour and gossip. It's the national pastime, and the cabal had been planting a host of 'hearsay' stories about me, claiming I was secretly supporting the breakaway Maxwell faction.

This was blatantly false. However, they had somehow discovered that, without my knowledge, members of the Maxwells had been using remote bush in Thula Thula as a hideaway at night during the fighting. The cabal then spread the word that I was harbouring the rebels. The story caught like wildfire.

But even worse, the malicious whispering campaign claimed that I was also supplying the rebels with guns and ammunition. Such rumour-mongering can have potentially fatal consequences. In a blink, my hard-earned reputation in the area was tenuous. I had been completely outmanoeuvred.

If Nkanyiso Biyela was alive, he would have guffawed at this nonsense. But he wasn't. His successor, his son Phiwayinkosi, was a good man of iron integrity but he didn't know me well and he was being force-fed false information by the bucketload.

I needed serious help to quash this rumour quickly. I phoned my old friend, the highly esteemed Prince Gideon Zulu, uncle of the Zulu king and head of the royal household and explained the situation. He was aghast and warned me of the potential danger I was in – as if I didn't know.

Thankfully he agreed to use his considerable influence, stressing that the first thing I had to do was contact the new *Nkosi* directly and tell him what was going on, while he used his contacts to find out the source of the rumours.

I phoned the young chief and assured him that if some of his enemies had indeed been on my land, it had been done so illegally. There had been no consent from me whatsoever.

He listened politely. I knew about the misinformation swamping him, and the fact that he was giving me time to defend myself over the phone showed unequivocally that he was a fair leader. I felt infinitely better.

'It's good you phoned,' he said. 'There's a meeting this weekend in Buchanana on this exact matter. Come and address us.'

I would far rather have had a private session with him where we could sort matters out face to face. Instead, I was going to have to confront the issue head-on. Being the only Westerner at a highly charged tribal gathering in the midst of a bitter fight was challenging enough – but to be accused of gun-running while people were dying was not good. Not good at all.

But I recognized the wisdom in his choice. He was giving me a platform to state my case. How I handled it was up to me. I thanked him, said I would be there, and then let Prince Gideon know of the meeting.

He tried to reassure me. 'I will have some of my people there and they will do some work in the background, but they cannot speak for you or defend you. You must speak for yourself and you must speak strongly.'

Then, if the situation could possibly have got worse, it did. I got wind that Thula Thula itself was also under threat. In post-apartheid South Africa, tribes were encouraged to claim back traditional lands that had been unfairly annexed by the apartheid government. The Biyelas had years before lodged land claims against Thula Thula and surrounding farms. The claims had failed legally and the matter had been amicably resolved on a social level with Nkanyiso Biyela. However, the cattle cabal, not content with just spreading lies against me, was also attempting to reactivate these discarded claims. Not only did they covet the Royal Zulu – they wanted Thula Thula as well.

I went to my office and began working on the most crucial address I would ever give. The future of Thula Thula depended on it. For if the cabal succeeded and moved into Thula Thula with families and cattle, our indigenous animals would be exterminated: including the herd. Nana and her family had at last found a place where they were happy. But because of the danger they presented to intruders, they would be the first to be shot if I failed at the meeting.

That thought sobered my fevered mind considerably and a plan started to take root. I knew the cabal was going to accuse me of harbouring combatants, thus I had to prove it was physically impossible to police every square inch in a reserve as vast as Thula Thula. I was certain that they had witnesses claiming combatants had been on my land. How could I know? If I knew everything that happened on Thula Thula, poaching would be eradicated overnight.

This meeting would be no clinical court of law and I had to provide graphic and practical proof to ordinary folk that would get me off the hook. My speech would not be dry legalese, but an appeal to reason.

Although the accusations could not be more serious, my good standing in the area would not be ignored by local leaders. It was well known that I abhorred apartheid and had worked closely with the national Zulu leaders in the years preceding the run-up to the first democratic elections in South Africa in 1994.

I decided that the first thing to do was get a translator. Although my Zulu was adequate, the fact that each question had to be laboriously translated from Zulu to English would give me more time to formulate answers. However, the translator needed to be acceptable to both sides otherwise I would face accusations that I wasn't answering the questions properly.

Ngwenya, my security *induna*, gave me the name of a local priest, whom he said was an esteemed member of the community, to translate for me. The priest, a kindly old man agreed and suggested that I come to his church for a ritual blessing.

There are a host of ministers in Buchanana, but most are not what you would call traditional men of the cloth. They mix Christianity with ancestral worship and animism. In short, this is a truly hybrid spirituality, uniquely African and drawing inspiration from every source imaginable.

I arrived at his church the next day. It was a simple shack with walls and roof of corrugated iron. Inside were a few rickety wooden chairs. One had been placed in the centre of the room where he asked me to sit down. A simple white cross hand-painted on the tin wall was the only decoration.

He then put a large zinc tub of what looked like river water by my feet, sprinkled some powders in it and began circling around me, chanting in Zulu, imploring both God and the ancestors to hear his calls. While he did so he tore pages out of a newspaper, set them alight, waved them around and then threw them into the water. The pages were thickly wedged together and continued burning while floating.

After several minutes he stopped and stirred the smoky water. It wasn't clean water to start with, and the liquid soon became a soggy mess of burnt-paper flotsam. Still chanting, he decanted the stuff into an old plastic water bottle.

'This is good *muthi*,' he said afterwards. 'When you go

into the meeting, you must drink from the bottle, and the people must see you do that. This meeting will then go well for you because you have been blessed.'

I thanked him, took the bottle and said I'd see him later in the week.

Five days later I arrived at the Buchanana village hall with David. The sun was not even midway in the sky but the air inside was like an oven and the simple brick and corrugated-iron building squatting on the top of a barren hill was bursting at the seams with people. There was no way the tiny windows could ventilate the seething room and the air inside was fetid and rank with sweat. Hostility hung just as thickly.

Outside many armed tribesmen who could not find a seat milled about. Men pointed at us as I drove up. One shook his fist; another brandished an *iklwa* – a traditional Zulu stabbing spear, named after the sucking sound made as the blade is yanked from a victim. I didn't feel too good about my chances.

There was a heavy police presence and I deliberately parked my Land Rover near their vehicles.

The cop in charge, a Zulu woman in a bright-blue uniform came across. 'Why are you here?' she asked, intrigued at seeing whites at a strictly tribal meeting.

'I'm speaking today.'

'Oh.' She stared at me with interest. 'Then *you* are Anthony.'

I nodded. 'How is it inside?'

'Hot,' she replied. Unfortunately, she wasn't referring to the weather. She was using the colloquial Zulu word for dangerous. In other words, Code Red.

She clicked her tongue, unhappy that my presence could spark more problems. 'Are you sure you still want to speak?'
I followed her gaze as she watched a crowd of men arrive,

one waving a dilapidated shotgun. 'I've already had to radio for reinforcements.'

The phalanx of police was due primarily to the smouldering faction fight and not because of me personally. Nevertheless it was disconcerting to know that even they thought this meeting could turn nasty at any moment.

'Yes, I will speak,' I replied with a bravado I certainly didn't feel. I knew I had been cleverly framed. Convincing hundreds of angry tribesmen in a state of virtual civil war of my innocence would not be easy, even with behind-the-scenes help from Prince Gideon.

We were interrupted by a messenger sent to fetch me. I followed him into the sardine can and sat in the front row just as an *induna* garbed in full warrior regalia finished off an extremely animated address. Suffice it to say, the gist of his message was that their enemies had spies in this room. The crowd growled, searching around for suspects.

The speaker, a senior chief, introduced me and asked the crowd that I be accorded a fair chance to put my case. Given the explosive mood of the meeting, this was no idle request.

I took a deep breath and, holding the priest's bottled *muthi*, stood and thanked the speaker whom I knew well. I could count on him if the going got rough. I then pointedly thanked the *Nkosi* for inviting me, as well as other councillors and headmen or anyone else I recognized, naming them one by one. In other words, I was shamelessly name-dropping. The priest translated.

I then put the *muthi* bottle on the floor next to my chair. There was no immediate reaction, but I could see that it certainly had got some of the crowd's attention. Perhaps they knew what it signified, and I was glad I had decided to bring it along. I needed all the help I could get.

Despite my apprehension, my voice came out strong, following Prince Gideon's instructions to the letter. This gave me some confidence and I pulled myself upright. Speaking as calmly as I could, I stressed that Zulu culture honourably entitled everyone to a fair hearing. I spoke in English as I wanted any questions to be translated, giving me precious extra moments to mull before I answered.

Just as I thought everything was going swimmingly, all hell exploded. 'Apologize!' screamed a loud voice, ignoring what I had just said. 'Apologize for what you have done.'

Other agitators took up the chant, trying to provoke the crowd. 'Apologize! Apologize!'

For a moment I was shocked, like a hare in a spotlight. Then instantly it all became clear; I knew what I had to do. Any apology would be a fatal acknowledgement of guilt and that's exactly what the cabal wanted. If I fell into that trap, giving in to a lame plea bargain, I would be finished. So I ignored the goading and waited for the speaker to restore order, which he eventually did. When it was quiet, he nodded at me to continue.

'I cannot apologize . . .' I said, which immediately incited more jeers from one section of the crowd. My eyes shot across. They had made the mistake of sitting together and now I knew exactly who they all were.

'I cannot apologize,' I repeated, 'because I have done nothing to apologize for.'

More jeers.

'A man – if he is a man,' I accentuated, 'will only apologize if he has done wrong and then he *must* apologize. Do you want me to lie to you? Do you want me to lie to the *Nkosi*? Do you want me to lie to this meeting? Are you asking me to give up my manhood and lie like a coward just because I am being threatened?'

These arguments may sound medieval in an air-conditioned First World courtroom, but in rural Zululand your integrity is central to your masculinity. That's the way it is. You may lie to outsiders, but not to your clan.

212

A wiry man with a wispy moustache jumped to his feet. 'But you are lying! You're lying as your words come out! I myself saw you giving guns to our enemies! It was dark but I saw you with my own eyes meeting secretly with our enemies. I saw you giving them many weapons.'

I knew him. He was a layabout and a poacher, and not a good one at that. And, wow! he was their key witness. I breathed a faint sigh of relief. Their prime source against me was a well-known petty thug with no standing in the community whatsoever. I knew the *Nkosi* and his advisers wouldn't miss that.

Unable to contain himself in the headiness of his newly acquired status, the *impimpi* – informer – had blown his cover by jumping up too soon. Now the crowd knew that the chief witness was basically unreliable.

Then the leader of the cattle cabal stood up and the hall went silent. A beefy man with a distinguished lantern jaw grizzled over by a peppercorn beard, he was a senior community member whose standing was rooted in cattle wealth. He spoke with authority, trying to undo the damage brought about by his *impimpi*'s premature accusation.

'Mr Anthony, I thank you for coming here to clear up some important matters. I know you are a man who does not lie' – he paused, clearing his throat for effect – 'and as you do not lie, do you deny that people were living with you on Thula Thula while they attacked our people and threatened our chief?'

In effect, the cabal head was saying he had eye-witnesses that combatants had been on my land – and daring me to dispute it.

'We all want to hear the answer to that question,' I replied slowly. 'That is why we are here.' I saw the leaders on the podium lean forward. 'But, I ask that I be allowed to finish what I have to say – everything – before anyone makes a judgement. Is this agreed?'

I needed those assurances desperately.

'It is so,' said a senior chief. 'Anthony will finish.'

'Good,' I said, then raised my voice. 'Then I deny that they were living with me. I deny it emphatically.'

The room erupted, so sure were they of my guilt. The cabal leaders were grinning wildly. I had been caught out. I was a liar.

It took a few minutes for the *izindunas*, headmen, to restore some semblance of order. Then, as promised, I was able to continue.

'However, I do not deny that men have been hiding on Thula Thula,' I said. 'I emphatically deny that I know them, or that they were living with me.'

The cabal leader again stood, shaking his head and grinning.

'This man says he does not know who is in his home, on his own land.' He turned to the crowd. 'Which man does not know his visitors?'

Laughter. The *Nkosi* raised his hand for silence. He nodded at me to carry on.

'As you all know, Thula Thula is a very big place. It takes many hours to walk fast from one side to the other. Anyone can easily hide there.'

'But you have workers patrolling on your land!' shouted the cabal leader, pointing a finger. 'And you still say you don't know your visitors?'

'I don't know,' I replied. 'But do you? Do you know who lives on Biyela land?'

'Of course we know! No man will dare stay on our land if the *induna* of the area does not know his name.' He laughed again, playing to the crowd, confident of victory.

I then signalled to David at the back of the room. A few moments later he came forward with Ngwenya who, impressed by the occasion raised both his hands head-high in traditional greeting.

I introduced him. 'This is Ngwenya, my senior ranger. We all know his family is well respected in this area.' I was pleased to notice several of the senior *indunas* nodding in assent.

I turned to one of the *indunas* who controlled the Ntambanana area, west of us. 'Biyela land in Ntambanana is off limits to anyone. No one can stay there. Is that correct?'

'It is,' he agreed. 'No one is there, no one may stay there.'

'Ngwenya and I have just been there and I can tell you now there are several people living deep inside the land. We found them and spoke with them, they have been there for weeks. The bush has hidden them. Just as it hid the men you said were on my land.'

Ngwenya nodded as I spoke.

'Is this true, Ngwenya?' asked the *induna*, suddenly standing up. 'Were you there? Are there people living there?'

Ngwenya nodded. '*Yebo*, it is as Anthony has said.'

'*Hau!*' The *induna*'s traditional exclamation of surprise echoed across the now silent room. 'Then they are trespassers.'

The cabal leader shrugged dismissively, but my argument had found traction and the tribal leaders were now looking at me expectantly.

'I repeat, I did not know anyone was hiding in the bush on Thula Thula. The same way the honourable *induna* did not know men were hiding on his property. Trespassers are trespassers; they are not visitors. They are not welcome.'

There was a murmur of assent from the crowd. Not huge, but still reassuring.

'What about the guns?' someone shouted from the back.

Now that was what the meeting was all about.

'Yes, we have guns,' I said. 'We have guns to protect ourselves from wild animals – you all know that. Why would we give away our guns and put our lives in danger walking in the bush with no protection?'

215

I was about to answer my own question but a tribal elder stood up first to defend me. This was a sure sign that the tables were turning.

'Mkhulu speaks the truth,' he said. 'I have spoken to his rangers and they all still have their guns. Their guns never leave their hands because they need them for their work. They wouldn't give them away to endanger their own lives.'

'Anthony lies!' shouted another cabal member in desperation. 'Everyone knows he is the one supplying guns to be used against *Nkosi*.'

OK, this was now getting personal and anger crept into my voice.

'No. Not everybody knows. This has got nothing to do with everybody. It's not "everybody" who's accusing me. It is just a few saying these terrible things and they say it recklessly without proof. All that's happening here is someone is trying to drive a wedge between me and the *Nkosi*; someone with another agenda altogether.'

'We don't believe you!' shouted the same man. 'Our people are dying because of you. We don't want you here living with us. You are white, and we do not trust you. You must take your family and go.'

I could hear the sudden intake of breath. Every head in the crowd swivelled, first to the *Nkosi*, and then towards me.

I suddenly felt tired. This is what it had all come to; in South Africa, when logic shrivels, the same dreary dinosaurs rear their vicious heads. But thanks to the racial slur, I now had the crowd's absolute attention.

'Several of the leaders here today knew my name long before I came to Thula Thula. They know that I worked with Zulu leaders during apartheid, even before some of you were born,' I added, invoking the deep Zulu respect for age.

'I had believed, and hoped with all my heart, that apartheid was dead. Yet this man wants to start it again here in our village.'

216

I turned to him, 'You will bring shame on all of us.'

At that moment the young *Nkosi* stood up. He stood straight as a spear, and at that instant I knew that he was a true leader.

'This has gone too far. We are not holding a trial here,' he said. 'Anthony's not on trial. This gun-running is a matter for the police. If anybody has proof, then take it to the police – not just make wild claims, which is what is happening here in this hall. I will speak to the police myself after the meeting. Anthony was a good friend to my father. This matter is dismissed.'

It was done and I breathed a sigh of relief.

That was the last thing the cabal wanted to hear. They had no proof of anything other than some rebels had been trespassing in the virtually inaccessible corners of Thula Thula. They knew the gun-running claims were complete hogwash; they knew how much I revered the *Nkosi*'s family. They knew that the only way to get at me was to incite the crowd into open revolt. They had failed and been publicly humiliated in the process.

Indeed, their bluff had been called by the *Nkosi* himself. The victory was sweet for me, and after the meeting many villagers, some carrying fighting sticks, shook my hand or waved, as if welcoming me back to the fold. Addressing this hostile meeting had in itself proved my innocence. Under Zulu tradition the matter could not be opened again. Thula Thula was safe.

Back at Thula Thula later, with Max comfortingly at my side, I looked out over the reserve and on the horizon caught a glimpse of the herd. They were on the move, safe and free to go where they pleased. The victory was sweet indeed, but that didn't mean the struggle was over. I had made some serious enemies, as I was soon to find out.

chapter twenty-five

Early next morning Marion Garaï of the Elephant Managers and Owners Association phoned. As usual, she had unusual news.

'Can you take another elephant? I've got a fourteen-year-old female that desperately needs a home.'

'What's the problem?'

'It's a real shocker. To give the short version, her entire family have been shot or sold and she's completely alone on a big five reserve.'

Big five reserves are so named due to their quarry's reputation as the most dangerous animals to hunt – elephant, black rhino, buffalo, leopard, and of course lion. An elephant may be a big fiver – in fact number one on the list – but a juvenile could not survive for long without the protection of its herd if lions are about. No lion would dare attack an adult tusker, but an adolescent would be relatively easy prey for a pride.

Then Marion added fuel to the fire. 'Even worse, she's been sold to a trophy hunter.'

She delivered that snippet almost as an aside, but she knew it would get me going like nothing else. It was something I simply couldn't fathom . . . what type of person would shoot a terrified teenage elephant, and a female at that? For a tawdry fireside trophy? For the pleasure of the kill? And what kind of reserve owner would hawk a vulnerable young animal for such a reason?

I have never had a problem with hunting for the pot. Every living thing on this planet hunts for sustenance one way or the other, from the mighty microbe upwards. Survival of the fittest is, like it or not, the way of this world. But hunting for pleasure, killing only for the thrill of it, is to me an anathema. I have met plenty of trophy hunters. They are, of course, all naturalists; they all know and love the bush; and they all justify their action in conservation speak, peppered with all the right buzz words.

The truth is, though, that they harbour a hidden impulse to kill, which can only be satisfied by the violent death of another life form by their hand. And they will go to inordinate lengths to satisfy, and above all justify, this apparently irresistible urge.

Besides, adding to the absurdity of their claims, there is not an animal alive that is even vaguely a match for today's weaponry. The modern high-powered hunting rifle with telescopic sights puts paid to any argument about sportsmanship.

I had to consider the implications of introducing a new elephant into the herd. On the credit side, Nana and her clan were settled and I was pretty confident she would accept another young female into her family. Only stable herds will do that; a maladjusted group of elephants will chase any newcomer off – or worse.

No matter the risks, the thought of a solitary elephant – still a teenager – terrified out of her wits, surrounded by lions and soon to be hunted grated deeply.

'I'll take her.'

'Great. I have a donor who'll pay capture and translocation costs.'

Predictably the hunter refused to relinquish his trophy. However, in a stroke of genius, Brendan decided to check the man's big game permit. You can say it was serendipity; you can say it was an act of God – whatever – but unbelievably the permit was due to expire that exact day. Even more wondrously, one of Brendan's ex-university friends worked in the permit office and we managed to block the reissue. At the eleventh hour, we saved the life of this orphan elephant.

The hunter was upset as he technically still owned the animal. He wanted his cash back. Thankfully Marion's donor again came to the rescue and paid him his blood money. A week later the juvenile was on her way to Thula Thula.

We hurriedly repaired the *boma* and David, Brendan and I prepared for another stint in the bush while our new arrival acclimatized. We even parked the Land Rover in the same position as when the original herd was in quarantine, wondering if Wilma our industrious bark spider was still around to weave her silky web on the aerial.

Max did a perfunctory check of the area and settled himself down. He knew we would be here for a while.

The transport truck arrived in mid-afternoon and backed into the loading trench. This time we had the levels right and the loading bay opened smoothly. We all craned forward for a good look. It was a good thing I didn't blink, for as the door opened the youngster sprinted straight into the thickest part of the *boma*'s bush. And there she hid for the next few days, coming out only in the dead of night to eat the food we were tossing over the fence. Whenever we crept around trying to get closer, she bolted to the far side as soon as she sensed us. I have never witnessed such terror in an animal. There was no doubt she thought we were going to kill her, just as humans had killed the rest of her family.

Using the techniques I had developed with the herd, I started to talk to her gently, walking around singing and whistling, trying to get her used to me as a benevolent presence. But no matter what I did she remained petrified, rooted to the spot in the densest part of the thicket.

For almost a week there was no change in her emotional tone or attitude so eventually I decided I needed to interrupt the process. Instead of trying to communicate with her, albeit in a roundabout way, I came up to the fence, picked a spot and just stayed there, saying nothing, doing nothing, just studiously ignoring her. Just being there.

Each morning and each afternoon I chose a different spot; always shifting fractionally closer to her hiding place and repeating the procedure.

The third day I did this prompted a reaction – but not quite what I wished. Instead of being soothed, which was the whole idea, she came out of the bush furiously, charging like a whirlwind at me.

I watched her come, amazed. I had thought such a lost soul would respond to warmth. The *boma*'s electric fence was between us and as there was no real danger I had three choices: I could stand firm and show her who was boss; I could ignore her; or I could back off.

Her charge, as ferocious as it seemed, didn't gel. I could sense that this poor creature, a couple of tons of tusk and flesh that could kill me with a single swipe, had the self-confidence of a mouse. She needed to believe in herself; to know she deserved respect and was a master of the wilderness. She needed to believe she had won the encounter. So I decided to back off with some major theatrics. I decided, counter-intuitively in an environment where the strongest survive, to let her know that in this instance she was the boss. It wasn't that hard to fake; if there hadn't been a fence I would've been running for real.

She pulled up at the fence in a cloud of dust and stared, dumbfounded – she had probably never seen humans run before. Any charge had probably been followed by the thunderclap of a rifle.

She watched, or rather smelt my retreat and then swivelled and ran back into the thicket with her trunk held high in victory – the first time I had seen her do that. She had seen off an enemy. More importantly, she had turned fear into action which, for the moment at least, was a huge improvement.

It worked well, almost too well. She now started charging whenever I came close. Each time I played the game, feigning fright and backing right off. I wanted to show her how powerful she was ... that she was queen of the bush. Elephants are majestic; they are not bullies or cowards. I had to let her rediscover herself.

She slowly starting getting her nerve back and even began coming out into the open during the day, wandering around the *boma*.

Whenever she emerged from the thicket, I tried to ensure I was around and she watched with beady eyes as I once more started talking to her and singing at random, alternating that with just being there quietly. During these encounters she never uttered a sound, whether she was intrigued, angry or frightened. To me this was uniquely sad. A trumpeting elephant is bush music. Yet this distraught creature was as silent as the air, even when coming at us full tilt.

Then one day she charged while we were pushing food over the fence. For the first time her hunger overrode her fear and she wanted to shoo us away. And for the first time she was trumpeting for all her worth. But instead of a clear, clean call she was honking like a strangled goose.

David and I looked at each other. Now we knew why she had been silent. The poor creature had destroyed her vocal cords, screaming herself hoarse for help, calling for her mother and aunts, lost and pitifully alone in the wilderness while lions circled. She really was a special case.

To try and lighten the mood we affectionately named her ET, short for *enfant terrible* – terrible child.

Even though she started tolerating me marginally more, she was still profoundly unhappy. Her fear and loneliness gloomed the entire *boma*. Sitting around the campfire at night, usually a time for talk, we too could feel it. Often we just crept into our sleeping bags and lay on our backs, staring at the stars.

Just as we thought we were winning, she had slid hopelessly back into an abyss of abject despair that not even shouting or the banging of cans could penetrate. Then she slipped further away and began walking endlessly in large figures of eight, oblivious to her surroundings. This sadness bordered on a grief too embedded to penetrate. She was so depressed I feared she might die of a broken heart, so I changed tactics.

I went looking for the herd. They were the only solution.

'Coooome, Nana, coooome, *babbas*!' I called out once I saw them. Three hundred yards away Nana looked up, trunk reaching into the air. A few calls later she sourced the direction of my voice and they all started ambling through the bush towards me, pushing easily through wicked thornveld that would rip human skin to shreds. As they advanced I marvelled at this magnificent herd, these beautiful creatures, fat, grey and glowing, and how content they were with new youngsters.

Now I needed their help. But first I was going to try something in the wilderness I had never done before: get them to follow me.

As they approached I gently footed the accelerator and eased ahead for about fifty yards and Nana stopped, perplexed at why I was moving off. Then I called them and, after milling about for a bit, she came on. As she got near I drove off again; again she stopped, confused.

Again I called 'Coooome, Nana!' willing her forward, calling out, telling her it was important, that I needed her. The words meant nothing, but would she get the emotion, the urgency?

Amazingly she started following, and eventually just kept on coming without me even calling, her family following fractionally behind. I looked in my rear-view mirror. There were nine elephants following me; I was for a fleeting instant the pachyderm Pied Piper. Nana loomed in the rectangular reflection, the others behind her, obliterating all else. Deep in the African bush I had a herd of wild elephant actually following me because I wanted and needed them to. It was all so implausible – and yet it was happening. God I loved them.

Three miles later we were at the *boma*. Unbelievably, the herd had stayed the course.

I stopped thirty yards from the fence and Nana came towards me, paused for a moment, and then saw the youngster. She looked back at me, as if, perhaps, to acknowledge why I had called her, then went to the fence and emitted a long set of stomach rumbles.

ET was as still as a tree, peering at the herd through the dense foliage, lifting her trunk to get their scent. For some moments this continued. Then suddenly, excited as a teenager at a funfair, she came out and ran to where Nana was standing at the fence. These were the first of her own kind she had seen in a year.

Nana lifted her python-thick trunk over the electric fence, reaching out to ET who responded by raising her own trunk. I watched entranced as Nana touched the troubled youngster who demurely acknowledged the matriarch's authority. By now the rest of the inquisitive herd had come forward and Frankie, who was also tall enough to get her trunk over the electric strand, did so as well. There they all stood, their stomachs rumbling and grumbling in elephant talk.

This went on for an animated twenty minutes as scents and smells were exchanged and introductions made. What happened next though left me in no doubt that ET's predicament was over. A solution found.

Nana turned and moved off, deliberately walking past the gate where she had originally pushed over the poles to get out. I had no doubt she was showing ET the exit and simultaneously letting me know to open the gate. I had asked for her help and she had taken her decision: 'Let her out!'

But with all the elephants around we could not get anywhere near the gate and could do no more than watch as ET moved along with them on the inside of the *boma* fence until she reached the far end and could go no further. She backtracked up and down the fence, desperately trying to find a way to join them and 'honking' in despair. It was heartbreaking to watch.

But would she allow us? No chance. Every time we approached the gate she thundered across, enraged at our presence, as if we were preventing her from joining the others.

Eventually she stopped, exhausted by her continuous stampedes, and we were able to move in and quickly remove the horizontal gate poles and electric strands.

Nana, who had been waiting nearby in thick cover watching all this, then came back out of the bush around the other side of the *boma* with her family following in single file. Deliberately and slowly, she once more walked past the now-open gate. ET rushed out of the thicket but again missed the exit and followed them on the inside of the fence until she could go no further. Her despair was wrenching but there was nothing we could do until she learnt that the gate was her sole exit point.

This time Nana didn't wait. She kept going towards the river and just as I thought we would have to close the *boma* for the night, ET backtracked to the gate and was gone, her trunk twitching just inches off the ground as she chased after the herd's scent in a gaiting run.

We switched off power to the *boma* fences and packed up. Half an hour later as we were driving home we saw them moving away across the open savannah. They were still in single file but already the pecking order had been established. ET was second-last, holding the tail of the elephant in front with Mnumzane behind her. He was resting his trunk on her back as they moved along. Comforting her.

Walt Disney himself could not have scripted a better ending.

chapter twenty-six

Françoise named our new boutique hotel the Elephant Safari Lodge and threw herself into making a success of it. To keep the bush atmosphere she limited accommodation to just eight luxury rooms spread out around a large thatched lodge on the banks of the Nseleni River. Most courageously she refused to bring in professional help, preferring instead to train Zulus from the next-door village for all positions. The Franco–Zulu communication challenges that ensued provided daily entertainment for David, Brendan and me.

'No TV, no newspapers, no cellphones,' she insisted, 'this must be a natural wilderness experience, an antidote to city life.' And it was, complimented by the fine food which she produced and presented with all her inherent flair. I balanced this against the knowledge that if I hadn't met Françoise, the guests would probably be sitting on log stumps around a fire with a sausage on a stick and using a bush toilet.

The lodge changed everything for both of us. It was a long day, starting with the early morning game drive and ending only when the last guest went to bed. I quickly learned that in today's world, if you want to survive as a conservationist, you had better learn all about wines and how to mix a good Martini.

All the while I knew the cattle cabal was still lurking in the background trying to disrupt the Royal Zulu game-reserve project, but being busy with the introduction of ET into the herd, I couldn't give it much thought.

Then my mother phoned from her office in Empangeni, her voice scratchy with worry. The Security Police had contacted her, trying to get hold of me, and the news they gave her was enough to terrify any mum. Police informers had infiltrated the homestead of a powerful local *induna* of an adjoining tribe who controlled an area to the east of Thula Thula and had learnt that assassins had been hired to kill me.

It had to be the cabal. In fact, according to police information, the rogue *induna* had openly said that if I was bumped off, he and his followers would be able to seize the tribal trust land. Even though it legally belonged to five different clans and I was just the coordinator of the project, they believed that without me involved they could then stake their own claim and torpedo the project. The scenario was reminiscent of the circumstances which led to the murder of conservationist George Adamson of *Born Free* fame in Kenya many years ago. He was killed by tribesmen who wanted the Kora reserve, where he worked with lions, to be cattle land.

The police even had the names of the assassins, but said they could not act as their information was only hearsay. However, it came from sufficiently reliable sources to be credible, hence the warning.

I know, and love, Zulu culture. It's part of my daily life. But I also know that if a person does not confront a problem instantly, it can balloon out of all proportion. Fierce blood feuds still flourish today for reasons no one remembers. There was no way around it; this threat had to be confronted head-on, and quickly. I had to pay the *induna* an early visit.

A good friend and extremely courageous old man, Obie

Mthethwa, deemed it was too dangerous for me to go to the headman's kraal alone and volunteered to accompany me. Obie was a senior councillor to the Mthethwa clan, one of the most powerful Zulu tribes and well respected in the area. He and I had become good friends over the years and his presence would be invaluable.

I told Obie the names of the assassins fingered by the police. He knew them by reputation. '*Tsotsis*,' he said spitting on the ground, using the Zulu pejorative for thugs. That afternoon we drove over rutted tracks deep into rural Zululand to the headman's home.

It was a picturesque village with traditional round thatched huts neatly set out on top of a hill. People were finishing their daily chores, herd boys bringing in cattle, mothers calling in children, everyone preparing for the night. The smell of the evening meals wafted across the village.

We were made to wait almost an hour and it was dark before being summoned into the kraal. This was an ominous sign and I took much comfort from the fact that Obie was with me. Then we were escorted to the *isishayamteto*, the largest thatch and clay hut, traditionally used for important business.

Shadows pulsed on the walls from a single candle flame which illuminated the room's simple furnishings, a table and a few flimsy wooden chairs. I noticed immediately the *induna* was alone. This was extremely unusual as advisers or councillors always accompanied him. We had seen some of them outside while we waited.

Where were they now? What was it he didn't want them to hear?

Then, as is Zulu protocol, we began asking about each other's health, the health of immediate families, and the weather. While all this was going on, I manoeuvred the back of my chair against the wall so no one could sneak behind me. I wanted to face whatever danger came at me head-first.

Eventually the *induna* asked the nature of our visit. Speaking in Zulu, I explained that the police had told me there was a contract out on my life and the hitmen hired to do the killing came from the *induna*'s tribe.

'*Hau!*' he exclaimed. 'It cannot be my people. They hold you in esteem, Mkhulu. You are the man who is going to bring them jobs with the new game reserve. Why would my people want to kill you?'

'I know that is true. But the police say their information is also true. They say it is not all of your people that want to kill me – just a gang of *tsotsis*. They believe that if they kill me, they can grab the land for themselves.' I paused for an instant and stared directly at him. 'But we both know that it is not my land. It belongs to other tribes as well, and killing me will not make it someone else's land.'

Again the headman appeared astonished and I was starting to wonder if perhaps the police information was off-target. He was either innocent or a virtuoso liar.

At that moment we heard a car pull up outside, followed by the traditional shout of identification. About ten minutes later four men walked in. They had come to report to their *induna*. He told them to sit and they squatted on the floor on their haunches, keeping their heads lower than their boss's as a token of respect.

As they settled down Obie grabbed my arm and whispered in English: 'These are the killers – these are the *tsotsis* whose names the police gave us.'

At first they did not recognize Obie and me in the dim light. But as their eyes grew accustomed to the shadows the sudden startled looks on their faces betrayed them.

I was wearing a bulky bush jacket and in my pocket was a cocked 9-mm pistol. My hand slid around the butt. I gently thumbed off the safety catch and pointed it through the jacket straight at the closest man's belly.

Obie leaned forward, grabbed my arm hard again and whispered, 'This is very dangerous. We have to get out. Now!'

But there was no way out. I looked directly at the *induna*, hand tight on my gun.

'The police have given me the names of the men out to kill me. Those names are the same as these four men.' I pointed at them with my free hand. 'Does that mean you know what the police are speaking about?'

The contract killers sprang up and started shouting at me. 'You lie – you have no business here!'

I jumped up to face them, keeping a firm grip on the pistol. Obie also stood up, squared his shoulders and glared at the assassins.

'*Thula msindu* – stop this noise!' he commanded with iron authority. 'This is the *induna*'s house. He must speak – not you. You must show respect.'

The *induna* gestured at us all to sit down.

'Mhkulu, I do not know where you get these stories from. I do not know why the police are lying about me. I do not know anything of what you say. All I know is that there is no killing list with your name on. Anyone who says so is a liar.'

The words were smooth, but there was no doubt his attitude had radically changed. He was now in full retreat, indirectly accusing me of calling him a liar – a heinous slur in Zulu culture.

'Then why is it that these men walk so easily into your house?' I persisted. 'Does this not seem suspicious?'

There was no answer.

'And what's more,' I added, 'the police know I have come to talk to you. My visit here has been fully reported to them and they await our return. If Obie Mthethwa or I do not get back home this night, they will know what happened here. They will find you and you will suffer the full consequences of your actions.'

Again, the *induna* did not reply.

I knew it was unlikely I would be able to shoot my way out, but I certainly would take a couple of these cut-throats with me in the attempt. Perhaps that would also give Obie a chance to make a break for it.

I focused on the candle, just a stride away on the floor. If anything started I planned to kick it over and plunge the room into darkness. The *induna* was also looking at the candle, no doubt harbouring the exact same thoughts. He then looked at me.

We both knew why.

The *induna* broke his stare first. I could see he was now unnerved – particularly as he now believed that the police knew we were at his kraal. He had been completely caught out by the arrival of the assassins and the fact that we knew who they were. All his earlier denials were now obvious lies.

The contract killers looked at their boss, unsure of what to do. The four of them could easily overpower us, but as experienced gunmen, they also could tell I had a primed pistol underneath my jacket. If they went for their guns, I would get the first shot off, straight at the nearest man. It was now up to their boss what he wanted to do.

The stand-off was tense and silent. Nobody moved.

I finally provided the *induna* with a way out.

'I am not calling you a liar. Maybe the police are, but that is a matter between you and them. All I want is your word of honour that I am in no danger from any man of your tribe – any man who answers to you.'

He quickly agreed, grabbing the escape line with both hands. He gave his assurance that I would not be harmed by any of his people, stressing again that there was no hit list.

That was all I needed. The main aim of the meeting had been achieved. The *induna* would be a fool to go back on his word of honour. He also knew he would be the prime suspect if anything happened to me – whether he was guilty or not.

As a parting shot I said our discussion would also be reported to *Nkosi* at the next council meeting. We then left. When we got in the car, Obie let out a large 'whoosh' of breath. We had just stared death in the face, and I looked at the old man with gratitude and respect. He had the courage of a lion and had put his life on the line for the purest motive of all – friendship.

Driving home through the dark, Obie – a natural raconteur – recounted the story over and again in the minutest detail, mimicking accents and actions with deadly accuracy. I laughed delightedly, adrenalin still fizzing with the manic relief of survival. I knew Obie would memorize the story and it would be told and retold around the night fires of his kraal, woven into the rich fabric of his tribe's folklore: of how we had called the bluff of one of the most powerful headmen and his *tsotsis* in the area – and lived to tell the tale.

With that, the cabal was now in full retreat. They knew the police had infiltrated them; that there was an informer in their midst. I also had assurance from one of their leaders that I would not be harmed. It remained to see whether he would keep his word.

chapter twenty-seven

I was keen to see how ET was settling in with her new family and spent as much time as I could out in the bush near them.

However, it didn't take long to experience the consequence of her inclusion. While Nana and Frankie were as content as always with me in the vicinity, ET went ballistic if I came near, especially if I climbed out of the Land Rover. She just couldn't believe that her matriarch was permitting a human – evil incarnate in her mind – to get close and she quivered on full alert, ready to charge at a moment's notice. This meant that I had to be as unobtrusive as possible. She may be a youngster, but she still weighed a couple of tons and was more powerful than a human could imagine, and I wasn't sure what Nana or Frankie's reaction would be if she attacked. This was uncharted territory for me, so there was nothing to do except be patient and let ET's malevolence dissipate.

On the plus side, she may have been mad as a snake at me, but she was absolutely ecstatic with her new family. And to see this previously depressed creature joyously bonding with the other youngsters, pushing, pulling and playing with all the physicality that elephants so enjoy, was simply phenomenal.

Mnumzane was still on the periphery, being shooed off if he got too close, and somewhat bemusedly watching the newcomer being accepted. I reckon I was his best friend – albeit by default – and whenever I drove past he would trumpet and chase after me. I always stopped, and he would then block the road, trapping me for as long as possible as he browsed around the Land Rover. I loved our 'chats' together but this didn't disguise his loneliness or unease. His newfound relationship with me, however expedient, was not natural and concerned me a little. Elephant bulls are always pushed out of the herd at puberty, and eventually they get over the rejection and join a loose affiliation with other bachelors.

However, we didn't have other bachelors, and to bring in a dominant bull to provide Mnumzane with a father figure was not something KZN Wildlife would consider. New rules set by KZN Wildlife demanded a larger reserve for elephant bulls, and it would have to wait for the Royal Zulu project to come to fruition. Mnumzane was thus stuck in no man's land living partly on his own and partly on the fringes of the herd.

One day, he was grazing a few yards off when I got an ominous radio call from the lodge. Penny our bull terrier was missing. She loved hanging out at the lodge where she was spoiled rotten by guests and we brought her down from the house most days. She relished swimming in the water-hole on the riverbank just in front of the lodge and would leap in regularly to cool off. As I have said before, her devotion to us and Françoise in particular was absolute. She was short for her breed but had the courage and character of a Titan.

I have always loved bull and Staffordshire terriers. They are the most tolerant, loving, friendly dogs imaginable, and you get a power keg of protection thrown in as a bonus. Unfortunately they don't like other dogs much and you have to watch that, but they can be taught and are more than worth the effort.

With Max at my heels I searched around the lodge, periodically yelling Penny's name. She normally reacted to my whistle, bursting out of the bush with a tail doing windmill facsimiles. But today there was only silence and I feared the worst. A dog AWOL on a game reserve usually meant one of two things: a leopard or a poacher's snare, where the poor animal would die a horrible, lingering death if not found in time. I forced the images out of my mind and walked through the bush in ever-widening circles carefully searching for her spoor. Nothing at all.

I eventually gave up, turned around and made my way down to the waterhole where suddenly I saw fresh spoor. I followed her tracks down into the riverbed and then some way upstream past some deep green pools. I shuddered, goosebumps on my arm.

The Afrikaners have a saying ''*n hond se gedgate*', which literally translated means 'a dog's thought' or gut feeling, that innate sense of premonition that all humans have in greater or lesser degrees. Looking at those sinister pools I felt something was wrong and I involuntarily reached down for Max's collar.

Then I saw it. With its knobby grey-green armour-plating barely detectable in the wind-rustled reeds, lay an absolute monster of crocodile. A flash of white caught my eye and just a few yards from it, lying motionless in a still backwater, was Penny. My heart sank into my boots. She had been snatched and drowned.

The crocodile was resting, about to submerge the corpse into its lair where it would decay. Despite its fearsome fangs, a crocodile cannot chew and unless there are two to tear a kill apart, a lone crocodile has to let its prey decompose into soft-rotted chunks before it can ingest it.

There was no way I was going to leave my loyal dog there. I edged closer. Crocodiles don't like loud noises; they like being surprised even less. I crept forward and when I was barely fifteen yards away, I jumped up, screamed and clapped my hands. With a whoosh of its huge tail it was gone.

I waited until it resurfaced some way downriver and then waded into the pool to retrieve Penny's body. Shocked and saddened, I carried her back up to the lodge and laid her gently on the lawn. Max, who had followed closely, pushed forward and sat silently next to her lifeless body.

Biyela and I buried her under a beautiful spreading buffalo thorn, the legendary *umphafa* tree which Zulus associate with the spirit world. It was just the two us. Brendan, who loved Penny, was on the other side of the reserve. Françoise was too tearful to come down.

'She liked to swim too much,' said Biyela as he laid his spade down. 'The crocodile was waiting for her.'

Knowing Penny, I wasn't so sure Biyela was right. Penny may have been domesticated, but she was still savvy to the bush. I couldn't see any croc stalking her. She was quick, smart and possessed survival senses long distilled out of desk-bound humans. Her death niggled at me; I really wanted to know what had happened.

The next day I went down to where we suspected she had been snatched and started unravelling the tracks, trying to fathom what actually took place. Reading signs of the wild is a dying art which few today have mastered. But I had learned something of it over the years, so I decided I'd stay at the river and turn over every piece of bush testimonial until the mystery was solved.

First checking that the monster crocodile wasn't around, I settled down on a rock and studied the evidence with silent stoicism, trying to get the bush to talk to me. Penny's tracks showed she had been pacing the riverbank. By the length of her stride, the scuff marks of her paws and the short turns executed indicated she was moving quickly and obviously excited. But the tracks were not at the water's edge; she was

237

a few yards up the bank, relatively safe with her turn of speed from any hungry crocodile. There was only one place where she actually went down to the water, possibly to take a drink.

Then I left the rock and walking carefully so as not to disturb the signs, picked up the crocodile's four-footed tracks from where it emerged on the bank, moving up towards the lodge to where it turned and slithered back into the water. Interestingly, Penny's tracks were a couple of yards above. She had seen it come out and had been stalking it, probably worrying it as it lumbered along the bank. This ruled out any surprise attack on her.

So I went back and carefully studied Penny's tracks at the only place where they led to the water's edge – initially where I thought she had gone in for a drink. Something didn't gel.

There were no signs of a struggle. And even more crucially there were no signs of the croc beaching itself in an attack, and no drag marks, not even in the mud under the water. Once a croc's jaws snap shut it's an inexorable slide to the water, an awful one-way ticket to hell which had to leave stark tracks of the victim's frantic struggle. Especially in this still pool.

Yet Penny's tracks indicated the exact opposite. Her footprints clearly showed that the sand had been scuffed backwards; that she had been charging into the river. It didn't make any sense at all.

And then it came to me. She hadn't gone to the river for a drink and been attacked by the crocodile. In fact, the exact opposite: the attack had happened the other way round. The croc hadn't gone for Penny at all. My mad, insane, beautiful dog had instead attacked the crocodile. She had deliberately rushed into the water and taken on a killing machine twenty times her size. Bush signs do not lie.

There are those who will say Penny was little more than

a dumb dog. I strongly disagree. I believe Penny saw a crocodile, recognized a threat and in her mind she was guarding our territory. With the limitless, impossible courage of her breed, she willingly gave her life to protect all that was important to her, all that she loved. In the same way that Max would soundlessly attack a spitting cobra, Penny went to her death doing what she considered her duty. Penny had perished in her own version of the Alamo or Thermopylae.

She was one of the finest and bravest creatures I have known.

Things, good or bad, never seem to happen singularly for me. They always come in triplicate.

Soon after losing Penny, Max was at the lodge dozing on the patio when he sat up sharply, sniffing the air. His nose followed the drift of the unfamiliar scent and quickly found its source. It was a bushpig, a hulking boar making his way rapidly across the lawn towards the lodge.

A bushpig is about two- to three-feet high, roughly the same size as a warthog and to the untrained eye the two are easily confused. But that's where the similarities end. A warthog has semicircular tusks and frightens easily. A bushpig is feral to its core and should be avoided at all costs in the wild. It's a real fighter, weighing up to 140 pounds and uses its lower incisor teeth with devastating effect on any creature that underestimates it.

Max didn't know about that. There was an intruder in his territory and the wiry hair on his back sprung up. Characteristically, he did not bark and at a sprint he cut the boar off, forcing it to confront this unusual threat. I say unusual because even a couple of hungry hyenas will avoid taking on a healthy adult bushpig.

In the wild there is no such thing as an idle threat, and stand-offs usually end with one animal tactically retreating so that 'face' is saved all round. There is no medical care in the bush and animals instinctively know that even a scratch can prove fatal if infected. Thus unlike humans who square up over something as flimsy as road rage, animals fight only as an absolute last resort. In this case there was no need for combat as neither could nor wanted to eat the other, and the bushpig was only a temporary trespasser. There was no need to take it further.

But they did. The big boar held his ground, refusing to back off and Max took up the challenge and began circling, looking for an opening. Then the boar did a little mock charge, and that was that. The fighting genes of Max's terrier forebears kicked in and he smashed into the big pig in a silent full-blooded charge. I was at the main house at the time, but fortunately David was nearby. Realizing the terrible danger Max was in, forgot his own safety and ran at them screaming.

Too late. The boar swivelled and rammed his shovel-shaped head under Max's gut, hoisting him high into the air. As Max toppled over the boar was on him, slashing with dagger-like incisors at his soft underbelly.

Max scrambled up and came at him again, fast and furious, but the boar, using his superior bulk bowled him over once more, hacking with lethal accuracy as Max rolled, desperately trying to regain his footing.

They parted briefly, the pig standing firm with Max, his pelt now slick with blood, circling warily, again looking for an opening. Both were completely oblivious to David's yelling.

Once again Max propelled himself forward and after another vicious melee the bushpig, unaccustomed to such determination from an obviously smaller opponent, retreated into the bush.

Seconds later Max proudly trotted back to David, ignoring the fact that his stomach had been gutted and his entrails were hanging out in ropes.

'Max, you're a complete bloody mess,' said David, shocked rigid. He picked the dog up, making sure the slithering intestines followed, and sprinted to the Land Rover. He didn't ease his foot once in the twenty miles to Empangeni, slamming on the brakes only at the surgery. The vet said it was touch-and-go when he began operating.

I visited Max regularly and a few days later he was back at Thula Thula, tail thumping away. Except for a fence of stitches in his stomach, he looked no worse for wear.

Incredibly, a few days later the third incident with our dogs occurred. This time it was Bijou, Françoise's little princess, who got herself into trouble. As I said earlier, Bijou defines the word 'pampered'. She prefers carpets to grass, and will not – or cannot – sleep on the floor. At Françoise's insistence, she only drinks bottled water ('still or sparkling?' the rangers mock when getting her a drink).

I say this only to emphasize how absurd it was for this cosseted mutt to decided to 'attack' a full-grown nyala bull grazing on the lawn close to the lodge's front door. Bijou, who stands an impressive six inches at the shoulder, rushed at the massive buck, yapping for all she was worth. David watched, laughing.

He suddenly choked on his guffaw . . . in an instant the tiny Maltese was too close; in fact, fatally close. Before David could intervene the bull lifted his head and in a blur rammed its long horns down on her.

Bijou lay still on the ground, little bigger than a crumpled white handkerchief and David's heart stopped. He knew his life was worth peanuts if he had to tell Françoise that Bijou had been killed on his watch.

Frantically chasing the bull away, David rushed over and picked the poodle up, checking for wounds. There were none, not even a splotch of blood. She's had a heart attack, he thought . . . then slowly she wriggled back to life. Bijou had simply fainted from fright as the horns pierced the ground on either side, missing by fractions. Today, Bijou still struts imperiously indoors but doesn't go outside much any more.

However, the numerous nyala grazing literally outside our bedrooms reminded me that we had a surplus of these magnificent antelope on the reserve and I decided we should sell about thirty off to other reserves for breeding purposes.

A phone call later and a game-capture specialist was on Thula Thula darting the animals, which we placed in a *boma* with plenty of fresh water and alfalfa until we had reached the sell-off quota. We would then load them into the customized van and he would deliver them to the buyer.

Brendan was overseeing the capture and radioed to say we had our quota and the van would be leaving the next morning. It had been a long day. I was tired and looking forward to an early night. Thus I was surprised to be woken by a radio call from Brendan at 11 p.m. 'You'd better come down. The most amazing thing has just happened.'

I cursed, pulled on some clothes and drove down to where Brendan and the team were waiting. The first thing I noticed was that the door to the *boma* was open.

'Where're the nyala? Surely you didn't load at night!'

I turned to the game-capture man who was standing with his staff staring at the open door. He looked as though he had seen a ghost.

'You're not going to believe what happened,' he said.

'Try me!' My patience was somewhat aggravated by lack of sleep.

'We were sitting by the *boma*, just chatting,' he said, 'when we heard the elephants come. A couple of minutes later Nana led the herd into the clearing and so we moved right off – some quicker than others,' he grinned, looking at Brendan. 'We thought she had smelled the alfalfa. We had twelve buck inside and we were worried what would happen

242

to them if the *boma* was flattened by the herd going crazy for the food.

'Then the herd stopped, as if on instruction. Nana walked alone to the *boma*. Just as we thought she would smash through the fence, she stopped at the gate. It wasn't locked because the clasps were folded and were secure enough. She started fiddling with the clasps and got one open, then the other, and then pulled open the door. We couldn't believe it, she actually opened the damn door!'

He looked around as the others nodded.

'Then instead of going for the alfalfa, which we thought was her whole mission, she stood back and waited. After a few seconds a nyala came out, then another, and before we knew it they had all found the gap and were gone.

'The weirdest thing is that as the last one fled, Nana just walked off and the others followed. They didn't even go for the alfalfa – a pile of prime chow and they just ignored it.'

I looked at him, smiling. 'Okaaaay. So what you're saying is that the elephants felt sorry for the poor old nyala. They came across the reserve just to release them out of the goodness of their hearts. Because they had nothing better to do. Good try. Now . . . what really happened?'

'I swear to God that's exactly what happened. Ask the others.' And with that they all started jabbering away simultaneously, backing up him and outdoing one another in verifying the story.

It took me a bit of time to digest it but there was no doubt they were telling the truth. There were elephant tracks all around the *boma* and Nana had thoughtfully dumped a steaming pile at the gate as a smoking gun. The lock clasps were also all smothered in trunk slime.

How or why this occurred remains a mystery for some, but it's a mystery only if you grant elephants' limited intelligence. Once you grasp that these ancient giants who have roamed the planet since time immemorial are sentient beings it all becomes clear. Nana, once a prisoner of the *boma* herself, had decided to let the nyala go free. It is as simple – or complicated, if you like – as that. There can be no other explanation.

The story was told and retold in the bush. Eventually the local media got hold of it and it spread to the international press: how a herd of wild elephants had freed a group of captured antelope. The significance of one species rescuing another for no ulterior motive seemed to interest even the most jaded journalist.

Of course, the next day we had to start all over again, capturing fresh nyala and this time we strung an electric wire powered by a mobile energizer around the Nyala *boma* to prevent another rescue mission. To me the trouble was worth it. I had never before felt prouder of my elephants.

chapter twenty-eight

Mistakes in the bush have a nasty habit of being irrevocable. As I have no desire to be a dead hero, I usually err on the side of caution by a healthy margin. Whenever I park the Land Rover near the herd, I always make sure I have a clear escape route. Or when I approach them on foot, I never venture too far from the vehicle.

But this time I was caught unawares. By the time I saw her coming, it was too late. ET was hurtling out of the bush like a missile and there was no way I could scramble to the safety of my vehicle in time. I was in big trouble and had no option but to defy every screaming instinct in my body and force myself to hold my ground and face the charge. Despite my mounting panic, some small voice kept reminding me that any attempt to flee would be a deadly mistake.

All of a sudden, Nana, who was about twenty yards off, moved across at surprising speed for her bulk and blocked the charge with the broadside of her body. The youngster stumbled, knocked off course. Clumsily regaining her balance, she meekly swung around and lumbered to the back of the herd while Nana resumed grazing as if nothing had happened.

I stared, barely breathing, pulling body, soul and nerves back together. That was certainly a first for me. In fact I had never heard of it before; a wild elephant blocking the charge of another to protect a human. Nana was radically changing the way I perceived her species. Over the past few weeks I had been wondering how to handle ET's constant aggression and here Nana was doing it for me, disciplining and teaching her not to hurt me.

Before ET's arrival I had planned to start cutting back on my visits to the herd. My sole purpose was to rehabilitate them in the bush so that they remained truly wild elephants, supremely at peace in their environment. That was why I was adamant that none of my staff ever interacted with them – in fact if they did, they were liable for instant dismissal. It was crucial that the herd learned to trust a human, but only one, which would stop them from attacking people but still keep them feral. Wild elephants that become accustomed to people generally can be extremely dangerous and unpredictable at times and almost always end up getting shot. For this reason I never interacted with the herd for guests.

My idea was that once the herd was settled I would gradually withdraw until there was no more contact. I believed I was almost there.

But ET was still a major problem. While the herd comfortably tolerated Land Rovers cruising past, ignoring them as they should, ET was doing the exact opposite. She regularly made threatening moves and gestures at the vehicles, which was alarming guests and upsetting the rangers. Wilderness bush walks, a favourite with our visitors, had become too dangerous to continue.

Consequently, I needed to spend more time with her. So instead of cutting back contact as planned, I was now forced to increase visits – with some alarming consequences, as I'd just experienced. I would have to be more careful in future.

I started working with her from my vehicle, approaching slowly head-on and watching her reaction. Invariably she would have a go at me, whether it was just two or three aggressive steps or a headlong run, angrily flaring her ears and lifting her tail. In the *boma* I had purposefully backed off whenever she did this, feigning fear to shore up her depleted confidence. That had worked at the time, but maybe a bit too well. Now I had to reverse tactics. She had to learn to respect me, and then all vehicles and humans.

Through trial and error I had learned several techniques on how to approach an aggressive elephant. One was to ignore it, which always worked wonders as it piqued curiosity and usually prompted a benign acknowledgement of my presence. But that would come later. In ET's case, I decided she needed to be challenged directly. Mind games would probably not work here. I had to confront her head-on.

Obviously I couldn't start on foot. Instead I would approach in the Land Rover, stop in front of her and wait, engine idling. Then as she started charging and got close I would jerk the Landy forward at her once or twice in rapid succession, just a yard or so, but usually that was all that was needed to make her stop and think again. To an elephant this is in effect saying, 'I'm not messing about here; I'm ready to fight – so back off.'

This move always broke her aggression. Then I would lean out of the window and say in a firm but comforting voice, 'ET, if you don't mess with me we can be friends.' I was in effect demonstrating my position of seniority in the herd's hierarchy.

I swear Nana and Frankie knew exactly what I was doing with their unruly adopted child. If not, how do you explain the one instance when ET came at me out of the blue from a thicket, once again catching me on foot without an escape route? On this occasion I hadn't seen her as I had approached cautiously thinking she was with the herd in the thick bush ahead when, unusually, she was on her own on the flank.

This time it was Frankie who reacted. She sprinted up alongside the galloping youngster and placed her tusks on ET's rump, forcing her hindquarters sideways and down onto the ground. As ET sprawled in a cloud of dust, Frankie stood over her until ET clambered up in that ungainly way that fallen elephants do and sulked off to join the others. To have Frankie, who was once the definition of aggression, protect me was little short of phenomenal.

The third full-blooded charge was broken by Nana in a somewhat bizarre way. I was about thirty yards away from the herd just sitting and watching when ET started stampeding towards me. But to do so she had to run right past Nana, who was grazing a little way ahead. She heard the youngster coming and tilted her head. As ET began building up a head of steam Nana lifted her trunk and held a pose, waiting. When ET drew level she reached out and touched her ever so gently right in the middle of her forehead with the tip of her trunk.

ET stopped dead, as if she had been whacked on the skull with a sledgehammer. Yet all Nana had done was almost caress her. I had never seen that before.

All this activity would attract the attention of other animals and on this occasion it was a bachelor herd of kudu, with their spiralled horns so beloved by trophy hunters, who watched with interest. They stood stock still except for their twitching oval ears, taking it all in.

The kudu bulls were a reminder to me to be constantly alert. Wildlife is perpetually aware, always ready to flee or fight in an instant. It's a life thrumming with eternal vigilance, absorbing every minuscule detail of one's surroundings, continually assessing degrees of safety and danger. It's knowing where or where not to be, perpetually analysing instinctual information so crucial for survival.

Every wild thing is in tune with its surroundings, awake to its fate and in absolute harmony with the planet. Their attention is focused totally outwards. Humans, on the other hand, tend to focus introspectively on their own lives too often, brooding and magnifying problems that the animal kingdom would not waste a millisecond of energy upon. To most people, the magnificent order of the natural world where life and death actually mean something has become unrecognizable.

I believed ET was making progress, and it appeared that working day after day with her was making a difference.

I was wrong; it was only effective when she was actually with the herd. She had developed another tactic to give vent to her overpowering instinct to kill me. Two junior rangers and I were following the herd on foot from a safe distance. I knew now that Nana and Frankie were implicitly on my side in disciplining the youngster, so I felt relatively safe.

But ET knew otherwise. She stood no chance against me with the matriarch and her deputy around, so she decided to become clandestine. So she broke away from the herd, surreptitiously moving off to the side as the rest moved on and waited in ambush. Before I knew it, I heard that awful sound as the bush came alive with snapping branches and she galloped into the clearing, dipping her head in the awesome way that elephants do when they start a charge – her prize at last within grasp without Nana or Frankie to stop her.

I looked at the out-of-reach Land Rover behind me, and shouted at the two young rangers, 'She's coming! Don't move! It's OK . . . it's OK! Just don't move.'

Running away can all too easily convert a bluff into something lethal and even though it's possibly the most frightening thing to do, a mock charge must be confronted at all costs.

'No! No!' I yelled at ET as she came on at us. 'No!' I raised my arms above my head screaming at her as she thundered on.

At the last moment she broke off, swinging away at a lumbering gait, trunk high.

Then despairingly I watched her turn a wide circle and turn back at us. 'She's coming again! Stand still . . . don't move. Don't move!'

But I was talking to myself. The two young rangers, having just witnessed their first-ever up close and personal elephant charge decided that to stand still for another was the most insane notion ever conceived. They disappeared so fast I thought they had been 'beamed up' to the top of the giant fig tree next to us.

That was fine for them, but it left me confronting a charging ET alone. Emboldened after seeing the rangers ignominiously bolting and clambering up the tree – the very scenario I was trying to prevent – she was now more determined to press home her advantage.

The moment I know when a situation gets hairy with elephants is when pandemonium switches into slow motion and the shrieking, mind-numbing fear leaches out of my body and is replaced by a blissful calmness. And so it was this time. I watched abstractly as I screamed at her until she was virtually on top of me. Then at the last moment she went swinging past. I can tell you that she very nearly didn't pull out of that one.

She kept running, joining the herd who were ambling across to see what all the fuss was about. Personally, I thought that Nana could have reacted a little quicker.

I looked up at the two tree-hugging rangers. 'Jeez! That was unbelievable!' shouted one from the top of the tree, giving me a thumbs-up. 'I can't believe you made it. I thought you were a goner. Well done.'

Yeah, thanks.

The herd was getting closer. The still agitated ET was with them, so I hurried over to the Land Rover and drove under the giant fig, deliberately calling Nana and Frankie to me. I smiled coldly at the arboreal rangers who were watching the elephants milling beneath them and gave a return thumbs-up. I was going to teach these two runners a bush lesson, all right. By fleeing, they had put all of our lives at risk.

I talked to the elephants for a short while, jokingly chiding Nana for not being there for me and sternly chastising ET for what had happened. Then I drove off, leaving the rangers hanging on to branches with the herd right beneath them.

On my way home I had a treat which more than made up for the trauma of the charge: a pair of foraging honey badgers jaunted past, just yards from the vehicle. I don't see them often, but they are among my favourite animals.

Bodies slung low to the ground, their thick fur is deep black except for the back which boasts a silver-white frost. The rich pelt is loose-fitting, allowing the badger to swivel its sinewy body almost 180 degrees out of a predator's grip and counter-attack with its pickaxe teeth and bear-trap death grip. No predator in its right mind would ever be brave or dumb enough to try and grab one.

Bluntly courageous, the honey badger, or *ratel* as the Afrikaners call it, fears nothing; not humans, not lions, not anything. They are absolute dreadnoughts and you mess with them at your peril. I once heard from a fellow ranger of a pair foraging among logs and hidey-holes that concealed food and walked right into a resting pride of lions. The badgers didn't even look up as they sauntered along while the scampering lions rapidly decided that *ratel* wasn't on the menu. It was bizarre to see the kings of the jungle jumping up wide-eyed with alarm as these ferocious little warriors buzzed past.

About three hours later I was relaxing on the front lawn with a beer when the rangers got back, sweaty and bedraggled. I didn't have to say anything.

Nor did they. They had learned their lesson.

chapter twenty-nine

It was spring again and the landscape sparkled in emerald and jade hues animated by the radiant colours of birds, flowers and trees. New life was everywhere, and everything seemed as it should be. Trees blossomed and the herds of buck, wildebeest and zebra were starting to put on weight, glowing with health as the pregnant females prepared to foal. But spring also brings the inevitable storms.

I felt the wind suddenly shift with a vicious gust and looked up to the sky. High above the eastern horizon bundles of cumulo nimbus towered into the stratosphere. A storm was gathering, a big one. I radioed Brendan and the rangers to warn them.

'It looks like a number. Let's get everyone in before it explodes.'

An hour later and we knew we were in for it. The wind had come up and it was as if a purple-grey blanket was being yanked across the heavens. It had been as hot as hell for the last two weeks and the rain gods were going to fix it their way.

The first peals of thunder rumbled in the distance and Max collapsed. He really hated thunder so I carried him inside where he sat staring forlornly at the wall. I made a mental note that if I ever had to burgle a home that had Staffordshire terriers, I would do so during a storm. Bijou was safely ensconced on her feathered pillow and I hoped

253

her usual late-afternoon pre-snooze nap would not be disturbed too much.

Outside it was still darkening by the second when a jagged white bolt of lightning seared through the sky followed by an almighty clap of thunder overhead. I walked to the bottom of the garden and looked out over the reserve which was quickly disappearing behind the grey sheets of water rolling in over the hills. Watching a spectacular Zululand thunderstorm advance is an unforgettable experience.

The first drops splattered on the earth, exploding like little bombs kicking up dust. Then the full storm hit us; within seconds foliage that usually stood firm gave up and the wilderness sagged under the soggy onslaught.

The pelting rain formed into puddles and then streams swept across the ground taking the colour of the rich soil with them. These hundreds of rivulets fiddled along: moving, stopping, starting and merging with others, flowing, swelling then, raging down to the lowest point – the Nseleni River, which bisects the reserve.

I watched, happy, as it continued to bucket down. The dams would be full again and millions of little clefts, dips, fissures and depressions would trap the moisture that sustained life. We could never get enough rain. Despite its picture-postcard beauty, much of South Africa in reality is a land of long droughts punctuated by rain.

The house lights behind me flickered and then went out which was par for the course with a storm, and meant the phones were gone as well. Through the windows I could see Françoise lighting candles, even though it was still mid-afternoon.

I went inside and wrapped my two-way radio in plastic. I knew from experience that it would be our only outside link for the night.

An hour and a half later and my contentment was beginning to be tempered by a touch of concern. If anything, it was raining harder than before and there were now brown streams surging across all the roads.

'Brendan, come in, Brendan,' I called on my radio.

'Standing by,' he replied.

'How's the river looking?'

'Not bad. It's coming up slowly but nothing serious.'

Brendan was at an outpost near the lodge keeping an eye on the Nseleni River. I have always longed for a gently flowing European-type river with steady banks, but this was Africa and our rivers are as volatile as nitroglycerine. One moment they're barely moving, the next they're a violent, muddy torrent that will sweep you twenty miles to the ocean in a heartbeat if you're careless enough to get caught.

The sections of fence where the river entered and exited the reserve were particularly vulnerable to flooding. Here we had built sacrificial barriers designed to break away in a deluge, but until they were replaced they left huge gaps through which the elephants could escape. This meant we would have to move fast as soon as the storm was over.

Two hours later it was almost pitch-black, the rain was still bulleting down and everything had changed. Brendan's voice staccatoed on the radio: 'You'd better come down and have a look. The river is getting seriously out of control.'

'How're the sacrificial fences?'

'Long gone.'

Françoise was sitting next to me. 'I'm going down to the river to Brendan,' I told her. 'It's come right up. I'll go past the lodge and do a check while I'm there.'

'I'll come with you,' she said, moving Bijou, who was now having her pre-nocturnal sleep, off her lap. 'I'm worried about the guests with no electricity. Some of them are real city people and I should be there with them.'

We grabbed raincoats and made a dash for the Land Rover, pulling out onto the road, which was now just a sloppy stream, causing the Land Rover to skid and slide all over the place. Above us almost continuous lightning illuminated in silver our savannah plains completely inundated with water.

As we rounded the last corner I got my first glimpse of the river. My heart jumped at the view of the seething torrent and I pulled over. 'Good God! Look at that – it's a monster!'

I reversed back and turned down the track to the river crossing, just above where we had been charged on the quad bike by Frankie, and played the headlights on the liquid mayhem roaring past.

A dead cow swept past in the gurgling waves, then another. 'This is unbelievable,' I said. Françoise just stared.

I slammed the Land Rover into reverse, but instead of going backwards the wheels spun loosely in the slimy mud and to my horror we started inexorably sliding forward, slipping down the slope into the hurtling river.

Just as I thought all was lost and we were going into the torrent, I instinctively swung the wheel and jammed the Landy hard against the right bank, wedging it into the soft soil.

'Get out quickly,' I told a wide-eyed Françoise. 'The Landy could slip away again. Let's go!'

She opened her door and disappeared from view as she fell into the mud. I clambered over to her side and helped her up. Then we slithered up the crossing back to the main track in the darkness, slipping and grabbing onto each other for support in the frictionless mud. Thankfully I had the presence of mind to bring the radio and a torch was clipped onto my belt. I called Brendan.

'Standing by. Where're you?' he asked.

'At the lodge crossing. The Landy's stuck at the water's edge. Can you get the tractor down as fast as possible? Or we're going to lose it.'

'Shit, what you doing there?'

'What do you think? I was about to go for a swim but changed my mind when I saw the dead cows.'

'Yeah, I saw them bobbing like corks. Even worse, I think I've also seen a body or two as well. Not sure, though, with the dark. Sorry but I can't get to you – our vehicles are up to the axles in mud. I'll try and work out how to get Gunda Gunda down.'

'Françoise is with me. We can't stay here, we're going to walk to the lodge.'

'OK . . .' He paused. 'Just remember the *ngwenyas*.'

Knowing Françoise was listening he had purposefully used the Zulu word for crocodiles. I silently thanked him.

The entrance to the lodge grounds was only about a hundred yards away, with the lodge itself another hundred after that. But between us and the entrance were two deep pools, one on each side of the road. Just yesterday Brendan and I had noticed that two huge crocs had taken up residence, one in each pool. Unusually, I hadn't brought a gun and now I really wished I had. Not to shoot the reptiles, but to frighten them off.

I surveyed the way ahead. The pools had overflowed onto the road between them and merged into a small lake. I knew exactly where the road went but it was swamped, about a foot and a half deep – easily enough to hide a crocodile in the dark.

We stopped at the edge and I played my torch over the water and found one almost immediately, its red eyes reflecting back at us. Then I saw the other. They were together and had left the deluge and moved away about thirty yards to a ledge on much higher ground. They were far enough away and, praying that the duo hadn't been joined by a third mate since we last saw them, I took Françoise's hand and we waded through the flow.

Emerging on the other side, it suddenly dawned on me

that even the crocodiles were instinctively seeking higher ground. How much bigger was this river going to get?

A few minutes later we were at the lodge which was in complete darkness. Françoise cleaned herself up and went to some of the guests who had left their rooms and were in the bar area putting on brave faces. I grabbed the security ranger and we walked down the expansive lawn towards the Nseleni valley. We were barely able to hear each other speak, such was the roar of the river, and then I felt water sloshing through my boots. These were no mere rain puddles.

A flash of lightning showed me the truth. The river, about a hundred yards away, was so swollen it had overflowed its banks and was starting to surge across the lawns. I immediately turned and ran back past the lodge down to near where we had passed the crocodiles in the pools.

As I suspected both pools were now completely submerged by a new river that had broken away and surged around the rear of the lodge grounds. And then I realized that we were completely cut off; the rampaging Nseleni River in front, and a flash flood at the back. This was why the crocs were seeking higher ground. The lodge was in danger of being engulfed.

I vaguely heard the radio cackle. It was Brendan: 'Come in, come in . . .' he was calling repeatedly.

I thumbed the button. 'Standing by. Sorry, I didn't hear the radio with the river noise.'

'We got the Landy out, but only just. I'm afraid we can't get to you. The river's jumped its banks.'

'I know. There's not much we can do, we're trapped at the lodge. We'll have to sit it out here. Stay in touch and let's conserve batteries.'

'Roger and out,' said Brendan and a few minutes later I saw his vehicle lights piercing the gloom a mile or two away as they headed back to the house.

I returned to the lodge where for three nerve-wracking hours I watched as the overflowing river inched closer and closer to the buildings. Thankfully the rain had stopped and just as I thought we would have to start getting my guests onto the lodge roof, the water stopped rising. We were safe. Françoise had found us an empty room. I had a warm shower, then told the night ranger to wake me if the river rose higher.

The next morning I was woken at dawn by Brendan on the radio issuing instructions to staff. The storm was over. Looking out of my window there wasn't a cloud in the sky . . . after all that drama last night. The sun was beaming and the river was dropping, but we were still cut off.

'Hi, Brendan, what's the damage?'

'Well, we measured six inches of rain and then the gauge overflowed. The Nseleni broke its banks for five solid miles. Our problem is, it didn't only take out the sacrificial fence, but another 500 yards on the eastern boundary as well. It's gone, like it was never there.'

'Where's the herd?'

'No idea. But if I know Nana, she's taken them to the top of the hills.'

'I hope so. That fence's going to take all day to repair and you still have to cross the river somehow to get to it.'

'Don't tell me. We're going to try and string a cable across, as it's still too wild to swim. I'll let you know how it goes.'

'OK, but put some guys on the lookout for the elephants. We need to know where they are.'

'Will do, out.'

Luckily when the herd was eventually sighted they were on the opposite side of the river to where Brendan was working, unable to access the gap in the fence even if they wanted to. I told Ngwenya to find a high spot and keep an eye on them.

The flash torrent behind the lodge had now dropped and a ranger drove my Land Rover down to rescue us – and not a moment too soon as I got the call I had always dreaded. It was Ngwenya.

'Mkhulu, Mkhulu! Come in! Come in quickly, the elephants are out. They are outside.'

I grabbed my radio and answered in a flat spin, 'Where? What's happened?'

'On the northern boundary. They're walking along the fence, but on the wrong side.'

The northern boundary was not too far away and thankfully on high ground. I jumped into the Land Rover and called Musa the fence ranger, instructing him to follow me on the quad bike and we sped off, skidding on the barely passable roads.

We arrived twenty minutes later and I saw Nana right away. But she and the others were inside the fence; what was Ngwenya on about?

Such was my relief that it took me a moment to realize that something was indeed seriously amiss. Both Nana and Frankie were pacing back and forth as agitated as all hell. Every few seconds they would stop and stretch their trunks over the top electric wires and shake the fence poles, the only part they could reach without shocking themselves.

I counted the herd as I always do. There was one missing, but which one? It had to be Mnumzane? No, there he was too, so I counted again.

Then I saw a movement on the other side of the fence that was attracting the herd's attention. There stood little Mandla, Nana's firstborn son. He was alone, and from his forlorn demeanour it seemed he had gone from panic into apathy and given up trying to get back to his agitated mother. The fence would hold, for the time being at least, but how were we going to get Mandla back in? The nearest gate was miles away, but a gate would be of little use because it was just as likely that Nana would go out as Mandla come in.

I drove closer and called out to Nana to let her know I was there. She looked over at me, staring hard. My mind sped, trying to find solutions. If we didn't get Mandla inside soon, the herd would break through the fence. There was no question about that; an elephant mother will do whatever it takes to ensure the safety of her babies.

Perhaps we could cut the fence, but then we would have the same problem as with a gate. I got out of the Landy, lit a cigarette and pondered the problem. How could we get Mandla in without letting the herd out? I looked at the electric wires and an idea started to form. If we cut the fence itself and then also the middle and bottom electric wires, Mandla could get in, leaving the top live wire intact to prevent the adults from going out. The question was, would the top electric wire alone be enough to keep Nana and Frankie at bay?

Nana shook the fence violently again. Suddenly I heard the sound of dogs barking . . . hunting dogs. Zulus traditionally hunt with indigenous hounds and there was a hunting party somewhere out beyond Mandla. Nana heard them too and she stopped rattling the fence, spreading her ears to absorb every sound.

The hunters were on their own land and in themselves not a problem. What concerned me was that if the dogs got the scent of Mandla and started harassing him, Nana would tear through the fence like a bulldozer.

We took the wire cutters out of the toolbox. The question now was how do we open the fence and cut the electric wires in front of Mandla with a herd of agitated elephants breathing down our necks?

I answered my own question: we cut the hole fifty yards

261

away. I then call Nana, she comes, Mandla follows on the other side of the fence, finds the hole, realizes he can get through and the drama is over.

Easy . . . right?

We moved away, cut the hole, folded back the fence and dropped the bottom two electric wires. The first part of the plan worked fine. Not so the second part: Nana refused to move away from Mandla and I spent a fruitless ten minutes trying to call her. It was a stalemate.

With the yapping of the dogs in the background getting louder I turned to Musa and asked him to go through the hole, backtrack behind Mandla and then make a noise to frighten him forwards toward the hole.

'He's just a youngster,' I said. 'Stay a good distance away and clap your hands to make him run to the hole. There is no danger.'

'*Yebo*, Mkhulu,' he said without enthusiasm.

'Good. We will speak on the radio and I will tell you exactly what to do.'

Musa was a good man but could be a bit of a show-off and often regaled other staff with fantastical stories of his courageous encounters with wild animals – including the elephants. 'I am not scared of them,' he would say, imitating Frankie's gait, using his arm as a trunk. 'They are scared of me.'

Well, now we would see.

He climbed through the fence and after giving him five minutes to get into position I called: 'Where are you?'

'I am here,' he replied, and I wanted to pull my hair out. Musa thought I could 'see' him through the radio. One can laugh at this, but it is just as easy for rural Zulus to laugh at how ignorant many technologically competent Westerners are in the wild.

'Okaaay. Where is here?'

'It is here,' he replied confidently. 'Here where I am.'

262

I promised myself I would strangle him later.

'Good, can you see the young elephant?' I asked.

'*Yebo*, Mkhulu. I can.'

'How far are you?'

'Close.'

'Good. Now clap your hands and I will call the mother at the same time.'

Silence.

'Musa why are you waiting? Clap your hands.'

Nothing.

'Musa! Clap your flipping hands!'

Then I heard clapping . . . well, barely. Painfully slow and methodical and so gentle it would not startle a flea. Worst of all it was happening right next to me, just on the other side of the fence. I looked around and there he was sitting on the ground in the middle of some shrubs slowly clapping his hands. He had gone through the hole in the fence and then hidden in the bush a few yards away rather than approach baby Mandla. So much for him not being afraid of the elephants.

'Musa?'

'*Yebo*?'

'I see you, come out from where you are.'

This made him doubly certain that I could see through the radio and he slowly emerged staring at me, then at the transmitter.

There was nothing left to do but continue trying to call Nana to come to where we had cut the hole and get Mandla to follow her. After forty minutes or so with me going hoarse calling, asking, begging and pleading, she ambled over. Mandla followed dutifully, found the hole, scampered into the reserve and it was over.

As he got back, every one of the elephants crowded around him, touching him with their trunks, fussing over him and rumbling their stomachs. It was humbling to watch the care and affection being showered on him after his ordeal.

I found out later that a flooded stream had taken out a small piece of the fence but left one electric strand still standing that was just high enough for Mandla to walk under – but too low for the rest of the herd. Once out, he panicked and couldn't get back.

I was so relieved to get Mandla back that I forgot to compliment Musa on his 'bravery' – about how scared the elephants, particularly Frankie, were of him. But I'm sure the yarns he told around the village campfire that night more than made up for that.

chapter thirty

Most rural Zulus believe that spirits, in countless forms and guises, are very busily involved in the destiny of man, that they take form in the plant and animal kingdoms, and that the rivers, skies and mountains are inhabited by supernatural beings.

They believe that after death there is no heavenly reward or hellish retribution, only a reassumption of the personality of an ancestor, from where one continues a never-ending role in the eternal symbiosis between the spiritual and material worlds. These deep-seated beliefs are poorly understood and too easily ridiculed by many Westerners who think they know best.

That is of course, until you turn out the lights. For there is nothing like darkness, nothing like experiencing night in the African bush with rural Africans who know strange stories to lead your spirit down the same roads. For surely it was not 'civilization' that eroded the spirit world, it was electric light at night, the light that took away the dark, blinded us to ghosts, angels and demons, and vanquished our ancestors.

It was nearly midnight and I was taking the lodge's night staff back up to their houses. There was a tree lying across the road. Mnumzane had come through the area earlier and he had a habit of doing that. Sometimes I used to think he was purposely closing roads. I mean, how come the trees were never pushed over away from the road?

I couldn't squeeze past the tree so I turned to go along the river road, a good alternative route, when one of the staff girls said to me, 'Mkhulu, why are you going this way?'

'Why not?' I replied. 'It's much shorter.'

'You cannot,' she replied quietly. 'Not this way, not now.'

'Why not?' I repeated.

'Do you not know of the *tagati* that lives here?

'No, I don't. Where?'

'In the big rock in the cliff at the river, it lives there, we cannot go near, please turn around.'

A *tagati* is a proactive evil spirit and the cast-iron rule for Zulus is that you don't have anything to do with them, ever. So, respecting the staff's wishes, I reversed and we took the longer road home. Later, I did some research and went back to find out what they were talking about.

The village *sangoma*, or diviner (often mistakenly called a witchdoctor), explained it to me: 'That *tagati* has been there for as long as anyone can remember,' he said. 'Long before Thula Thula, long before the white man came, and he will be there long after we are all gone. It is his place; do not go there.'

'Why not?' I asked.

He looked at me in a strange way. 'Why would anyone want to go to a *tagati*?' he asked querulously. 'You do not know *tagati*, be very careful.'

Well, of course I went there. A few times, in fact, and try as I might I didn't see or feel anything. I think. Well maybe, if I stretch my imagination far enough, and add a dollop of fantasy. On one occasion when I was there for a while studying the rock I could have sworn I picked up a little something, a little uneasiness, but it was inconsequential and I forgot about it.

In deference to my staff who had all been talking disap-

266

provingly about my visits to the place, I started to pay respect to the superstition and only went past if I had to. It was near one of our roads after all.

Then one evening at dusk I was slowly driving along the river road, looking for foreign plants of all things, when I got an uncomfortable sensation of sorts, and unconsciously looking up, found myself below the same concave rock I had been warned about.

Surprised by this illogical intrusion into my practical contemplations, I stopped, and as I did so a strange feeling came over me and I experienced a dim awareness that all was not right. The feeling slowly grew as I sat there spell-bound. Suddenly I became aware of a presence I can only describe as one of absolute malevolence. An involuntary alarm seized me and I went into goosebumps all over. Then slowly the sensation dissipated, almost as if it was taken up by the rock itself.

Not being superstitious at all I was shocked at my reaction and looked back at the rock, still drawn to it. I swear there was still a little something there, a tiny residue of what I had just experienced. And that's when I recognized it. The residue was what I had picked up on my previous visits, when I thought I felt a little something but wasn't sure. I recovered myself and left very perplexed, too embarrassed to tell anyone about it, and eventually put it out of my mind.

A few weeks later I decided I had to go back. I wanted another's opinion. Not from a Zulu for I already knew what they would say, if I could even get them to go. I wanted a Westerner's opinion. David would be the one. So I waited for dusk and then said to him, 'Come with me, I want you to see something.'

We drove down the river road just as it was getting dark and I stopped below the rock and turned the motor off.

'What are we doing here?' David asked.

'This place . . .' I said, 'that rock, what do you think of it? Take your time.'

David knew we were here for a reason and looked around unhurriedly, and then I watched as his gaze slowly went up to the concave edifice as if drawn there. My skin started to prickle as he did so, and after a while he turned to me. David, who is as tough as they come, smiled strangely and said to me quietly, 'Let's get the hell out of here – now.'

We stayed silent until we were almost back at the lodge and then he laughed and said to me, 'What the hell was that?'

'A *tagati*,' I said, laughing back, 'a bloody *tagati*, that's what it was.'

Sangomas rule the roost in rural Zulu society, not overtly, but behind the scenes, where they are very influential and highly respected. Many are charlatans who manipulate superstition for their own ends, but there are those who are legitimate, practising an ageless art which is as far removed from Western science as you can possibly get. Any interview with a good sangoma is a more than interesting experience.

A *sangoma* is born, not made. One cannot just decide to be a *sangoma*, you have to be chosen or otherwise accepted under unusual circumstances, and historically this takes place at a very early age. Sometimes the *sangomas* will even arrive at a home and announce to the parents that their child is a *sangoma*, perhaps the incarnation of a deceased *sangoma* and tell them who. This is a great honour for the family and not so long ago they would even give up the child who then goes away to live with these spirit doctors for indoctrination, taking on the mantle of *sangoma* for the rest of their life.

Sangomas, unlike *inyangas* who are herb doctors or medicine men, deal exclusively with the spirit world. Typically an interview will have the *sangoma* go into a trance, com-

268

municating with the ancestors, principally your own ancestors; your long-dead family members. Messages will be passed to you from one ancestor or another, advice given and sometimes the future foretold.

If you have an ailment it must be divined by the *sangoma*. This is the opposite of Western medicine where one must tell the doctor the symptoms. With a *sangoma* you may not say what is wrong with you. It is the *sangoma* who must make the diagnosis entirely without your help. Their reputations depend on it.

I once gave a *sangoma* a lift and in return he offered me a session which I accepted out of interest. I happened to have a back pain which he diagnosed. It is uncanny to sit there with an ailment and have it identified and be given the cure via an ancestral-induced trance.

Since then I have attended several such trances and the results can sometimes be absolutely remarkable, though it is not for the faint-hearted since *sangomas* tell it like it is.

Françoise had an idea that overseas guests would be interested in this, so we made an arrangement with a local *sangoma* to receive lodge guests who wanted to 'have their fortunes told'. He started doing well with the extra fees he was receiving and the guests loved it.

The next thing we knew he was showing off a brand-new, shiny briefcase which he carried with him wherever he went. We spoke to him, explaining that his image and regalia of skins and beads were important for overseas guests, and that he must always hide his new briefcase when they arrive. He agreed most reluctantly, because, as he explained, it was such a beautiful briefcase and the guests would be most impressed.

As his income increased his accoutrements grew to include a new cellphone which he strapped to his belt with Zulu beads. We also had to reason with him about that because he had taken to making calls in the middle of his divinations, explaining to his clients that this special phone didn't need wires.

With Françoise and me it is very much 'when in Rome', so we respect the local beliefs. Periodically when staff get sick too often, or there are unusual mishaps, we will call in a respected *sangoma* to put *muthi* or protective spells around the reserve, and it is important for us to be seen to be doing so. For without white magic, they believe *tagati* will get bold, take human form, and ride through the night on the back of a baboon striking terror and spreading evil.

But there are many other lighter and sometimes humorous manifestations of the ancestors and other spirit presences at Thula Thula, such as the infamous *tokoloshe*. A *tokoloshe* is an evil, mischievous little demon, in character somewhat like Loki, the Norse god of chaos, but much smaller in size. *Tokoloshes* are the minions of a *tagati*, and they are sent out all over Zululand every night to create mayhem. Almost every Zulu on Thula Thula has his bed mounted on bricks, two or three under each leg. This is to prevent the tiny *tokoloshe* from bumping his head while he scampers around the floor, and thus earning the sleeper unwanted attention. It is said that only innocent young children can see a *tokoloshe*, who also causes bad dreams.

I have always found it interesting that if you take a Zulu to task about the *tokoloshe* they will often make light of it, laughing at the notion derisively, but go into their room and sure enough, there will be the bricks under his or her bed.

Witchcraft has a more sinister side though. One day I was with Brendan and a ranger called Zungu, watching smoke rising from half-a-dozen places around the village.

'What's going on?' Brendan asked Zungu.

'Today they are burning out the witches and wizards,' he

said matter-of-factly, as if it were an annual event. 'Some have even been seen riding baboons at night.'

'Are they killing them?' Brendan asked worriedly.

'No, no, in the old days they would kill them, now they burn their houses and all their belongings, and chase them away from the village. Some may be beaten but they do not kill them. But they must go,' he added with a note of conviction in his voice.

'What do you mean, they are witches, how do they know they are witches or that witches even exist?'

'Everybody knows they are witches,' he replied comfortably.

Brendan decided not to give up and pushed forward with a line of questioning that had way too much Western logic in it.

'But what would happen if they said your mother was a witch and came for her too,' he asked.

'They wouldn't.'

'Why not?'

'Because everybody knows she is not a witch.'

'OK,' said Brendan, nonplussed. 'If they have done such bad things, why aren't they taken to court?'

'Because the court will ask for proof,' said Zungu.

'That's a good thing,' said Brendan. 'Surely there must be proof of wrongdoing before punishment.'

'There is no proof,' said Zungu. 'Of course there is no proof, and there can be no proof with witches, that's why they are witches.'

Brendan walked away shaking his head. What Zungu was saying made some sense though. What judge would ever believe that a man died of a snakebite, or crops had dried up because a witch had put a spell on the household?

The news of my strange communication with elephants, coupled with my refusal to allow anyone to kill even a deadly snake or scorpion had spread, and many in the village considered me to be somehow mysteriously connected to the animals. I mean, what sort of person would shun normal life and live in the African bush preferring to commune with elephants, rather than his own kind?

Now, if I can just tame a big baboon . . .

chapter thirty-one

'Here, Mkhulu, here!' shouted Bheki, leaning over from the back of the Land Rover into the driver's window. 'Left, left!'

I yanked hard on the steering wheel, bumping roughly off the lip of the rutted track, then swerved to keep the wicked overhanging thorns from raking the rangers standing in the Land Rover's back.

Max, who had his head out of the passenger's window, spilled across the cab and onto my lap.

'Straight, straight!' shouted Bheki, thumping on the roof to get my attention. Ducking the barbed branches and navigating from his elevated position he directed me through the tangled bush and a few jarring minutes later we arrived at the carcass.

It was a wildebeest, albeit barely recognizable as the corpse had been messily butchered. But that was not why we were here. Lying close to the carcass was a dead vulture and further afield I could see another. Both of them had their heads hacked off.

One of the most accurate indicators of a vibrant game reserve is a healthy vulture population. I remembered when we first arrived at Thula Thula searching vainly for breeding pairs. If you don't have large numbers of game you're not going to have resident vultures. In those early days these great, graceful scavengers used to flock in from the Umfolozi game reserve, tiny specks in the sky surfing the thermals at incredible altitudes as they searched for carrion.

Today, with our healthy game population, we had plenty of breeding pairs ensconced in their nests at the top of the great trees lining the river, raising their chicks seasonally and generally doing well for themselves. But now out of the blue, vultures had become top of the poaching hit list and for bizarre reasons that no conservationist could ever have guessed. The once-belittled vulture had become an extremely potent good luck totem among the *sangomas*.

The reason was simple: money. A national lottery had recently been introduced with huge weekly payouts. If you guessed the six winning Lotto numbers you were an instant millionaire. Most of us know that playing a lottery is pure luck. But in Africa, predicting the winning numbers has become a mysterious art verging on the occult. A growing number of South Africans believed that there was only one way to scoop the pools, and that's to consult your ancestors. And who was the vital link between mortals and spirits? Why, the *sangomas*, of course.

This is not just primitive rural superstition; ancestral guidance is practised by all kinds of people, from illiterate herd boys to multi-degreed university professors. If you don't understand the power of this belief, you will never truly grasp the rich albeit often incomprehensible spirituality of Africa. According to some unscrupulous *sangomas*, the most powerful Lotto *muthi* was dried vulture brain. So as the race to become an instant millionaire heated up, the humble vulture was being poached almost to extinction in some game reserves.

Muthi is a collective Zulu term given both to magic spells and to the foul-tasting potions prepared by *sangomas*. It can be good *muthi*, or bad *muthi*, the latter always associated with witchcraft. Dried vulture brain was considered to be very good *muthi* indeed. So much so that *sangomas* told their gullible clients that if they placed a slice of it under their pillows at night, their ancestors would whisper the winning Lotto numbers to them in their dreams.

One of the most inconceivable aspects of vulture *muthi* is how someone blindly places so much faith in something so manifestly unreliable. Thousands of desperately poor peasants, totally ignorant of basic gambling odds, were placing all they could afford into a lottery in which there were precious few winners. Each week, millions lost their hard-earned wages, with or without vulture brains under their pillows.

This translated into big business for *sangomas*. A tiny sliver of vulture's brain cost about ten US dollars, which is a lot of money in outback Zululand. Yet despite there being only a few winners, visits to *sangomas* skyrocketed. And no matter how much they lost, villagers continued forking out wads of cash for more vulture brains, which they religiously placed under their pillows, waiting for their ancestors to murmur the magic numbers.

The end result was distressingly obvious: people squandered lifesavings and vultures continued to die – so much so that in some game reserves breeding pairs were becoming increasingly rare. In fact, the true Lotto winners were the *sangomas*.

We clambered out of the vehicle, dodged a series of tall brown termite mounds which had blocked the Land Rover's passage and closely studied the gory remains of the wildebeest, looking for the cause as we always do with an unnatural death. Other vultures, attracted to the carcass like iron filings to a magnet, either circled above or gathered atop nearby trees, disturbed by our presence.

For obvious reasons, a contagious disease fatality is our biggest fear as it can spread in a blink to other animals. We first checked for nasal discharges, tick loads, injuries, and what the overall condition of the animal had been prior to its demise. This wildebeest had been fit and healthy and the cause of death, while not immediately obvious from the hacked remains, seemed to be a bullet.

Bheki and Ngwenya put down their rifles and were moving in to turn over the body so we could inspect the other side, when something made me stop them.

'Poison,' I said, slowly realizing what had happened. 'I think there is poison here. Don't touch the body until we inspect the vultures.'

They looked up surprised, but said nothing and stepped back, following me as I walked to the first headless bird.

I kept a close eye on Max, ordering him to 'heel' often enough to let him know he must not leave my side, not even for a sniff of the dead creatures. A noseful of strychnine, insecticide, or whatever it was they were using would certainly do him no good.

I had never been that close to a white-backed vulture before. With a seven-foot wingspan it is a big, impressive bird by any standards, but how undignified and ignominious it looked in death. This superb sultan of the skies lay there headless, sprawled awkwardly with one huge wing jutting into the grass. There was not a mark on it and judging by the distance from the wildebeest carcass it must have died very quickly, perhaps even while trying to take off. It was the same with the other one, which had managed to get a little further away. After a thorough search of the immediate area we found four in all.

The wildebeest carcass must have been loaded with toxin to cause death that quickly. Any smaller a dose and the bodies would be dropping miles away and the poachers would never find them.

We walked back and stood leaning against the Landy's hood, surveying the carnage. The rangers also remarked that the wildebeest's tail had been sliced off.

'They have died strangely. There is witchcraft here,' Ngwenya said ominously.

A wildebeest's tail is much prized by *sangomas* who use it as the Zulu equivalent of a magic wand. Ngwenya was correct in believing witchcraft was behind this killing, but for the wrong reason.

'Yes, there is witchcraft here,' I said, confirming his suspicion, 'although not in the way you think.'

I then told them the story of dreams and vulture brains, of the *sangomas* and the Lotto, and waited for their reaction.

Bheki was first to respond. 'I have heard of this. Far away up in the north near Mozambique, but never here.' He shook his head. 'We do not do this.'

'But it is with us now,' said Ngwenya. 'These people do not think. If the vultures die, who is going to clean up all the dead animals in the bush? Disease will come from the rotting meat left behind. It will be bad.'

Ngwenya looked around. I could sense with all the talk of disease what he was thinking. 'The poison is still here, we must burn everything – the wildebeest, the dead birds, everything, or more will die,' he said, pointing at the vultures circling above. 'And tonight the hyenas and jackals who think they have a feast will also die. We must do it now or . . .'

'No. Not yet,' interrupted Bheki. 'The thieves can see the birds above us from faraway and they'll come back to check for more. Let us rather hide now and we will catch them later today.'

'Good idea,' I agreed. 'I have also heard that these vulture poachers act as *impimpi* – informers – for other poachers. If we don't catch them this time, the elephants and rhino will be in serious danger as well.'

I looked at my watch; it was already early afternoon, and there was always something else that needed tending to on the reserve.

'I have to go now, but radio me so I know what is going

on. But whatever happens, do not let any more birds – or anything – eat the meat.'

'Of course, Mkhulu. We will find you here later.'

A couple of hours afterwards I was driving along looking out for either Mnumzane or the herd when a gunshot barked a couple of miles away. I braked hard . . . then the calm voice of Ngwenya staccatoed over the radio.

'Mkhulu, Mkhulu, come in, Mkhulu.'

'Standing by.'

'We have them,' Ngwenya said, jubilation incongruously creeping into his usual phlegmatic voice. 'Two of them.'

'Already! Well done. OK, stay right there – I'm on my way.'

As I passed the housing quarters an idea came to me. Perhaps we could play the *sangomas* at their own game . . .

I drove to the storeroom next to the garage and selected several items, placed them in two large hessian bags and loaded everything on the back of the Land Rover. Then I went into the kitchen and took three packs of beef ribs out of the fridge, wrapped them up and shoved them under the driver's seat where Max couldn't get at them.

Then I radioed two other Zulu rangers, one a middle-aged man whose impressive gravitas would ideally serve my purpose, told them to change into civilian clothes and where to meet me.

Finally I called Ngwenya and asked if he had quizzed the poachers about the poisoned carcasses.

'Negative,' came the reply.

'Good,' I said relieved. 'Don't say anything about the vultures or the poison. Just pretend you're arresting them for killing a wildebeest. I'll explain when I arrive.'

I picked up the two other rangers and on the way we stopped at the lodge where I raided the curio store.

As we drove to where Bheki and Ngwenya were waiting, I explained to the two rangers what had happened and what

I wanted them to do. I then showed them what was in the bags. The older man stared and started laughing; he grasped the plan instantly.

'How is your hyena call?' I asked the younger ranger.

'At school I was the best,' he said modestly.

Imitating animal sounds with uncanny accuracy is a skill many rural Zulu youngsters acquire and tonight we would put it to good use. A hyena, some believe, has supernatural characteristics. When you observe these magnificent creatures up close, their loose-limbed canter and eerie nocturnal howl, you can see why this myth continues.

Zulus are natural actors who enjoy a show and this was going to be fun for them. But it was also serious and their acting had to be both simple and convincing. I left them under a tree to discuss their drama tactics and drove on to join Ngwenya and Bheki.

The two culprits were squatting on their haunches, hands cuffed behind their backs while Bheki and Ngwenya sat around the carcass, their presence deterring the gathering flock of vultures from descending on the poisoned meat. The surrounding trees were now heavy with their presence.

The poachers were in their early twenties and both adopted the air of feigned apathy and despondency that I have seen in every poacher we have ever caught. Given half a chance, though, they would be gone like rabbits and if they still had their guns they would be shooting. In fact, where were their guns, I wondered? I didn't see any.

Ngwenya greeted me and I gave them some water. It had been a hot thirsty day keeping vigil.

'*Yebbo*, Mkhulu,' he said before taking a long draught from the canteen. 'It was easy. They walked up and sat down and we came from behind. I fired one shot in the air and they surrendered. There is their gun and a machete.'

I looked at the old but well-maintained Rossi .38 revolver lying on the grass.

'What's going on?' I asked surprised. 'They can't shoot a wildebeest with a revolver.'

'We questioned them and they told us half lies, half truths,' said Ngwenya. 'They are not locals. They work for a *Sangoma* in the north and say their job was only to collect the tail – which they don't even have. They say the wildebeest was shot by two professional poachers also hired by the *sangoma*. The poachers took most of the meat and left them here. The revolver is just for protection. They are very inexperienced these two, but dangerous.'

'So, these are the magician's assistants?' I said out loud. 'Where is their transport?'

'They have none,' said Bheki. 'They will walk and then take a bush taxi home.'

'And the vulture heads?'

'As you said, we didn't ask but they had a sack. We left it in the bush close by. Don't worry, it is safe,' replied Ngwenya.

'Good.'

I then lowered my voice to a whisper. 'It's a waste of time taking this to the police, just a wildebeest and some vulture heads. So today we will teach them a lesson they will never forget. They are a *sangoma*'s lackeys and they will take a message back to their boss that neither they, nor anyone else can ever come here again. We will fight this with our own witchcraft. Here is the plan.'

Bheki and Ngwenya listened with big smiles as I outlined some impromptu Thula Thula *muthi*. Then, according to plan, they strode across to the two poachers, stood them up and marched them into the bush.

I called the two back-up rangers who came in carrying wood and we lit a small fire about twenty yards away to boil the beef ribs in a three-legged cast-iron pot. They then took out the skulls of a crocodile and large baboon from the bags that I had brought from the storeroom, placing one on either side of the wildebeest corpse. The older man pulled a hyena skin over his shoulders and wrapped beads from our curio shop on his arms and legs. To finish off the special effects he stuck guinea-fowl feathers through his hair and swished about the all-important wildebeest tail.

For my plan to work, it was essential that I be out of sight. This was no place for a white man. I hid the Land Rover in a small copse and then walked back to the clearing with the younger ranger where we secreted ourselves behind a tree with a good view. The twilight was perfect for the surreal atmosphere I wanted so I radioed Ngwenya and told him to bring the poachers back, blindfolded.

As I put my radio down I heard a sudden crack of a branch behind. I almost leapt out of my skin. The herd! They were here. I was just about to radio Ngwenya to move off at speed when a shadowy silhouette caught my eye. It was a bachelor herd of large kudu bulls, their spiralled horns corkscrewing above thornbush.

'Whew!' Both the young ranger and I exhaled noisily with relief. If that had been Nana and her family, the whole plan would have backfired spectacularly.

We watched in the gathering murk as the two poachers were led to the wildebeest carcass where their blindfolds were removed. They stood blinking, taking in the new surroundings and as they saw the skulls by the carcass they flinched almost in unison and started backing off. Both crocodile and baboon skulls are malevolent symbols in a *sangoma*'s arsenal. Their spontaneous reaction was good news for it signalled that our charade was working.

'Sit!' ordered Ngwenya, as he pushed them to the ground.

'But why is *he* here?' one asked, looking across at our ranger sitting fifteen yards away, covered in a hyena skin. I grinned with satisfaction; they definitely believed that they were in the presence of another *sangoma*.

'This is his place. All of this area around here right up to

281

the mountains is his,' replied Ngwenya with an imperial sweep of his arm. 'He is here because many of his family have died here today. The vultures, they are all his children. Some say he flies with them.'

Ngwenya spoke slowly and deliberately with cold anger. He then gazed up at the vultures in the trees, nodding meaningfully. I felt like awarding him an immediate Oscar.

'What does he want from us?' one asked, his voice quavering.

'What do you have that belongs to the impotent man you work for? Or is it a woman who controls you?' Bheki suddenly roared.

'We have *muthi* to protect us,' said one hurriedly. 'It's here in our pockets. We will return it to him when we go back together with his gun.'

Bheki reached over and searching their pockets retrieved two small pink and white river stones wrapped in snakeskin. He walked over to our '*sangoma*' and handed him the *muthi*, along with the revolver.

Then, swift as leopards, he and Ngwenya moved in, held the first man down and using their razor-sharp bush knives sliced off a lock of his hair and a tiny piece of fingernail. They did the same to the second poacher and placing both men's hair and fingernails on a leaf, ceremoniously gave it to our '*sangoma*' who was sitting with his back to them. For *muthi* to be truly effective the *sangoma* needs either to have some body part of the targeted person or at least one possession. And the poachers knew it.

They were now petrified. They believed they had trespassed on the turf of a powerful *sangoma* who now possessed their hair and fingernails as well as their master's possessions – the stones and gun. This was juju at its most malevolent. They sat staring straight ahead, rocking mindlessly on their heels, just like trapped animals, I realized.

Our '*sangoma*' called out in what I thought to be an

impressively haunting tone and Ngwenya went over and came back with the semi-cooked ribs which he placed in front of them.

He untied their hands. 'It is over. Now you will eat meat from the *nyamazane*. The meat is good and you have a long journey ahead of you.'

He may as well have hurled a spear at their hearts. The poachers assumed they were about to be poisoned, just as the vultures had been. After all, didn't this strange omnipotent *sangoma* in a hyena skin who held them captive actually fly with vultures? Weren't they his children?

They clamped their mouths tight, moaning through their noses in abject horror. They were completely taken in and I felt sorry for them, uneducated and unknowing as they were, but we had to play this out fully if we were to have any chance of protecting our vulture population from obliteration.

'You refuse to eat? You have killed his children, now you refuse his hospitality!' Ngwenya thundered, shoving a chunk of meat towards one of the poacher's mouths.

The poor man was beside himself with terror, spitting and coughing, twisting his head this way and that. Then he broke, wailing uncontrollably with terror that they had been forced to collect the vulture heads and that they were sorry for what they had done. And above all, how could they know the vultures were the children of the '*sangoma*'?

Bheki waited a little longer and then instructed them to stay where they were while he and Ngwenya walked back to the '*sangoma*', deliberately leaving them alone.

Just as expected, the poachers bolted, running blindly into the darkening bush as fast as they could go. Bheki fired two shots into the ground to speed their journey. They wouldn't stop until they were miles away and I hoped they made it home safely. In fact, I needed them to make it in one piece so they could report back to their *sangoma* that his stones and gun as well as their hair and nails were now 'owned' by a powerful rival whose ancestors resided in vultures.

As soon as we were sure the poachers were well out of earshot the young ranger and I came out of hiding, laughingly congratulating our 'sangoma' as well as Bheki and Ngwenya for their superb performance that would have rivalled any of Hollywood's A-listers.

'We didn't even need the hyena call,' I said, slapping the young ranger on the back.

Then I asked the all-important question. 'What do you think? Did they believe it?'

'They will never come back here again,' replied Bheki. 'They believed everything.'

We gathered the four dead birds with the wildebeest, stacked wood up high and burned them all to cinders. Ngwenya then fetched the poachers' bag of vulture heads. We counted seven, all liberally covered in salt. Some were more than a week old.

As the vultures' bodies flared in the blazing wood, I began thinking of the huge Lotto winnings that perhaps I was watching go up in smoke. Even if I didn't win the Lotto, the look on Françoise's face would be worth a million bucks were she to find stinking vulture heads under my pillow.

chapter thirty-two

The afternoon breeze barely stirred the bush. Mnumzane was browsing languidly at the side of the road and I was about ten yards away, hanging around the Land Rover saying whatever came into my mind, both of us content in each other's company. It was one of those days where you just felt like hanging out with friends, basking in the warmth of sunshine and companionship. As usual, I did all the talking and he did all the eating. But something had changed and I couldn't quite put my finger on it.

Max, who by now was used to having Mnumzane around, and in turn was totally ignored by Mnumzane, was under the Landy making a bed for himself, digging a hole to get to the cooler earth just below the surface.

I had come to see Mnumzane because one of the rangers had told of a huge ruckus among the herd that morning complete with prolonged trumpeting and screaming which could be heard a mile away. I had just checked on the herd, who were grazing a few miles off, and they seemed fine. Mnumzane too seemed calm . . . but there was something else; his once palpable insecurity seemed to have vanished. He seemed to have a new-found sense of self-assurance.

He walked over to me and I studied this huge bull elephant now standing not ten feet away. There was no doubt that he seemed more confident, more deliberate. Towering almost five feet above me, I needed every ounce of warmth and reassurance he dished out so liberally when we were together.

He then lifted his trunk towards me. That was extremely unusual. Mnumzane seldom put out his trunk, and if he did, he didn't really like me to touch it, unlike Nana and Frankie who were quite comfortable with being tactile. He then turned and moved off into the savannah. That too was different, for I was always first to leave our bush sessions with Mnumzane invariably trying to block my way by standing in front of the Land Rover.

Later on, as the setting sun cloaked the hills in reds and gold, the elephants visited the waterhole just in front of the electric strand at the lodge. This was always a treat for the guests, to watch these lords of the wilderness up close, and it was then I saw exactly why Mnumzane was now so self-assured.

The herd was drinking and splashing around when Mnumzane emerged imperiously out of the bush and with head held high he moved swiftly toward the waterhole. Now that's strange, I thought. Usually he skulks around the periphery. What's going on here?

Nana looked up and saw him and – to my intense surprise – with a deep rumbling she moved off, calling the herd away.

Too late. Mnumzane, picking up speed, singled out Frankie – the herd's prizefighter – and smashed into her so hard that the blow thundered across the bush, smashing her back-wards and very nearly tossing her over.

Seeing what had just happened to their champion, the other elephants started scurrying off with indecent haste. I caught my breath as Mnumzane swung to face Nana, ears spread wide, head held high.

She quickly placed herself between the threat and her precious family and then turned and started reversing towards him, which is not just a sign of subservience, but also bracing herself to best absorb the pending meteoric impact. I winced as she took the colossal charge on her flank; ten tons of combined elephant bulk clashing at speed is like watching two Abrams tanks collide. I felt stunned, winded in sympathy just watching.

Satisfied that he now had the respect he believed he deserved, Mnumzane eased over to the water and drank alone, as was his right as the new alpha elephant. From now on he would always drink first.

Mnumzane had come of age.

Things changed on the reserve after that. Mnumzane no longer gave way to vehicles or anything else for that matter. He would stand in the middle of the road and finish whatever he was doing before moving off in his own sweet time. Any attempt to move him along would result in a warning, which was always heeded. Nobody wanted to be charged by the new big boss of the reserve. Everybody quickly learned bull elephant etiquette, namely to stay the hell away from him, or else.

Despite all that, to me he was still the same old Mnumzane and our bush meetings continued, although less frequently as he didn't trumpet or call me any more. I was a lot more careful when I was with him and if I got out of the Land Rover I would try to make sure that at least the hood of the car was between us. That didn't always work, as sometimes he still wanted to stand next to me. I just loved this magnificent creature and was so pleased to see his insecurities and fears gone. He had had a tough time growing up without a mother or any father figure and at last he had a role.

'You are a mamba,' I said to him at our last chance meeting. 'You are surely now a real *Mnumzane* – a real boss.' He stood there motionless as I flattered him, gazing with those big brown eyes, as if accepting the compliment.

Mnumzane may be the dominant bull, but Nana was still

boss of the herd. Not long afterwards there was another clash – this time between Thula Thula's two indomitable matriarchs.

'Lawrence, Lawrence! Come *queekly*, look what's happening!'

I dashed out of the house. At one end of the garden was Françoise; at the other was Nana. She had found a weak link in the fence and had broken into Françoise's precious herb and vegetable patch. Along with her children Mandla and Mvula, she was gobbling every shrub in sight.

'Tell her to stop! Take her away!' ordered Françoise.

Farting against thunder would have been a more viable option. Seeing the big grin on my face, she turned to Nana and shouted: 'Nana you stop this, I cannot buy zees herbs anywhere. I need zem for my guests. Stop! *Merde!*'

It was a stand-off: Françoise and Bijou weighing perhaps a combined 125 pounds versus Nana, Mandla and Mvula, together topping the scales at perhaps ten tons.

Seeing that I would be of no use whatsoever Françoise rushed into the kitchen and came out with some pots and pans. Before I could stop her, she started banging them together like a demented bell-ringer.

First to respond was Bijou, who thought the sky must be falling and bolted for the safety of the house. I had never seen her deign to run before and was impressed at the speed her fluffy little legs could muster. This left Françoise on her own.

Nana looked up, startled at the clanging, then shook her head and stamped her drum-sized front foot like a dancing Zulu warrior, glaring at Françoise who glared right back, shouting at her to leave. After a while Nana got accustomed to the sound and simply continued eating.

Seeing her percussion wasn't having any effect, Françoise went off and came back with the garden hosepipe. We have good pressure at the house, so from a safe distance behind a

288

fence she opened the nozzle and started spurting water like a firefighter at Nana who again shook her head and stamped her foot back at her.

Eventually Nana got used to the high-pressure fountain and started trying to catch the spray. That was it for Françoise, who heatedly told me and other nearby rangers barely concealing their mirth exactly how useless we all were. She stormed back into the house shouting 'Merde' repeatedly.

Once things had calmed down I picked up the hose and relaxing the pressure valve gently offered it to Nana and she came across and let me fill her trunk before going back and totally wiping out the garden.

The next morning Françoise had an electrician over to fortify the fence and the garden from then on was rendered impervious to anything with a trunk.

Whenever the herd comes up past the house, even though they can no longer raid Françoise's garden, they inevitably pass a 100-yard-long dam we call Gwala Gwala, just off the road, where they like to bathe in the shallows. But elephants can break things just by being there, and on more than one occasion the dam overflow wall has had to be repaired. My rangers told me this had happened again and I went down to have a look, Max at my heels.

Sure enough, even from a distance I could see they had entered the dam on the overflow wall and their combined weight had collapsed it. It was no big deal, the labour team could fix it in a day and so I decided to park off for a while, enjoy the peace and quiet and see what was going on.

There is always plenty of life around water and a couple of hours spent at a dam are infinitely worth making time for. The season's first tadpoles were out, schooled together in tight underwater clusters, some as big as soccer balls rolling gently just under the water, while in the reed banks orange dragonflies hovered and darted.

A large *shongololo*, the impressive six-inch long African millipede with its thick black body and orange legs came out of a crevice in the gabion retaining wall. I put my hand out and it climbed on and kept walking right up my arm as they always do. Eventually I pulled it off and let it down gently – in fact, very gently, for if you scare them they excrete a foul-smelling substance which even soap and water won't readily remove.

Plenty of insects indicates an abundance of life, and the still surface of the brown water was continually marbled by barbell and tilapia rising to feed.

Nearby a bent old acacia robusta leaned over the water, laden with hundreds of weavers' nests hanging like straw-coloured fruit from its branches. These beautiful bright-yellow birds were busy building their seasonal homes, and as usual there was at least one domestic argument going on.

It's the male's job to construct the nest and he is watched carefully by his mate who takes her role as self-appointed quality control officer very seriously indeed. The poor little guy, who had probably spent three days collecting reeds and slaving away to get the nest just right, was hopping from branch to branch, twittering and complaining. His wife had just been inside for the final inspection and was now pecking at the support knot that tied the nest to the branch. This meant one thing: the nest had been rejected and he was grumbling bitterly as the condemned home came away and fell into the water, joining dozens of other similarly discarded abodes. His new home had failed the test and he was now going to have to start from scratch, or lose his mate.

I took off my cap and, using it as a pillow, stretched out on a nearby grass bank and dozed, surrounded by paradise.

A gut feeling is a strange and advantageous thing. It comes from nowhere and is often illogical. Yet it is very real, and in the bush infinitely valuable. While I was dozing, a distant feeling of latent fright suddenly impinged on my serenity. It took me a few moments to recognize it, and when I did I instantly came awake and frantically looked around.

Everything seemed peaceful. Max was at the water's edge having a drink, and he would have given a warning if there was any danger. But what was it that had caused this worry to engulf me?

I checked and rechecked the calm surroundings repeatedly, but absolutely nothing was awry. I was about to rest my head on my cap again and very nearly missed it. Moving across the dam surface was an almost imperceptible ripple. That's interesting, I thought sitting up again. What is it?

It seemed so innocent, so slight that it was barely worth worrying about. But something nagged and then my gut feeling kicked in again. I looked harder and went stone cold. For hidden in the murk-brown water under the barely visible ripple was a huge crocodile, its great tail propelling it towards Max. The ripple was generated by the tip of its nose nudging microcosmically out of the water.

I jumped up yelling at Max and rushed towards him. 'Max come here; come here, Max . . . Maaaaaax!'

He stopped drinking and looked at me. He had never heard me screaming manically at him before and as he wasn't doing anything wrong he must have concluded that my ravings had nothing to do with him. He put his head down and continued lapping.

I scrambled over the wall, grabbing at a small loose stone to throw at him to regain his attention, then slipped and fell, cutting myself on the sharp rocks and losing my missile. I got up and continued running towards him, but by now the crocodile was almost at the bank's edge. Still Max continued lapping, oblivious to the terrible danger.

Then at the last moment, realizing that I actually was screaming at him, Max turned and sprinted up the bank with me fractionally behind – both fleeing for our lives; me

291

wittingly, him not. I have seen a croc launch itself out of a river before and it's pretty low on my list of preferred ways to die.

Those awful moments before I reached the top lasted forever. As we made the safety of the ridge I turned and saw the water swirling around the huge shape of the monster surfacing exactly where Max had been drinking. It was probably twelve feet long.

We were safe and I sunk down on the ground to recover both my sanity and my breath. I reached out and put an arm around Max who gave me a big wet lick, obviously pleased that I wasn't crazy any more. Then facing forward again he suddenly saw the croc, tensed and came on full alert. It was so lucky I had my arm around him for he started towards the monster. I just managed to grab his collar in time. I immediately thought of my brave Penny and how she died. The bush signs were right; she did go for the croc that killed her. Foolhardy or not the courage of the bull and Staffordshire terrier is truly unlimited.

It was Max's drinking that had done it. Crocodiles are attracted by the sound of an animal's tongue lapping. Their killing technique is simple: stay underwater, get close, then launch a vicious surprise attack from the depths. And they are very, very good at it. You have precious little chance of escaping death in the jaws of hell itself. With crocs there are no prior warnings.

We were alive due to a gut instinct. Nothing more, nothing less.

Fifteen minutes later the reptile surfaced on the far side of the dam, slowly pulling his bulk out of the water and crawling up the bank. That's what I had been waiting for. Now at least I could get a good look at it.

It's difficult, if not impossible, to sex a crocodile from a distance but I took him for a male, an old one from the dark colouring on his back. And judging by his hunting technique, he certainly was a cunning old fellow. He was a new arrival on the reserve and must have come down the river, perhaps during the recent floods, and walked the two miles to claim Gwala Gwala dam for his home. As such he had joined the extended Thula Thula family and was now entitled to protection and to be left alone to live out his natural life. There were plenty of barbel in the dam to support him between the occasional bigger meals – though hopefully not Max or me. He would be happy here.

chapter thirty-three

'Boss! Boss come in, come in!'

It was David on the two-way radio.

'Standing by. What's up?'

'There's a big mistake here,' said David, using the word 'mistake' in the Zulu context to mean a major problem. 'I'm up from the Kudu River crossing. You better get here quickly.'

'Why?'

He paused.

'We have another dead rhino.'

'Shit! What the hell happened?'

'Rather come and see for yourself. You're not going to like this at all.'

Puzzled, I picked up my .303 half expecting an encounter with poachers – as had happened after our first dead rhino – and ran for the Land Rover with Max at my heels. What was it that David wouldn't tell me over the radio?

The crossing was about twenty minutes away and driving along my focus was snapped by Mnumzane loping off across the veldt to the left of me. Despite my haste I stopped. Something was wrong; I could sense it from where I was sitting.

I called out, but instead of coming to me he lifted his head, spread his ears and deliberately moved off. Every new elephant reaction intrigues me and normally I would have trailed him to find out what was going on, but David was sitting on a crisis.

Ten minutes later I reached David. He was squatting on his haunches in the shade of a young umbrella thorn tree, staring sombrely at the ground. I pulled up next to him and got out.

'What happened?' I asked, looking around. 'Where's the rhino?'

He stood up slowly. Then without a word he led the way down an old game path and into a clearing. In the middle lay the gray carcass. It was a female. From the look of it, her death was recent.

Her horns were still intact. That surprised me, for I had expected them to be butchered off, the first thing poachers do. I walked up to the immense motionless body, automatically looking for bullet wounds. There were none.

I then scrutinized the corpse for signs of disease or other causes of death, while David stood by silently. Except for some nasty fresh gashes on her armour-plated hide, she had been strong and healthy. In fact, even in death she was so imposing that I half expected her to suddenly rise up.

I was so transfixed by the grim scenario that I hadn't taken in my wider surroundings, and as I looked up I was shocked. A tornado could not have done more damage. Bushes were crushed and trees lay sprawled and splintered all over the place. The earth itself had been gouged up, as if a bulldozer had lost its driver and careered around recklessly flattening everything. Nothing made sense; no rhino could cause such havoc. What the hell was going on?

I instinctively looked to the ground for answers. Rhino spoor was everywhere, heavy and mobile in its tread, yet unnatural in its twisting and turning patterns. Then elephant tracks jumped out at me; big heavy pachyderm spoor, the aggressive earth-wrenching footprints of an enraged bull in full cry.

Mnumzane!

I tried to suppress the dawning realization, hoping against hope I was wrong.

'He killed her, boss.' David's words whispered into my thoughts. 'She put up a helluva fight but she was no match for him – never could be.'

I nodded, not wanting to believe it. But the tracks told the story as clearly as if they were on celluloid.

'I once saw an elephant kill a black rhino at a waterhole in Namibia,' David continued, almost as if speaking to himself. 'He hammered the rhino so hard it shot back thirty feet and went down and died right there, its ribs smashed in, collapsed over the heart. And then the elephant put his front foot on the body and stood over it rolling it over back and forth as if it was a plaything. The power was just unbelievable.'

He stared at the corpse in front of us. 'I know she is a white, and nearly twice the size of a black rhino. But still, she stood no chance.'

A slight flicker in the bush to my left caught my eye. Max had also seen it and following his gaze through the foliage I caught sight of a camouflaged rhino calf silently watching from a nearby thicket. It was Heidi, the dead animal's two-year-old daughter. A rhino will fight to the death under most circumstances – but with a youngster, that's an absolute given.

'What a mess up!' I fumed, my words echoing harshly through the bush. 'What the hell did he do that for? The bloody idiot!'

'We . . . we're not going to shoot him, are we?' said David and for the first time I realized why he had been so downcast.

Shoot Mnumzane? The words shocked me rigid.

In most South African reserves, aggressive young male elephants, orphaned by earlier culls and reared without sage supervision of adult bulls, have gratuitously killed rhino before. And when they did, retribution by reserve owners was swift and harsh. Rhinos in South Africa are rare and very expensive. Elephants, on the other hand, are more plentiful and comparatively cheap. Past records indicated that elephants which killed rhino before would do so again. Thus to protect valuable rhino, an elephant that kills one effectively sentences itself to death.

Through one senseless violent act, Mnumzane had made himself an outcast . . . an untouchable. I now couldn't keep him; nor could I give him away for love or money. Who would want an elephant that killed rhino just for the hell of it? On most game reserves an owner in my position would immediately set up a hunt and end the problem there and then.

'No,' I said trying to reassure myself. 'We're not going to shoot him. But we really have a bloody big problem on our hands.'

I paused, trying to get my head around it all. 'Let's unpick this slowly. Firstly Heidi will be fine, she's big enough to survive without a mother and she will herd with the other rhinos.'

'Secondly we have to retrieve the horns,' interrupted David. 'The word will get out and they're too much of a temptation for poachers. I'll get the men and we'll cut them out, clean them and put them in the safe.'

I nodded. 'Good thinking. I'll phone Wildlife and let them know what happened. They're not going to be too happy with the way she died but I'll speak to them about that as well. The carcass will stay here and there'll be plenty of hyena and vulture activity for guests.'

David started to say something, then paused. 'Boss . . .' again almost whispering, 'you're sure we're not going to shoot Mnumzane?'

The million-dollar question. One I didn't have an answer

for, so I decided to wing it. 'I'll go and find him and see what I can do. I need to spend time with him and try to work something out.'

David looked at me, unconvinced, but it was the best I could come up with. We both stood and took a long hard look at the hulking grey carcass and then left in different directions. He was going to get the team to dehorn the once-magnificent creature. I was going to have a serious chat with Mnumzane.

As we left I saw the calf trot out of the thicket she had been hiding in and stand vigil over her valiant dead mother. Mnumzane had really messed things up big time.

It was another hour and a half before I found him browsing near the Gwala Gwala dam. I approached slowly, pulled up about thirty-five yards away, got out and leaned on the Land Rover's hood unsheathing my binoculars. I didn't call him, but he knew full well I was there. Instead he chose to ignore me and continue grazing which is exactly what I wanted. A swift scan of his body with the binoculars showed the scars of battle.

Congealed blood revealed he had been gored in the chest and there were deep grazes and scrapes on both his flanks. This had not been a brief encounter; the battle had been fierce and long, probably only because he was not used to fighting. A veteran brawler of his size would have ended it with one thundering charge.

There also must have been plenty of opportunities for the rhino to escape, but with a calf, that word was absent from her dictionary. She held her ground as her gallant species always do and paid the highest price for her stubbornness.

Eventually he finished eating and looked at me.

'Mnumzane!' I called out sharply, focusing on connotation and intonation rather than volume. 'Have you any idea of what you have done, you bloody fool?'

I had never used that furious tone with him before. I

needed him to understand I was extremely angry about the death of the rhino.

'This is a big problem, for you, for me, and for everyone. What the hell got into you?'

He stood motionless as I berated him, his stare static and it was only after I drove off that I saw him move away.

From then on I tracked him daily, staying near him as much as possible, but if he approached I deliberately drove off. I could see that bugged him.

Then through extreme good fortune I found him near the scene of the crime. I immediately drove to the rotting remains of the rhino still festering on the ground and making sure I was upwind of the intolerable smell and in a good getaway position, I gently called him.

Obviously pleased to hear my usual genial tone of voice again, he ambled over towards me. I let him keep coming until he was right at the kill, and then leaned out the window and lambasted him in a firm and steady voice, stopping only when he uncharacteristically turned and walked off in the opposite direction.

There are those who will say that all of this is nonsense; that of course elephants don't understand . . . that I was wasting my time. But I believe Mnumzane got the message. He never hassled another rhino again, let alone killed one. Our relationship returned to normal and Mnumzane would again emerge for a chat in the bush again, like in the old days.

He even, on occasion, came up to the house to say hello and there was no one more relieved than David.

Shortly afterwards David knocked on my door, looking a little doleful.

'Can I come in, boss?'

'Sure. What's up?'

'My mum and dad are leaving the country. They're going to England. Emigrating.'

You could've knocked me over with a twig. David's family came from pioneer Zululand stock and were well respected throughout the area. This must have been a big decision for them.

David noticed my astonishment and smiled, almost embarrassedly.

'That's not all. I'm going with them.'

This time I nearly did fall over. If I couldn't visualize David's family in England, I could do so even less with him. He was a man of the bush – something of which there is precious short supply in England. The wild was his element.

'You're sure it's not khaki fever again?' I asked smiling, remembering the last time he had left us was for a pretty English tourist who fancied hunky game rangers. That only lasted a month or so before he came charging back, asking for his old job.

He laughed. 'Not this time. It's going to be hard for my mum and dad to adjust in a foreign country. I'm going along to help out.'

I nodded, knowing how close he was to his family.

'Anything we can do to make you stay?'

'Afraid not, boss. It's been a terribly difficult decision and as much as I'm going to miss Thula Thula and you guys, I have to go with my folks.'

'We're going to miss you too.'

He left later that month. It was a melancholic day as I shook his hand for the last time as his 'boss'.

Being David, with his inextinguishable cheerfulness, he soon landed on his feet in Britain and joined the British Army. He was selected for an officer's course at the world-famous Sandhurst Military Academy and did a tour of combat duty in Afghanistan as an officer – where I believe his outdoor skills and natural leadership skills helped make him a superb officer.

chapter thirty-four

There hadn't been a snakebite on Thula Thula for nearly sixty years. The previous owners had been here for fifty years without incident and we had been bite free for the eight years we had been here.

This is not surprising, for although Thula Thula, like every African game reserve slithers with serpents of all types and sizes, these intriguing reptiles avoid man for three very good reasons. Firstly, they don't want to get stomped on and will move away long before you get near them; secondly, humans are not their prey; and thirdly, they have long since learned that we will kill them for no other reason than that they exist.

The only exception to the first proviso is the puff adder. It relies on its dull yellow-brown and black colouring as camouflage, and will not budge however close you come. It has a thick body, averaging about three feet in length, and because it is so aggressive it is responsible for more deaths in Africa than any other snake. Every veteran ranger has at some time stood on – or almost on – an immobile puffy, only noticing afterwards that he or she has just missed a deadly injection of venom. They just don't move, sometimes even if you stand on them. But they do bite, faster than you can jump.

Dispelling myths about snakes opens the minds of visitors to appreciating and perhaps even befriending these fascinating creatures that are so vital to the environment, particularly in keeping down rodent populations.

There is, however, one snake that is a law unto itself.

'We've just lost two zebra,' said John Tinley, the veteran ranger from KZN Wildlife's Fundimvelo reserve next door who had stopped in for a cup of tea one day. 'Both dead, right next to the waterhole, fat and healthy, no sign of disease and not a mark on them.'

He looked at me waiting for comment, testing me.

'OK, what happened?' I said, taking the game out of it.

'Black mamba,' he replied, blowing on his hot tea. 'Killed both of them. Stone dead.'

'You're having me on,' I said sitting up. 'A mamba killed two adult zebra?'

He clicked his fingers. 'Just like that. They were history when we got there. They must have frightened the damn thing, or stood on it . . . or something.'

'You're sure?' I asked, amazed at what I was hearing. A zebra can weigh 600 pounds. 'Two of them?'

'The spoor doesn't lie. There isn't another snake that leaves marks like that. You may have seen the fire. I burned the bodies. Don't want anybody or anything eating that meat, not even hyena.'

As soon as he was gone I got on the phone and after a couple of calls I sank back in my chair. He was right, a mamba can easily kill a zebra; in fact it can kill almost anything – lion, towering kudu bulls . . . even giraffe have been dropped. As for humans, one mamba packs enough venom to kill up to forty adults.

It grows up to fifteen feet long and is as thick as a man's arm. It's also the fastest snake around, sometimes hurtling along with its head three or four feet above the ground. To complete the picture, it's not actually black; more of a metal grey. However, the inside of its mouth is pitch-black, hence

302

its name. The sight of a mamba almost gliding with its coffin-shaped head raised several feet above a grassy plain is the ultimate game-viewing experience.

Several days afterwards, I was in my office when I heard Biyela shouting at the top of his voice.

'Mkhulu, come quick! Mamba!' The word galvanized me and I grabbed my shotgun, locked up Max, and bolted outside to find Biyela standing at the rear of the house, backed up against a storeroom wall, pointing.

'Mamba!' he shouted again.

I put my finger to my lips to get him to lower his voice. He nodded, thankful for the presence of the shotgun and pointed to a small fenced-off courtyard which housed general bric-a-brac.

'It went in there.'

'You sure it was a mamba?' I asked, aware that for Biyela all snakes are automatically mambas.

'Ngempela – absolutely.'

As a rule we never kill snakes. Even with a black mamba we try for a catch and release into the bush. But if something so lethal looked like it was going to escape into the house, I wouldn't hesitate to shoot it. The last thing I wanted was several slithering yards of venom surfacing in one of the bedrooms or settling down behind some sofa cushions.

We edged closer and suddenly Biyela grabbed my sleeve and we watched the tail disappearing – of all places into our open bedroom window.

'Damn!' I exclaimed as I started running back around to the front door with Biyela hot on my heels.

We rounded the still-open front door at a dash and bolted through into the bedroom and stopped dead. Edging in, we cautiously scanned the area immediately around us, then the floor of the room, and then the poles spanning the thatched roof above us. Nothing, nothing at all. It had gone. We searched everywhere, under the bed, in the cupboards, behind the curtains. Everywhere. It had completely, but completely disappeared.

'This is unbelievable. A mamba in our bedroom and we can't find it? A bloody mamba for Pete's sake! Where the hell is it?'

'They are like ghosts,' Biyela replied.

Dismayed, I suddenly I heard Françoise chatting outside with some of the staff. 'What do you mean there's a mamba in my bedroom? Where's Lawrence?'

'Hi. I'm here in the lounge!' I called out, trying to sound unconcerned.

She walked in with Bijou scampering at her heels. 'What's all this nonsense about a mamba in our bedroom?'

'Well . . . maybe. I think there was one but now . . . well, maybe it's gone.' I nodded sternly as if I was in total control of the situation.

'You're not sure if there is a mamba in our room?' She stood on tiptoes peering over my shoulder through the bedroom door. 'Well, OK oh great white hunter. I'm sleeping at the lodge tonight and if you are so sure it's gone you can stay here. Just make sure your will is up to date.'

Then Bijou, who had somehow slipped past us, started growling from the bedroom and I instinctively knew she had found it. Or worse, maybe the deadly snake had found her.

I hurtled back into the bedroom. In the middle of the floor was the poodle . . . and rearing itself directly in front of her was . . . not a mamba but a full-grown Mozambican spitting cobra. A *mfezi* – Max's favourite adversary. But unlike Max, who would quickly circle a reptile before striking, Bijou was no snake fighter.

The snake was in the classic attack position: head raised and hood flared, hypnotically focused on this bite-sized ball of fluff before it. Luckily, emboldened by our arrival, Bijou started prancing about and yapping for all she was worth, denying the lethal serpent a fixed target.

Now while an *mfezi* has enough venom to kill a man, it plummets way below a mamba on the snake Richter scale. Relief poured out of my system.

A black mamba, as mentioned earlier, is actually grey, almost the exact same top colour as a *mfezi*. From the tail slithering into the window Biyela and I had somehow mistaken one for the other. But my relief that it was 'only' a deadly Mozambican spitting cobra was soon tempered by the fact that if anything happened to Bijou, Françoise's wrath would ensure I'd be on my way to the North Pole without a sleigh.

'Lawrence! Do something!'

Adjusting my glasses closer to my face for protection against venom spray, then shutting my mouth (recently opened for a retort) for the same reason, I edged around the poised snake, scooped up the excited poodle and delivered her still yapping to Françoise.

Biyela then handed me my trusty snake-catching broom and I moved in cautiously, not wishing to antagonize Mr Mfezi any more than absolutely necessary. I manoeuvred the broom painfully slowly towards the erect serpent, which – as they usually do – allowed the bristle-head to be eased under its body. For some reason the reptile is not threatened by the broom. However, the momentum of the broom moving forward gently 'trips' the upright snake – which is only balancing on the bottom half of its body – onto the broom's head. Once it collapses onto the broom head, it's a simple matter of lifting the broom up by the handle with the snake still coiled on the far end and carrying it outside. I then released it a good distance from the house.

Hallelujah! Bijou was saved and I was accorded mega domestic hero status with Françoise. I was also pleased that a couple of trainee rangers had witnessed the capture and afterwards I went over the broom technique again with them, stressing that it only worked with cobras and they had to be upright in the attack position before you could edge the broom underneath the lower part of their body.

Unfortunately a few days later the impromptu lesson had serious unintended consequences.

'Code Red! Snakebite at the main house!' the rapid-fire call cranked out of the Land Rover's radio as Brendan and I were parked out in the bush with the herd, watching Mandla playfully wrestling with the much larger Mabula.

Brendan's reply was cool and calculated, just what was needed to calm the panic. 'Who was bitten, where, and what type of snake?'

'It's the new trainee Brett. We think it may be a black mamba. We're trying to find it so we can do the identification.'

As the voice trailed off I felt sick to my stomach. Black mamba! Flooring the Land Rover's accelerator I rushed back to the house in a blur, unable to get a word in among the frenetic radioactivity.

The drive from Thula Thula to the hospital in Empangeni was about forty minutes, way too long in case of a full-dose mamba bite, which can kill in half that time. Also, we didn't keep mamba serum on the reserve. In fact nobody keeps it on hand, for the simple reason that it goes rotten after a short time. Sometimes the serum could kill you as surely as a bite.

'God, I hope it's not a mamba,' I prayed. 'And if it is, then not a big one.'

But I knew that didn't matter, for even a day-old hatchling mamba packs enough venom to kill a full-grown man.

I pulled into the parking area behind our house in a billow of dust, leapt out and ran over to where the rangers were gathered around a large dead snake, hoping against hope that it wasn't a mamba.

It was.

'Who took Brett to hospital?' I asked.

'Nobody. He wanted to pack a suitcase, but we're going to take him now,' came the absurd reply from another trainee.

'What! Does he know it was a bloody mamba?'

'Yes, but it was only a small bite on the finger.'

'Only on the finger! For Pete's sake – it's a mamba! It doesn't matter where it bit!'

I couldn't believe what I was hearing and yelled at Brett, who had just appeared from his room carrying a suitcase as if he was going on holiday, to hurry.

I then took a deep breath, the last thing I wanted to do was panic the kid. 'Brett,' I said quietly. 'Please don't run as it will only increase your heart rate and spread the venom. This is a mamba. OK? Show me the bite.'

He gave me his hand and there on the finger was the fang wound. I exhaled with relief. Just one puncture.

'Did it hook into you?' I asked.

'No. It just struck at me and moved off, but my finger is getting as sore as hell.'

With no purchase to inject venom and only one fang in one finger Brett might – maybe just – have a chance.

'Are your hands tingling?'

'Yes, strange you should say that. So are my toes.'

Tingling in the extremities are the first symptoms of a mamba bite, a sure sign that venom was in his system.

'That's from the bite. You must go right now. Just slow everything down – your breathing – everything down.'

I then turned to the driver. 'Go like hell,' I hissed, making sure Brett couldn't hear me. He nodded and sped off.

I looked at my watch, six precious minutes had passed

since the bite and we had no way of knowing how much venom was in his body. If it was anything more than just a scratch we had to accept that he would be dead before they got halfway to town. I put the horrible thought of the phone call I'd have to make to his family out of my mind.

'What happened?' I asked Bheki.

'*Ayish*, that young man doesn't listen. We were here when we saw the mamba in there.' He pointed to the small courtyard behind our bedroom window.

I stared at the courtyard, the same one where Biyela had seen a snake earlier that week and it suddenly dawned what had happened. There were two snakes that day. Biyela had been absolutely right. It was indeed a mamba he had seen going in to the courtyard. It must have came face to face with the *mfezi*, which then bolted out of the courtyard and climbed into our window to get away, straight into the growls of 'brave' Bijou. The mamba had been operating from the courtyard ever since.

'*Yehbo*,' said Biyela who was standing next to Bheki, as if reading my thoughts. 'It was a mamba I saw, not an *mfezi*. We became confused.'

'And then?'

'Brett took a broom to the mamba. I told him this snake was too dangerous and that you only use the broom for *mfezi* but he did not listen. I tried to stop him but it was too late and the mamba bit him. Now maybe he will die.'

'Who shot the mamba?'

'I did. It was very angry and moving everywhere.'

'Well done.'

Ten minutes later I picked up my cellphone and dialled the driver.

'How's Brett?'

'Sweating and salivating. But he's still coherent and it's not far to the hospital. I'm just about flying at this speed.'

'OK, let us know when the doctor is with him.'

As bad as it sounded, I knew from that rudimentary diagnosis that Brett had a slim chance. He was in for a rough ride, but if the bite had been lethal he would have already started vomiting and losing muscle control, the final fatal symptoms.

Ten minutes later we heard from the driver that they had arrived at the hospital. Brett was rushed into intensive care and stayed there for two days fighting for his life. And it wasn't even a bite, just a fang fractionally nicking a finger.

We have often seen mambas since that incident, all of them just carrying on with their lives but that bite will go down as our only snake crisis in over half a century. And it's a story the trainees will never forget.

chapter thirty-five

Nana's oldest daughter Nandi's swollen stomach was attracting a lot of finger-pointing.

Named after King Shaka's influential mother, Nandi – which means 'good and nice' – had stamped her own definitive temperament on the herd: dignified, confident and alert. As a teenager, she had been with the herd in the famous breakout the day after they arrived at Thula Thula, and had now blossomed into a twenty-two-year-old adult. She was inheriting from Nana the hallmarks of a potential matriarch. And she was very pregnant.

The father, of course, was Mnumzane and with Nandi ballooning like a keg we were expecting a big healthy baby. The whole of Thula Thula was waiting for the good news.

Johnny, a likeable new ranger, was first on the scene when it happened. Blonde, good-looking in a boyish way, he had recently joined us and his easy smile made him popular with the staff. He radioed me and, surprisingly, didn't sound that happy. 'We've just found Nandi down near the river but we can't see the baby properly. The herd's gathered around and won't let us anywhere near her. They're acting most peculiarly.'

'Where are you exactly?' I asked, heading for the door and taking the portable radio with me.

'Just before the first river crossing on the lodge road.

Take the back route otherwise you won't get past the elephants.'

It was mid-morning and the sun was already blistering down. The mercury was topping 100 degrees Fahrenheit and soaring as I leaned over and groped for my cap on the Land Rover's floor. Being fair-skinned, I had learned the hard way to watch myself in the merciless African sun. Max sat in the passenger's seat, head out the window, tongue out lapping at the passing scents.

I found Johnny and Brendan easily enough. Just as Johnny had said, fifty yards away stood the herd gathered in an unusually tightly knit group.

'What's going on?'

'We don't know,' said Johnny. 'We can't get close enough to see anything. But they've been there for a while now.'

I walked off into the bush, keeping my distance, trying to find a spot from where I could get a peek through the obviously flustered herd. At last I got a glimpse of the brand-new baby on the ground in the middle.

The fact it was lying down sent alarms jangling. The infant should already be on its feet. All wildlife in Africa stands, albeit tottering, almost instantly after birth, and for a good reason. A vulnerable baby on the ground is asking for trouble, an easy snack for predators. Even elephants, with their formidable bulk, move away as soon as possible from a birth spot where the smell of the placenta will attract lurking carnivores.

I needed to find out what was going on so I started approaching on a slow zigzag path, carefully watching to see how close they would let me come. I got to about twenty yards away when Frankie caught a glimpse of me and rose to her full height, taking two or three menacing steps forward until she recognized who it was and dropped her ears. But she held her position and from her demeanour I could tell she didn't want me any nearer. Once she was sure

311

I had got the message, she turned back to the baby lying in front of her.

I could now at least see what was going on, and my heart sank. The little one, invigorated by the elemental energy that surges in new life, was desperately attempting to stand up. Time and time again it tried, patiently lifted by the trunks of its mother Nandi, its grandmother and matriarch Nana and its aunt Frankie. But, heartbreakingly, each time as it rose half up it fell back, only to start trying to get up again. This had obviously been going on for a while and my heart went out to the baby and the desperate family.

It was blazing hot and with absolute rotten luck the baby was lying in the middle of the only open space among the trees, right out in the blazing sun. To compound matters, it was also off the grass, lying on hot sand.

There was nothing to do but wait, watch and hope, so I sent the rangers off on other duties, got myself a bottle of water from the Land Rover and found a shady spot as close as I could to the elephants. I called out so they all knew I was with them, and Max and I settled in for the duration.

I took out my binoculars and managed to focus in on the baby. She was a girl and the problem was starkly evident. Her front feet were deformed; they had folded over themselves in the womb and each time she tried to stand, she was doing so on her 'ankles'.

An hour later and the little one was exhausted and her attempts to stand were becoming weaker and less frequent. This did not deter her mum and aunts who, if anything, renewed their efforts with each failure. By worming their trunks under the little body, they lifted the baby up and held her on her feet for minutes at a time, then gently let her down, only for her to crumple to the ground again.

Elephants always find deep shade on hot days and stay there. Their humungous bodies generate a lot of heat so keeping cool is a priority. Looking up at the sun I cursed; it was firing full-strength and these poor animals were in its direct blast. Yet none shied off for the shade of the trees, barely twenty yards away. There they stood in the midday solar furnace guarding the baby, even the younger elephants, which were doing little more than watching. Nor did any leave for a long draught of cool water at the river less than half a mile away. Their sail-like ears, their natural radiators were flapping overtime, fanning as much air as they could, attempting to regulate their overheated bodies.

It was only then I noticed that the baby was permanently in the shade of its mother's and aunt's shadows. Not just because they happened to be standing around her, but because they were taking conscious care to do so. While the sun arced through the sky I watched amazed as they all took turns to act as an umbrella, slowly shifting their positions to ensure the struggling infant was always out of direct heat.

Three hours later and the baby started to succumb. She didn't want to be moved any more and trumpeted pitifully when family trunks lifted her yet one more time. She was fatigued beyond measure.

Eventually Nana stopped and they all just stood there, waiting with the baby lying motionless in front of them. I homed in with the binoculars and could see she was still breathing but fast asleep.

Wildlife can absorb adversity that would destroy a human without a blink. This little elephant had gone through the trauma of birth and spent half a day in a blazing new alien environment and hadn't even had her first drink. Yet she was still alive, still fighting.

But she must be nearing the end and somehow I had to get her away from the herd. They were doing the best they could, but this little creature needed sophisticated medical care. With the best will in the world, Nandi and Nana could not fix the baby's feet. Her only chance was with us – and even that was tenuous. But how could we get her away from the herd? An elephant's maternal instinct is extremely powerful. We could not remove a baby from its mother simply by driving up and snatching it. The retribution would be cataclysmic.

So what could we do? Short of opening fire and trying to scare them off with bullets, which would destroy my relationship with them forever, there was no other way. Perhaps if it was just Nandi . . . but certainly not with Nana and Frankie around as well.

So there we sat, Max and I, pondering the great mysteries of the elephant world. In the late afternoon, when the day cooled fractionally, the elephants started again worming their trunks in tandem underneath the baby, trying to lift her onto her feet. They kept it up until nightfall, agonizingly failing each time.

I drove the Land Rover in closer and beamed the headlights onto the scene to help them, watching in awe as the elephants never gave up. They had been trying for nearly twelve hours now. Their persistence was absolutely phenomenal. The Marines may have a saying 'leave no one behind', but these elephants could even have taught them a thing or two.

Towards midnight the baby was pitifully weakened and I resigned myself to the fact that not only was she not going to make it, but there was nothing I could do. I called out a goodbye, saying I would be back, then drove back up to the house and went to bed, expecting the worst when I woke.

When I returned the next morning as dawn broke, incredibly the herd was still there, still trying to get the now almost completely limp body to stand. I couldn't believe it; the dedication of these magnificent creatures was beyond comprehension. My respect for them and what they were doing was infinite.

The sun started climbing and by 10 a.m. I knew we were

314

in for another steamer. And still they continued. But what more could they do? I knew the baby was finished.

A few minutes later, Nana backed off a few paces for the first time and stood alone, as if assessing the situation. She then turned and walked off without stopping. Her trunk dragged, her shoulders stooped, a portrait of dejection. The decision had been made. Nana knew that they had done what they could. She knew it was all over. Despite their best efforts, the baby was unable to stand and thus wouldn't survive.

The rest of the herd followed and were soon out of sight on their way to the river to slake their arid gullets. They had been on wilderness ER for more than twenty-four hours without drink or rest. Few humans could match that.

Yet Nandi stayed behind. As the mother, she would be there to the end, protecting her baby from hyenas or other predators. She manoeuvred her crippled daughter in her shadow and stood still, head down, exhausted, resigned to her firstborn's fate, but determined to protect the infant to its last breath.

I studied the baby through the binoculars, certain she was now dead. Then almost imperceptibly, I saw her head move. My heart pounded with excitement. She's still alive, barely, but still alive! And with the herd gone, another crazy plan came into my head.

I sped to the house and loaded a large open container on the back of the Landy, filled it with water, and threw in a bag of fresh-hewn alfalfa. Brendan summoned the rangers.

'OK, guys,' I said, 'this is what's going to happen. I'm going to try and reverse right up to Nandi, give her a sniff of the water and alfalfa, and then slowly move off to try and draw her away from the baby. She hasn't had a drink or anything to eat for twenty-four hours and she's been baking in the sun solidly. She's starving and thirsty, so she may just follow me. There's a sharp corner in the road about thirty yards off, and if she follows me there she won't be able to see the baby. That's when I want you guys to sneak in from the other side, get in as fast as possible, load up the baby and then speed off.'

I paused for a moment, scanning their eager faces. 'But if Nandi sees you taking her baby, there won't be enough of you left for me to bury. So if you're not comfortable with this, don't come with me. It's bloody dangerous. I really mean that.'

There wasn't a moment's hesitation. 'We're in,' was the unanimous reply.

I nodded my thanks. 'OK. I've phoned the vet and he's on his way with a drip as the baby will be dangerously dehydrated. I have also put a mattress in the back of the truck for her.'

We quickly drove down, got into position, went over every aspect of the plan once again and then tested our radios. 'We've only got one chance,' I reminded them. 'As I said earlier, if Nandi catches you near the baby you're in big trouble. Reverse in so you can drive out of there forward if she sees you. One driver, two in the back to load the baby.'

I at least had some protection as Nandi knew me and I was carrying food and water, but how she would react with her lame baby right there was anybody's guess. However, for the rangers, it was a different story entirely. Nandi didn't know them and on top of that they were stealing her baby. They could expect no mercy.

I got in the Land Rover and started reversing towards Nandi, calling out to her as I got closer to let her know it was me. Her first reaction was uncharacteristic. She moved between the baby and the approaching Landy and then charged, trumpeting loudly to scare me away, kicking up a cloud of dust. She had never come at me before so I stopped and leaning out of my window started talking to her soothingly. As she walked back, I gently started reversing again, only to prompt another noisy stampede. I kept talking and the third time I reversed, her charge had no steam at all and as she turned away I saw her physically jolt as she got the unbearably intoxicating scent of fresh water and food. She stopped and turned.

'Come, *baba*,' I called gently, 'come, beautiful girl, come on. You're hot; you haven't had anything to eat and drink for twenty-four hours. Come to me.'

She paused and then tentatively took a few steps forward, ears straight out, hesitantly checking everything, and then walked up and dipped her trunk into the trough and sucked in a yard of water which she squirted messily into her mouth, spilling it everywhere in her haste. Then her screaming thirst kicked in and she started drinking insatiably off the back of the vehicle and I moved forward very, very slowly. Without hesitation she followed, slugging bucketfuls as we moved along. She still hadn't stopped when we were around the corner, out of sight of her baby. I couldn't believe how thirsty she was.

'Go, go, go!' I whispered into the radio. 'I can't see you so neither can she. Let me know as soon as you've done it.'

I continued talking to Nandi, calming her with my voice, keeping her distracted, and then for what it was worth I told her what we were doing. 'Unless I take your baby, she's going to die. You know that and I know that. So when you get back she won't be there, but if we save her, I will bring her back to you. That I promise.'

I have no idea if she understood anything, but intonation and intention can communicate far more than mere words. At least I felt better that I had told her what we were doing.

A few minutes later, a breathless call came through. 'We've got her. She's alive – just – we're moving off.'

'Great! Well done, get her up to the house. I'm going to stay with Nandi for a while.'

Nandi drank every drop of water and then tucked into the alfalfa. When she finished, she looked at me in acknowledgement and walked back to where she had left the baby. I reversed, following her and watched as she started nosing the ground. With her superb sense of smell she would have immediately caught the scent of the rangers. After sniffing around for a few long minutes, she stopped for a while and turned and slowly moved off in the direction of the herd.

I know that if she had smelt hyena or jackal there was no way she would have reacted so calmly or left the scene so quickly. She would have followed the scent with a vengeance, never letting up.

I waited until she was out of sight and radioed the rangers. 'How's it going?'

'She's still alive. She's on the lawn and we've been spraying water to cool her down. The vet is putting in the drip now.'

'I'll be there shortly. Well done, guys.'

My hands were still shaking. I couldn't believe we had done it. Thanks to my intrepid rangers, we had taken a baby elephant from her mother.

Now all we had to do was save its life.

chapter thirty-six

When I arrived back at the house the baby was lying motionless in the shade on the grass and the vet was connecting the second drip sachet into a bulging vein behind her ear.

'She's barely alive and very dehydrated,' he said. 'The next few hours will tell if she makes it.'

I walked off and made a few phone calls querying what milk substitute a wild orphaned baby elephant would take. We needed the exact mixture, and having got the formula from Daphne Sheldrick's famous animal orphanage in Kenya I sent a ranger into town to buy the ingredients as well as some jumbo-sized bottles and the largest teats on the market.

While I did that, Françoise started converting the spare bedroom, right next to ours, into an elephant nursery, scattering straw in bales on the floor and putting down a firm mattress for her to sleep on.

'She'll be comfortable here,' she said with more confidence than I felt. 'We will name her Thula.'

I nodded. It was a good name.

I went back to the baby and inspected her front feet crumpled in on themselves.

'She's huge,' said the vet. 'In fact, too big. That's why her feet were squashed back, folded over in the womb. She was simply too big for the womb and her feet had nowhere further to grow. But the bones aren't broken and the muscles are intact and loose enough to manipulate into the correct position. Hopefully they'll straighten out with some exercise.'

He walked around her. 'Her ears are also worrying me a touch. They've been burned raw by the sun and sand and she may lose the fringes. I'll prescribe some ointment.'

Just then Thula lifted her head quite strongly. A drip is a wonderful thing with wildlife. Sometimes it works so powerfully it's like watching a resurrection and so it was with Thula who was suddenly springing back from the dead.

'She's certainly feeling better,' said the vet. 'Let's move her to her room and hopefully she'll get some sleep. When she wakes, give her a bottle.'

Holding the drip we carried her to her new room. She instantly fell asleep on the mattress.

'I'll tell you what is amazing,' said Johnny, coming over to Françoise and me. 'It only took two of us to lift her on to the pickup. We were so scared of the mother coming back that we loaded her in seconds. But when we got back here she was so heavy we couldn't get her off the truck at all. It eventually took four of us. That's adrenalin for you.'

Johnny our new ranger stayed with her and would do so around the clock until she was healed. Orphaned elephant babies need the constant companionship of a surrogate mother otherwise they rapidly decline, both physically and emotionally. Johnny, who had only joined us a few months back, was going to be just that – a chore he accepted with relish.

The next morning Thula took her first giant-sized bottle from him and drank the lot.

The following day she was much stronger so Johnny fashioned a canvas sling and hung it from the towering marula tree on the lawn. We gently carried Thula out and she protested vigorously as we slipped the sling under her stomach, lifting her up while Johnny eased her deformed limbs forward. We then lowered her with her feet in the correct position.

Our plan was simple: we had to strengthen her front feet or else she would die. And there she stood, wobbling like a wino at first, but gradually gaining some balance. We repeated this procedure several times between meals and by evening she was standing steadily with the aid of the sling.

I whistled softly. Perhaps we could save her after all – perhaps I would be able to keep my pledge to the herd. The progress this tough little infant had made in one day alone was inspirational.

The next morning she started taking uncertain steps supported by the sling and by the third day she was walking unaccompanied, albeit slowly with plenty of fall-downs. Yet she never complained; she always seemed cheerful, almost laughing in an elephantine way as she struggled to get up. Her courage was absolute. Her cheerfulness amid constant pain was simply unbelievable.

Within a week, although limping badly, this gallant little creature was hobbling around the lawn with Biyela following behind carrying a large golf umbrella to protect her from the sun. She had captured our gardener's heart; from now on it seemed his mission in life was to keep the sun off her frazzled skin.

As the days went on she got stronger and was regularly taking the bottle, a vital part of hand-rearing a wild elephant. Unlike baby rhinos which will trample over you to drink from a bottle, orphaned elephants can be extremely difficult to feed. They subliminally want to suckle from their mother, so you have to persuade them that they are doing just that. The trick is to hang a chunk of sacking from the ceiling to simulate the mother and then stand the baby next to it and introduce the teat from underneath, just as if she was suckling.

But if that didn't work, it was back to muscular force-feeding, and feeding times sometimes redefined the word chaos in our house. Johnny would back Thula into a wall, put his arm around her neck and ram the bottle into her mouth, squirting the vitamin-enriched milk into her system while she fought him every inch of the way. And at 270 pounds she could fight all right. Johnny often came off worst, landing flat on his bum spraying milk all over the place while Thula bolted for the door to seek consolation from her new best friend Biyela and his omnipresent umbrella. Biyela would then follow her around the lawn, glaring at us as if we were serial elephant-abusers.

But the fact that she took the bottle regularly was a huge plus. This, I believe, was due to her essentially being a happy creature and the caring environment we had created around her. Françoise in particular lavished constant attention on her and Thula adored her in return, following her around the house like a giant love-struck puppy. The only problem was that she broke everything she could reach; a coffee mug on the table was instant history and we soon learned that anything not nailed down would be trashed. If she didn't pull it onto the floor with her trunk, she bumped it off its perch with her bulk.

As she got stronger, the limp receded and apart from having some trouble lying down, she was healing beautifully. Indeed, her biggest problem in life was now trying to unravel what that strange appendage flapping in front of her face was all about. An elephant's trunk pulses with about 50,000 muscles. Thula was endlessly fascinated by hers; she flapped it about as a human baby would do with a doll.

Although I instructed everyone that she should never be alone I could have saved my breath. Johnny was always there and off-duty staff members regularly came up to the house to make a fuss of her. Everyone loved her indomitable spirit and Thula flourished under this utter devotion from her new family. Despite constant pain as her feet slowly straightened out, she always seemed to be smiling. Even Max, who would fight any creature for no reason other than that it was there, followed her around the lawn on her daily walks, his tail wagging like a feather in a gale.

One late afternoon, a sunset in paradise, I was walking her through the bush outside the garden, acclimatizing her to the longer grasses, thorns and trees that would be her future home, when suddenly I saw the herd appear at the top of the road. They had decided to come to the house for one of their periodic visits.

The timing could not have been worse. I was well outside the electric wire and to be caught with Thula in the open by her mother could be calamitous. I might even be regarded as a kidnapper. If I abandoned Thula and made a run for it there was no doubt they would whisk her off, and she would die. Her little – by elephant standards – feet were totally ill-equipped for life in the bush. A stroll around the garden as opposed to what she would be expected to do with her family was like comparing climbing a hill to Everest. It would be a slow death sentence even if Nandi lagged behind with her.

The only thing going for me was that the herd didn't know Thula was alive. They had come for a social visit – not to find their baby. I had to move fast.

'Come, Thula! Come, my girl!' I called anxiously, looking over my shoulder and made for the gate about a hundred yards away as fast as I could urge her. Luckily I was downwind and the herd didn't scent us while Thula stumbled along behind. If the wind had been blowing the other way, it could have provoked a stampede from the herd. Ahead Biyela was frantically pointing at the oncoming elephants with his umbrella, desperately calling Thula to hurry.

We made it to the gate – just – and I passed Thula on to Biyela, and then turned to watch the herd coming up.

They drew level a few minutes later and Nana's trunk shot up like a periscope, the tip switching until she fixated on where Thula had just ambled out of sight behind a hedge of wild strelitzia. She turned, her stomach rumbling. Nandi and Frankie joined her, scenting the air, analysing floating molecules Thula had left behind. They were like detectives at a crime scene and eased forward just inches from the electric wire.

I went to Thula's room, made sure she was closed in with Johnny and called a ranger to double-check the fence's current. I then waited, guiltily hoping they would leave. I was copping out, pretending nothing was happening.

Twenty minutes later they were still there and I felt I could no longer ignore them. They were entitled to know what we had done.

But how? If I let them see Thula it might prompt something so primordial we could not handle it; if elephants believe their babies are in danger they're uncontrollable. Their maternal instinct is ironclad. So what could I do to pacify them but still keep Thula with me until she was ready to be returned to her family fit and strong?

I didn't know. But I felt that at least I should let them know their baby was alive.

I went to Thula's room, took my shirt off and swabbed it over her body, put it back on and wiped my hands and arms all along her. I then walked back down to the fence and called them.

Nana came over first and as her trunk swept just above the single electric wire in greeting I stretched my hand out as I usually do. The response was remarkable. The tip of her trunk paused at my hand and for an instant she went rigid. Then her trunk twitched as she sucked in every particle of scent. I offered both hands and she snuffled up my shirt and vacuumed every inch. Nandi the mother and Frankie the aunt stood on either side, trunks snaking as they too got the olfactory messages that Thula was alive and close by.

All the while I talked to them, telling them how we helped Thula cheat death, what was wrong with her feet and why she had to stay with me for a little longer. I told them we all loved her because she was so brave and happy. I told them that they could be proud of their newest little member, who was fighting so gamely for her life. I then told them, for some completely random reason, that even Max – the ultimate canine curmudgeon – had befriended her.

I have long since lost my self-consciousness at chatting away to elephants like some eccentric. As I spoke I looked for signs that something of what I meant was getting across. I needn't have worried. We had come a long hard road together, this herd and I, and talking to them had been a crucial part of that process. And why not? Who am I to judge what elephants understand or otherwise? Besides I personally find the communication most satisfying. They evidently liked it too, responding with their deep stomach rumblings.

Eventually they read whatever they could from my shirt and these three magnificent elephants stood there before me like a judicial panel assessing the evidence.

After much deliberation they moved off and I could tell that they were relaxed and unconcerned. I'm not saying this lightly as I have seen unhappy elephants. I am familiar with many of their emotions. When they left, I know that they were happy. I know that they could have stormed the fence, electric or not, if they had been otherwise. I felt a glow ignite inside me. They trusted me, and I knew I could not let them down.

The weeks passed by and Thula was doing well, revelling in the affection and care ladled on her by Françoise and Johnny. So much so that Bijou became insanely jealous, constantly barking at the hulk towering up above like the original mouse that roared. Thula ignored the yapping poodle with impressive regal disdain.

Inside the house she was Françoise's shadow, particularly in the kitchen where she would dip her trunk in anything Françoise was cooking. I remarked that this would be the first elephant who would want her marula berries marinated in garlic.

Still she broke everything. The rangers' weekly shopping trip to town now included lugging mountains of crockery to replace Thula's damage. But what could you do? How could you get angry with a gallant creature that never gave up? That never complained? That refused to lie down and succumb?

Outside, Biyela was her hero. With his multi-coloured golf umbrella constantly covering her, the two became inseparable. In fact Biyela started sulking if she remained in the house for too long.

Indeed, for all of us, Thula was our talisman. She exuded an energy and vitality that tapped into the ethos of the reserve: that life was for living.

Then one morning Johnny called from her room and I went through to find her struggling to get up.

'She can't stand,' he said, pushing and pulling to try and get her on her feet. I climbed in and helped. Eventually after much squealing and protesting we had her up and she tottered briefly then limped outside.

Biyela and his umbrella appeared as if by magic and as we followed I saw that it took far longer for her to loosen up. So did Biyela, and I watched as he spoke softly into her weakly flapping ears. I then realized she wasn't just stiff in her feet; she was in acute pain – not just the pain she had bravely fought before. Her right hip also seemed to be troubling her. This was serious and I called the vet.

'Short of doing X-rays, which is impossible, I can't tell you what's wrong,' he said. 'Nothing is broken but she has badly inflamed joints in her front feet and hip, probably caused by the way she walks.'

He then prescribed some anti-inflammatories and instructed us to ease off on long walks.

The next morning it was the same. She couldn't stand up. The same happened the following. My concern rocketed.

A week later she wouldn't drink. Johnny, unshaven, wild-haired, despondent and soaked in the milk he was trying to coax her to take, summed it up. 'She's just not interested any more.'

I looked at Thula who was in the corner facing the wall, apathetically swinging her little trunk back and forth. She was also suffering from thrush, which as any mother knows is an extremely uncomfortable yeast infection in a baby's mouth, and she hated the pungent ointment we spread over her tongue and gums each day.

Johnny was exhausted so I took the bottle from him and tried to ease it into her mouth, with no success. Then Françoise, whom Thula truly loved, tried. She was gentle with her, but Thula still wouldn't take the bottle.

As Johnny said, she wasn't interested. From a feisty little fighter, she suddenly seemed to have given up. I had no idea why, except that perhaps the pain she had endured in her courageous quest to live was now simply unbearable.

The next day she took a quarter of a bottle – a fraction of what she needed – but the fact she had even taken that gave me heart. I prayed that her indomitable spirit would resurface triumphant.

That evening she was on a drip. The vet had come out of her own volition. Thula had also captivated her.

Two days later, despite drips and encouragement from the entire staff which would rival cheering at an international rugby match, she sunk into bottomless apathy.

Early the next morning a disconsolate Johnny told us she slipped away during the night while he was with her.

Thula's death affected everybody, particularly Françoise. I have never seen her sob so bitterly. We've had lots of animals living with us over the years and we were close to them all but with Thula it was different. Her cheerful disposition, her refusal to surrender until the last few days inspired everyone. She had shown us how life could be joyous despite pain; meaningful despite brevity. How life should be lived for the moment. The pall of sorrow she left behind was for many days impenetrable.

Her body was taken out into the veldt by Johnny to allow nature to take its course.

I later went out alone, found the herd and led them to the carcass. They gathered around. This time I didn't speak; I didn't have to tell them what had happened. For a moment I held my head in my hands; I had let them down. When I looked up, Nana was outside the vehicle's window, her trunk raised in her familiar greeting pose. Next to her was Nandi. They then moved off.

The remnants of Thula's skeleton are still there and every now and again Nana leads her family past and they stop, sniffing and pushing the bones around with their trunks, toying with them in an elephant remembrance ritual.

chapter thirty-seven

Cape buffalo are the quintessential African animal. The quandary for the uninitiated tourist is that a buffalo looks like and seems like a cow, an African cow perhaps, but a cow nevertheless, and why would anyone want to spend valuable safari time staring at bovines?

But for the aficionado of African bush there is nothing that quite compares, nothing that better symbolizes Africa, and there is no animal more regal, more unpredictable, or more dangerous. I had always wanted to introduce these magnificent beasts to Thula Thula and today was the day.

It was 4.30 a.m. Dawn was streaking with the first shards of light as we were taking delivery of a prime breeding herd of Cape buffalo. We had been up since 2 a.m. preparing the ramp, positioning vehicles and drinking coffee with excited rangers and a few lucky guests from the reserve. The state vet was there and the seals on the truck door had long since been broken for the animals to be freed but for some reason they were refusing to come out.

Then everything went wrong. Firstly, the state vet announced with all the officiousness he could muster in the very unofficial bush that two of the cows were dead and a formal investigation may be required. That stunned us. Apart from our concern for the welfare of the buffalo, they were very expensive and to lose two was a big blow. Secondly he complained that the truck was late; the herd did not want to come out; and that ours was not the only game delivery that he had to attend that morning. In short, he was a busy man and the lack of enthusiasm of the buffalo to leave the trailer was impinging on his valuable time. And it was obviously our fault.

By now Hennie had had enough. In between trying to persuade the buffalo to disembark and convincing the un-happy inspector that their reluctance was nothing personal, he climbed down off the trailer roof with deliberately aud-ible curses and walked back to his vehicle dialling his wife to say he would be late. That was when the bull finally left the truck . . .

Without warning a huge bull came thundering out of the back of the trailer and instead of disappearing into the bush, inexplicably made a U-turn that would give a Spanish matador the heebie-jeebies. But this was no mere *toro*; this was a one-and-a-half-ton Cape buffalo in its prime. And it was spitting mad. For the briefest moment he took in his surroundings and then focused on the ample figure of Hennie ambling off.

'Dear God no!' I thought and watched awestruck as the bull charged at Hennie in revenge for his uncomfortable journey.

'*Oom! Oom!*' screamed a young Afrikaner ranger, calling Hennie by the reverential 'Uncle' title Afrikaners give their elders. '*Die bull kom!*' The bull is coming!

It sure was. Hennie glanced over his shoulder, dropped his cellphone and ran for his life.

I knew he wouldn't make it. Hennie was a large man, the distance too far and there was no time for us to get a gun out, nevermind load and fire an accurate shot. An eerie stillness blanketed the scene unfolding in front of us – a real-life horror movie in surreal slow motion.

Wisely abandoning any hope of opening the vehicle's door in time, Hennie angled for the bonnet to try to duck out of the way of the horned juggernaut. Despite his lack of fitness and ungainly step he had built up a head of steam and was pounding along a lot faster than I thought possible. But that's adrenalin for you. With the bull inches behind he somehow reached the vehicle's bumper and they both sprinted around the front left corner as one, the beast's wicked horn-tips hooking viciously at his back.

It was so close I was certain Hennie had been pierced. But he somehow emerged with the buffalo less than a snort behind him, then ran the width of the pickup and managed to twist again around the bumper and dash for the tailgate.

'Go, *Oom*!' the ranger again cried at the top of his voice, shattering the silence. And with that we all came out of our collective trance and started shouting: 'Go, Hennie, go!' trying to distract the beast.

It must have worked as the buffalo overshot a fraction on the next turn and suddenly there was a glimmer of light between the two.

'Go! Hennie' we screamed louder.

Somehow Hennie managed to gain another precious half a yard as they sprinted like Olympians around the vehicle again.

Bulky as Hennie is, he was still nimbler on the corners and on their third lap he was able to yank the driver's door open and dive in. He slammed it shut and scrambled to the passenger side as the buffalo could skewer a vehicle door like a can opener, but it wasn't necessary. As far as the beast was concerned, Hennie had vaporized into thin air. He gave up the chase.

Well, not quite. Hearing our cheering, he turned to face us all standing on the back of the Land Rover, as if we were watching gladiators at the Coliseum. That certainly put a damper on things. This angry beast could easily flip the Landy.

Breaking into a trot he hurtled forward, head down and

331

I braced for the impact. Thankfully it never came as the snorting ton of horn and sinew missed by inches and continued straight off into the bush. With that a cheer went up . . . even louder than the one we roared for Hennie.

Hennie then climbed out and crouched with his hands on his knees catching his breath in rasping gasps. As he did so, the rest of the buffalo herd scrambled out of the back of the trailer into the bush.

Game rangers are a tough bunch and the gallows humour started immediately.

'Hey, Hennie, I missed that. Do it again, will you?' shouted one.

'Why are you breathing so hard?' called another. 'Oxygen is free.'

A third walked over to him and shoved a cold beer into his hand. 'Well done, *ou maat*. God was with you today.'

That was true. Hennie gulped the brew down without checking what time of day it was. As he did so I noticed the rip in his trousers. The bull's horn had actually pierced his clothing on the first turn. It was that close.

Bheki, Ngwenya and Vusi, who was now a section ranger, came with us as we went to inspect the two dead females. The state vet had to give his report, but to us the tragedy was right there in a mound of unmoving flesh. We weren't sure how they'd died. But one thing we did know was that we had some angry muscle out there charging through the bush.

'*Ayish*, Mkhulu, that bull is something,' said Vusi, echoing my thoughts. 'Hennie was lucky. We must be very careful as these cows will be the same, maybe worse.'

'I agree. Let's cancel all walking safaris for a while. And, Bheki, warn all your guards and the labourers to stay well away from them. Tell them all what happened here today.'

I knew that the story would be embellished upon – exactly

what I wanted. We had to let this herd settle down, which I knew they would.

But Hennie's close encounter with permanency got me thinking about something else I had been trying to avoid.

Life and death go hand in glove. Death is cyclical, witnessed more in the natural order of the wild than anywhere else. And my thoughts turned back to Max who was now fourteen years old and too old to accompany me into the bush he loved so much. The old warrior, who had survived poachers, snakes and feral pigs double his size, had succumbed to chronic arthritis in his hind legs. As I left him in his basket early that morning, he tottered about in a vain attempt to come with me. A year back he would have been in the front seat of the Land Rover. Now he could barely walk. And the sight of Hennie running for his life brought this home with unimaginable sorrow.

It's funny how these things happen so quickly. It seemed just yesterday that we were out and about on our adventures. I had been told by Françoise and a few close friends that I had to face up to the fact Max was no longer bulletproof. He was very old and in pain and not going to last much longer, but it was just too dire for me to consider. I countered that with the best veterinary help I could get but recently he had all but stopped taking food and sadly I knew his time was coming.

Even so, I was surprised to see Leotti the vet's car parked in the driveway so early in the morning as I got back. She was sitting next to Max's basket in the lounge. With her was Françoise. She seemed on the verge of tears.

Max tried to get up to greet me and fell over. He tried again . . . he wouldn't give up.

Leotti, who had treated Max throughout his numerous escapades, including regular *mfezi* fights, looked at me and shook her head.

'Françoise phoned me about this. Lawrence . . . I know you love him but' – she gestured at my loyal friend – 'it would be cruelty for this to carry on.'

She stood up. 'I will be waiting outside.'

As she closed the door Françoise put her arms around me and squeezed for a moment. Then she too left.

I sat down next to my beautiful boy, lifted his rugged spade-shaped head onto my knee and he looked up, licking my hand as he always did. Even in his dotage he was still a superb creature.

He and I sat for about ten minutes, just us together. I told him how much I loved him, how much I had learned from his courage and loyalty and that the life in him was eternal. He knew exactly what was happening, we were too close for him not to, and I braced myself and called out to Leotti.

She came in. The syringe was ready and she administered that loneliest of all injections as I held him.

I was inconsolable.

chapter thirty-eight

About a month later I woke at 6 a.m. with something shaking my shoulder. It was Françoise.

'So,' she said in that delightful way the French have of being as direct as an arrow, 'exactly when are we are going to get married . . . *mon chérie*?'

I rubbed the sleep out of my eyes. This was serious talk at this time of the morning and I had to engage my brain quickly.

'Married? We are married. We're married under common law. In fact we've been married longer and happier than most people I know. Almost two decades – a lifetime,' I added with a yawning grin to rob any unintended offence.

'Well, I don't understand this common-law business you always talk about. You just say that to do me out of a real wedding,' she replied, throwing a cushion at me with a laugh that didn't fully disguise her intent.

'I know. That's because you turned me down.'

'Turned you down? When, exactly?'

'So you don't remember? That shows just how important it was to you.'

She looked baffled. I moved in for the kill.

'It was years ago when I first asked you to marry me. You didn't even reply.'

'Rubbish! I must have been asleep and you've made up all this incredible nonsense.'

Despite the easy banter we both knew that the eternal

battle of the sexes was in full cry and I was thankful when the two-way radio blared at that moment, giving me a pretext to rush off into the reserve. We'd been together for eighteen years and all of a sudden the marriage 'thing' was rearing its head. It wasn't that we weren't happy. Françoise was absolutely fantastic, and we had been crazily in love since the moment we met, but my theory in life is that if things ain't broke, why fix them?

I kissed her as I left. She responded cheerfully . . . and I breathed a sigh of relief. Once again, all was quiet on the Western front.

A month later I had to go to England and while away my mother called, asking when I would be returning as she wanted me to meet some government officials that would be visiting Zululand. I gave her the date and she phoned back to say the meeting was confirmed. I let Françoise know and a few days later caught the flight home.

I arrived on a Saturday morning and after greeting the herd, who came as always to meet me at the fence, walked up to the house.

Françoise went off to prepare the lodge for the VIPs and I dressed in my best khakis . . . well, OK the ones with the least holes in them, a little disgruntled that I had to put on a smiling face for some officials barely hours after returning from an exhausting trip.

I walked to the front entrance of lodge, battered bush cap in hand, and peeked inside. It was packed to the rafters. There was a wedding going on. This was nothing unusual as we often do functions for overseas couples wanting a romantic Zulu wedding in the bush. I turned and walked out, bumping into my mum. I kissed her hello.

'Where are your VIPs? We can't meet them here. There's a wedding going on.'

She nodded, with a strange smile on her face. Something was up.

'Hang on . . . who is getting married? Anyone we know?'
'You are.'

There must be some innate male defence mechanism that kicks in at moments like this. I heard the two words she said, but neither registered.

'OK, well let's take the government people to the conference centre, out of the way of all this stuff.'

She shook her head, still with that strange smile. There were no government officials. My mum linked her arm through mine and we walked into the thatched lounge. Everyone stood and started clapping.

I had plenty of time to register what was happening because it unfolded before me as abstractly as an elephant charge, taking place in surreal slow motion despite its thundering reality. This was an ambush, a joint operation planned by both Françoise's family and my own. I recognized her best friend from Paris sitting with the Anthonys in pride of place. They must have been in on this for some time; you don't fly out from Europe just like that.

My staff were also dressed in their Sunday best standing in rows facing the minister at the podium, smiling and clapping. They too had been co-conspirators. The only person surprised was me – although stunned would be a more apt description.

Now my mother is the dearest person in the world to me. If it was anyone else I would have at least put up an argument. But she had me firmly by the arm, only surrendering her grip when I was at the podium and shaking hands with the minister.

There I stood, smiling and nodding at guests, feeling like an absolute idiot, knowing that they knew I had been utterly outmanoeuvred. I looked down at my shoes which gleamed back at me. Even they had been shined in a way I had never seen before. I then looked up to see Ngwenya and Bheki in their finery nudging each other and grinning hugely.

For the polygamous Zulus, what was taking place was contrary to their way of life and they were never going to let me live this down. Indeed, my Zulu friends are genuinely mystified why I don't have multiple wives. You white men are so stupid, they would say. Everybody knows one woman is too strong for one man. Two are even worse as they will gang up against you. You must have three, as one will always be fighting with the other two to take the pressure off you.

Chauvinism? Sure, but then every woman I've told this story to has battled to hide a knowing smile. Well, at least for the first proviso.

My train of thought was broken by appreciative murmurs from the crowd as Françoise walked in. I turned as she came up the aisle looking absolutely gorgeous and as her beautiful eyes fixed on me everything came together and made perfect sense. I was willingly caught up in her magic and totally agreed to the surprise proceedings. It was all just so right.

'Look,' she said as she arrived at the podium and pointed across the river. Mnumzane was there browsing quietly.

'He loves weddings,' she said, smiling. 'He seems to arrive for so many of them. Now he's at ours.'

A ring magically appeared and when asked if I took this woman to be my wife, a chorus rang to the rafters: 'He does!'

And I did.

We never have loud music at the lodge, but that night the bold rhythms of Africa throbbed across the reserve in celebrations that went on until the early morning.

chapter thirty-nine

Something strange was going on with Mnumzane. It happened out of the blue. A young ranger was on a game drive with two guests, a married couple, when they rounded a sharp corner and unexpectedly ran into him coming in the opposite direction.

He started ambling over. The ranger panicked and reversed too fast, smashing into a tree. They were stuck with Mnumzane coming straight for them. To the frightened ranger's credit he didn't reach for the rifle. Instead he told his passengers to sit tight and make no sound as Mnumzane strode up to the vehicle. I know first-hand that this is one of the most frightening sights imaginable. A six-ton bull literally breathing down your spine is something else all right. Then he lightly bumped the Land Rover and his tusk actually grazed one of the guest's arms. Somehow the man didn't scream.

Showing great presence of mind, the Zulu tracker jumped off his seat on the front of the vehicle and sneaked around to the other side, surreptitiously helping the guests off the vehicle. They all fled into the bush. Mnumzane fiddled around the Land Rover for a bit without causing any damage, and then moved off. Once they were sure he was gone, they crept out of their hiding places and drove at speed back to the lodge.

From initial accounts, Mnumzane was just being inquisitive

rather than aggressive. The ranger also played the incident down, so I didn't take it too seriously. I only got the full story months later when I was phoned by the couple.

After that encounter, Mnumzane started on occasion approaching our open guest game-drive vehicles. But again, the reports I got was that he was never angry, just curious. It was not dangerous as the rangers would merely drive away as soon as he approached. The bigger problem was that this was totally out of character; he simply was not behaving as an elephant should. Elephants automatically ignore us humans as long as we don't move into their space.

Then I discovered the reason for his sudden interest in game-drive vehicles. Prompted by a few pointed questions, a staff member told me that two of our young rangers had been teasing the bull, driving up and playing 'chicken' with him, daring each other to see who could get nearest then speeding away when he approached. They had seen me with Mnumzane before – totally without my knowledge as my interactions with him were deliberately kept private – and thought that they would also try to get up close. It never occurred to these two idiots that taunting the ultimate alpha male from a game-drive vehicle that normally carried guests on viewing safaris was teaching him a terribly bad habit. Both rangers had resigned before I found this out and hopefully they have since embarked on careers far removed from wildlife.

The most non-negotiable rule on the reserve was that no one was allowed to have any self-initiated contact with the elephants. Anyone who disobeyed that law would be instantly dismissed. Perhaps my biggest failure was to trust that all my carefully chosen staff had the same ingrained ethics and common sense that David and Brendan had shown. Sadly, that does not always hold true.

A little later a trainee lodge manager left without notice. The dust had barely settled as he sped from the reserve when I heard that he too had been using a game-drive Land Rover to approach Mnumzane, trying to imitate my call. These were the worst possible scenarios. Mnumzane had always been a very special case and the continuous teasing by strangers was dangerously altering his attitude to humans. He considered the shouting and revving of engines as a direct challenge and as a result game drives were forced to move off whenever they saw him. My concern was mounting.

I had also just bought a brand-new white Land Rover station wagon. The faithful old battered bush-green Landy had now gone around the clock a good few times and had to be retired, her innards due to be cannibalized for other vehicles. It was a sad day for me. The well-weathered seat, the simplistic dashboard, the worn-smooth gear stick, the bush-smell of the cabin . . . I loved her.

Taking delivery of this spanking new vehicle, I decided to do a test drive in really rough terrain to see if she was as rugged as my old Landy. She performed beautifully off-road, but eventually a tight copse of trees forced me to make an extremely tight 360-degree turn. I had just about completed this when suddenly I felt unaccountably apprehensive.

An instant later Mnumzane towered next to me. He had appeared silently from the shadows as only an elephant can and was just standing there. I looked up into his eyes and my heart skipped a beat. His pupils were cold as stones and I quickly called out his name, repeatedly greeting him. It took ten chilling seconds before he started relaxing. I completed the turn, talking continuously to him as he gradually settled down and let me go.

I drove off with a heavy heart. Things were not the same any more. Perhaps his aggression had been because he had not recognized the new vehicle. I fervently hoped so. But he shouldn't be approaching any of our vehicles, let alone acting aggressively towards them. My entire interaction with

Mnumzane was based on an intensely private, personal interplay between us, whereas now for the first time since arriving at Thula Thula he was being teased by rogue rangers.

Then in another incident our lodge manager Mabona was driving up to the house when Mnumzane appeared from nowhere and blocked her path. Doing exactly as she had been trained, she cut the engine and sat motionless. Mnumzane moved to the back and leaned on the car, shattering the rear window. The crackling glass surprised him and he backed off, giving Mabona enough time to turn the key and accelerate away.

After this we hacked out a dozen or so outlets on the road to the lodge where vehicles could rapidly reverse and turn if necessary. I also had all encroaching bush on the track cleared so we could see Mnumzane before he got too close.

This worked. The game drivers were avoiding him and the road to the lodge – the reserve's most travelled route – had easy escape routes. Mnumzane now had no contact whatsoever with any human except me. Best of all, any idiotic ranger activity had now been completely rooted out.

In short, everything started returning to normal.

But I was still worried. I began spending more time with him again, trying to reassure him and get him to settle down. With me he was always the same friendly accommodating giant that I loved. He seemed OK.

However, my senior rangers remained unhappy and shook their heads when I told them this. 'That's only with you,' they would say. 'He trusts you, but it's very different for the rest of us.' They wouldn't go near him and all walking safaris were stopped if he was anywhere in the area.

A few weeks later a journalist and good friend asked to film me interacting with Mnumzane. I very rarely do this and eventually agreed only on condition that the camera crew's vehicle was out of Mnumzane's sight and no one spoke during the entire episode.

We found him and I drove forward and got out of my new Land Rover leaving a young ranger in the back of the vehicle. I called out and Mnumzane started ambling over. I had some slices of bread in my pocket to throw to the side when I wanted to leave. I had recently taken to doing this with Mnumzane ... much as I dearly love him, when on foot I would only turn my back on him if he's distracted.

As he approached I studied his demeanour and decided he was fine. We had a wonderful ten minutes or so inter-acting, chatting about life – well, me doing that while Mnumzane contentedly browsed – and as I decided to leave I put my hand in my pocket for the bread. However, it had hooked in the material of my trousers and I looked down trying to yank the slices out.

At that moment it was me, not Mnumzane, who was distracted. He suddenly moved right up against me and I got the fright of my life. For not only was he almost on top of me, his entire mood had changed. Something behind me had disturbed him, possibly the young ranger in the Landy and he wanted to get at him. There was malevolence in the air.

I hastily threw the bread on the ground and thankfully he moved over to snuffle it up as I retreated.

By the time I got back to the film crew my heart was pounding like a bongo drum. I knew his temper was on a knife edge; something had changed with him.

I would soon realize by how much.

A few weeks later I was taking some VIP visitors on a game drive in my Landy as the sun was setting and we spotted Heidi, the rhino orphaned as a calf by Mnumzane years ago, slinking into the bush. We were crawling along at five miles per hour when out of the twilight the herd appeared, crossing the road fifty yards ahead.

'Elephant,' I said, switching on the spotlights.

It was the first time my two passengers had seen an elephant, let alone a herd, and their excitement attested, as always, to the ancient bewitchment of Africa. I switched off the engine to let them savour the moment, perhaps one they would not experience again.

Then I saw Mnumzane bringing up the rear. I knew he was now in musth, a sexual condition where a bull elephant's testosterone levels shoot up by an incredible fifty times and this is when bulls can become dangerously unpredictable, especially when following females as he was doing now. I never dared interact with any bull in musth. It was just too volatile. Anyway I was with guests, so it was out of the question.

Nana was leading her family towards Croc Pools and I waited for about five minutes to make sure they were well off the road before I started the Land Rover and again moved forwards.

Suddenly the man in the passenger seat started shouting: 'Elephant! Elephant!'

The yell shook me rigid. What was he on about? The elephants were gone. I strained my eyes searching the headlight-illuminated track in front, unable to see anything.

'Elephant!' he shouted again, pointing to his side window.

It was Mnumzane, barely three yards away in the dark. Prompted by the loud noise he stepped forward and lowered his massive head right onto the window as if to see what all the shouting was about and with instant dread I saw his eyes. They were stone cold and there was malevolence in the air.

Mnumzane then prodded the window with his trunk, testing its resilience. Realizing that at any second he was going to shatter through and in the process crush my passenger, I slammed the vehicle into reverse while desperately pleading with the two men to calm down. All I managed to do by reversing was to skid Mnumzane's tusk across the glass, snagging it at the edge of the door with a jarring bang. He lifted his head and trumpeted in rage. With that I knew we were now in grave danger. As far as Mnumzane was concerned, the car had 'attacked' him. In retaliation, he swung in front of us and hammered the bull bar so hard my head smacked the windscreen as we shot forward like crash-test dummies. Then he put his huge head on the bull bar and violently bulldozed us back twenty yards into the bush only stopping when the rear wheels jammed against a fallen tree.

I opened my window and screamed at him, but it was tantamount to yelling at a tornado in the dark. I watched in horror as he backed off sideways to give himself space to build up speed then lost sight of him as he moved out of the headlights. At least the guests had stopped yelling. All three of us were now deathly silent.

There was only one way out. As he set himself up for the charge I revved until the engine was screaming and dropped the clutch, trying to wrench the Landy out of his way. Too late. He came at us out of nowhere in an enraged charge. The shock of the colossal impact jarred my teeth as he smashed his tusks into the side of the Landy just behind the back door and then heaved us up and over.

Ka-bang! The Landy smashed down, landed on its side, then flipped over onto its roof and into a thicket as he drove on with his relentless attack. Another almighty charge flipped us back onto our side.

My shoulder was lying on the grass through the broken side window and the guest in the passenger seat was practically on top of me. My head hurt terribly from the strike on the windscreen as I tried to gather my senses. I wasn't injured but my biggest concern was that this wasn't over. In fact, our ordeal was in its infancy. Bull elephants have a terrifying reputation of finishing off what they start. To confirm this, just inches away Mnumzane stomped around the upturned vehicle in a rage.

I had to snap him out of his red mist and amid all the confusion I somehow remembered that elephants that have been exposed to gunfire sometimes freeze when they hear shots. I also knew that it could go the other way, that the gunfire could prompt a final lethal attack, but I had no choice.

Twisting around, I drew Françoise's tiny .635 pistol from my pocket just as the Landy shuddered with another titanic blow. I pointed at the sky through the broken windscreen and fired . . . again and again and again. I fought the compulsion to fire all eight shots in the magazine. My last-ditch plan was that if he got to us I would shoot the final four slugs into his foot and hope like hell it hurt enough to divert his attention and we could somehow get out and run for our lives.

To my eternal relief he froze. It had worked. As he hesitated I called out to him but I was trembling so much my voice was way off-key. I gulped lungful after lungful of oxygen until everything steadied and tried speaking again. As my voice calmed, he recognized me and his ears dropped; the anger visibly melting from his body.

I then told him it was OK, that it was me, and he had frightened the hell out of me – that he didn't need to be angry any more. Thankfully he recognized my voice and slowly came right up to where I lay on my side in the cab. His feet, practically the size of dustbin lids, were literally inches from my head. All he had to do was lift his foot onto the flimsy cab and that would be it. I aimed my puny gun at his foot and then watched entranced as he pulled out shards of the shattered windscreen, then gently reached in and put his trunk onto my shoulder and head, touching me, smelling me all over. All the while I talked to him, telling him we were in terrible danger and that he must be careful.

He could not have been more gentle. Eventually he walked off and started browsing on a nearby tree as if nothing had happened.

'The radio, the radio!' whispered one of the guests. 'Call for help!'

I reached for the mouthpiece only to find that the radio had been smashed off its hinges. In the darkness I found it and fumblingly reconnected the wires and got it going, whispering a Code Red, describing where we were and what had happened, and then turned the volume right down. I didn't want any loud responses to unsettle our precarious situation with Mnumzane.

Françoise took the call and relayed the bush version of a Mayday to get to us fast. Luckily there were rangers on a night-time-viewing safari close by who had heard the shots and they were with us in minutes. But whenever they approached, Mnumzane started challenging their vehicle, keeping them away.

I knew they carried a rifle and whispered strict instructions into the radio that despite how bad everything looked, under absolutely no circumstances was Mnumzane to be shot. They must just wait until he left.

But he wouldn't leave. Each time he came to the vehicle, one of the guests would panic and frantically climb over chairs to the opposite side of the Landy station wagon. This was prompting his interest and he would walk round and bump the vehicle making the poor man scramble back again. It was horrifying lying there absolutely helpless in the dark with this giant stomping around outside hitting the vehicle. Every now and then I would call out to him and he would come around to my side and stand quietly for a while, and then go back and continue worrying the guest. On top of that he kept circling our upturned vehicle, chasing off the rangers coming to our aid.

Then as I started to despair, I heard the ranger anxiously calling out on the radio, 'The herd is here, the whole herd is here . . . They're coming straight towards you. Oh my God, they're going to your Landy, what must we do? Over.'

'Nothing,' I replied, relieved. 'Just wait.'

This was good news, not bad as the ranger thought. Leaning forward out of the vehicle I could just see Nana and Frankie followed by the herd and I called out to them repeatedly.

But unusually they ignored me completely. Without breaking stride, they walked right past us and then, to my astonishment, surrounded Mnumzane, jostling him away from us. He could easily have butted them off – he certainly had the strength – but amazingly he didn't. From my cramped horizontal position on the ground I could hear their stomachs rumbling. I have no idea what the communications were, but moments later Mnumzane stopped his aggressive vigil over the wrecked Land Rover and left with them.

When they were about fifty yards away the rangers sped up, climbed on top of the Land Rover and pulled us out via the smashed side windows, one by one. Thankfully, incredibly, no one was hurt.

As we drove off I watched the elephants walking with Mnumzane, the undisputed dominant bull, submissively in tow. Given that adult bulls are loners, it was most unusual to see him herding with them. I had no doubt Nana understood what was going on and that she and Frankie had intervened to get him away. Not only for our good but for his. She had probably saved our lives.

But as we passed by some forty yards off, Mnumzane lifted his head sharply and took some angry steps towards us. That he again showed aggression towards the safari

Land Rover concerned me infinitely more than my wrecked vehicle. I had a big problem on my hands.

Back at the lodge Françoise gave me a fierce hug and ushered the guests to the bar. One, a lifelong teetotaller, gulped down three double whiskies before uttering a word.

Despite the drama, no one had a scratch.

My brand-new Land Rover was not so fortunate. The bemused insurance company took one look at the wreck and assigned it to the scrapheap. They had never before paid out a claim for an 'elephant incident'.

chapter forty

Our traumatic escape had me going in a dozen different directions trying to figure out what to do. Predictably the 'I told you so' brigade kicked off with a vengeance with some wildlife experts saying that Mnumzane should be put down immediately; that he was an accident waiting to happen; and that if I didn't do it now, someone was going to get killed.

Once again I rose to his defence and justified the series of events, saying that all he had done was come to my vehicle as he had done hundreds of times before. He had then become confused by strange voices shouting and being in musth he had lost it when the Landy suddenly reversed and hit his tusk. The proof was as soon as he heard my voice he stopped his craziness and actually came to me, pulling out the windscreen fragments and snuffling his trunk over me to check if I was OK.

I refused to shoot him and instead started to put into place other measures to ensure his and everyone else's safety. The rangers were experienced enough to take care of themselves. It was the lodge staff driving back and forth that concerned me, so we cleared out every inch of bush and shrubbery for thirty yards on each side of all roads between the house and the lodge. Now if he was anywhere near the track he could be seen from a long way off. At night I had a ranger drive well ahead of any staff vehicle with a spotlight to check if he was around.

But there was no need as he had gone deep into the bush alone and stayed there, almost as if atoning for his outburst.

The herd, on the other hand, were just being wild elephants, doing things that contented elephants do such as pulling down whole trees for grazing, wallowing in mudbaths and providing great game viewing. Even ET had settled down and I took solace from this success. After a few weeks of no trouble I dared to start thinking that Mnumzane had learned something from the incident and could be saved.

Then early one morning I was radioed by a safari drive ranger to say that he had a breakdown and had left the Land Rover in the bush to go and get parts. When he returned, the vehicle had been smashed off the road and overturned.

'Stay right there,' I radioed back with a deep sense of foreboding. 'I'm on my way.'

But even before I got there, I knew what had happened. Mnumzane's spoor was all over the place. He had found the stationary vehicle and destroyed it, flipping it upside down and smashing it off the road. Despondently I surveyed the damage.

A safari Land Rover is an open vehicle to facilitate game viewing. It has no roof, and if turned over like this one had been, people could get killed. Mnumzane had attacked an empty Landy for no reason and therefore would surely attack one with passengers in it as well.

I fruitlessly tried to find justifications; anything to put off the inevitable but there was no way out. It was over and I knew it. He was completely out of control. In fact, in virtually any other reserve, he would have been put down immediately after killing the rhino never mind also flipping the Land Rover, and now it was a guest game-drive vehicle as well.

I took a slow lonely drive home and called a friend.

'I need to borrow your .375,' I asked, numbed by the words coming out of my mouth.

'Sure, why?' came the reply.

'Nothing major, thanks. I'll have it back by tomorrow.'

'No problem.' Then he paused, 'Are you OK?'

'I'm fine, I'll see you later.'

I put the phone down, appalled at my decision but I knew in my heart we had reached the end of the road. If I left it any longer someone was going to die.

My .303 would probably suffice but the task was difficult enough as it was and I didn't want to make any mistakes. I wanted maximum firepower so I drove into town, collected the rifle and eight rounds of 286 grain monolithic solid ammunition. Without telling anyone, I went out onto an adjacent property, marked a tree and fired three shots, sighting the rifle to make sure it was perfectly on target. An hour later I found my big boy grazing peacefully near the river.

At the sound of my car he looked up and came ambling over, pleased to see me as always. Feeling absolutely treacherous, I got out, readied the rifle on the open door and took aim, his familiar features looking completely out of place in the telescopic sight. As he arrived I was still standing there, wracked by emotion, unable to pull the trigger . . . tears flowing freely.

I couldn't do it. I stuffed the rifle in the car as he stood by, warmly radiating greetings in that special way he had. I gathered myself and said goodbye to him for the last time, telling him we would see each other again one day. A few moments later I drove off leaving him standing there, palpably bewildered by my hasty departure.

The next morning two sharpshooters I had earlier phoned arrived. I watched as they sighted their rifles on a target in a riverbed. This is absolutely essential when hunting dangerous game – you have to ensure your rifle is absolutely on target. These were retired professional hunters, now conservationists who knew exactly what they were doing.

'So you're not coming with us?' asked one of them, an old friend of mine. 'You sure you don't want to do this yourself?'

'I tried. I know him too well.' My voice was dead.

'Yeah, I heard about that. It's amazing, what happened.'

'He's now completely lost the plot,' I said, not wanting to go into the details.

'I understand,' he said, giving me a brief pat on the shoulder.

An hour later I was standing outside on the lawn looking over the reserve that I loved so much when I heard two distant shots. As the finality of it came crashing home I was seized by a terrible loneliness, both for my beautiful boy and for myself. After nine years of friendship I had failed. He had gone to join his mother whose violent death just before he came to Thula Thula he never really recovered from.

I forced myself to go to where Mnumzane's immense body was lying, the hunters nearby. I was pleased he hadn't fallen badly, lying on his side as if asleep.

'It was painless. He was dead before he hit the ground,' said Peter. 'But we had a bit of a fright at the last moment as he suddenly came at us and it was touch and go. There's something wrong with that elephant. You made the right decision.'

I looked at the magnificent body, the ground and sky still pulsing with his presence.

'Goodbye, great one,' I said and got back into the Landy and went to call the herd, to bring them, to let them see what I had done.

What I had had to do.

chapter forty-one

'These things always seem to happen in threes,' I thought mournfully a couple of days later, pondering over the deaths of baby Thula, Max and now Mnumzane in the space of little over a year. The bush, though, is a great place to regain perspective and I was comforted by the belief that although they were gone physically, they would always be part of this eternal piece of Africa. Their bones would always be in this soil.

With the exception of elephants and crocodiles which can live a man's three score years and ten, animals generally do not live long. In the wild, everything is continuously regenerated. Lions only live about fifteen years, as do impala, nyala and kudu. Zebra and wildebeest can reach twenty and giraffe a little more. Many smaller animals and birds live very short lives indeed; insects sometimes only weeks.

Each spring the bush comes alive with pulsating new life as Thula Thula morphs into a giant nursery, tended by thousands of caring mothers of all shapes and sizes, all bringing a new generation into the world. And they need to, for regardless of its vitality, wildlife succumbs rapidly. Despite its infinite beauty, the wilderness is a hostile environment and only the fittest, wisest and luckiest reach old age. Death is an integral part of life. This is the dominant bush reality and I like it that way. It's natural, uncluttered by materialism or artificial ethics and it helps me to maintain a wholesome perspective of my own existence and that of my friends and family.

I was sitting on a termite mound near a grove of acacias, still deep in thought when a Land Rover approached and Vusi, who had been my 'guinea-pig' ranger in initiating walking safaris with elephants – or running safaris, as was sometimes the case in those experimental days – got out. A powerfully built man with steely self-assurance whom I had just promoted to senior ranger, he told me he had just driven past Mnumzane's body.

He paused for a moment, looking at me directly. 'There was only one tusk.'

I instantly snapped out of my reverie. 'What do you mean only one! Where's the other?'

'It's gone. Stolen.'

'How did that happen?' I was shocked to the core.

'It was there yesterday evening. I saw it myself, and today it's gone.' He continued staring at me, a rare gesture for rural Zulus whose culture demands that eyes be averted. I think he was as shocked as I was.

'We searched for hundreds of yards around the body. Then I had every inch of the fence checked and there are no holes cut by poachers. Nobody broke in last night.'

I stared back, astounded.

'Also I advised security and every car today has been searched. I didn't want to tell you until I was sure.'

'That's unbelievable,' I said, thinking back to our early poaching days, 'I mean . . . who the hell took it then?'

'It's still on the reserve,' replied Vusi confidently. 'It's one of the staff and it has been hidden somewhere here. Someone with a vehicle. I saw the lights near the body last night, but it was gone before I got halfway.'

Just then Ngwenya walked up carrying the second tusk over his shoulder and lowered it heavily onto the ground.

'There is something that will interest you,' said Vusi,

abandoning the topic of the theft. 'Feel here,' he knelt down next to the magnificent piece of ivory, his fingers running lightly over its length. 'There is a bad crack.'

I crouched next to him. I had always known that the tip of Mnumzane's tusk had a slight crack, but as this is fairly common among elephants, I didn't worry much about it.

But then I followed the path of Vusi's fingers with my own and whistled. On closer inspection the crack was much bigger and deeper than I had realized; in fact the tusk was splayed right open at the end and the blackened interior was visible. A tusk is just an extended tooth. And just as with a human, a break like that in a living tooth is a magnet for infection and absolute torture, as anyone who has ever had an abscess will attest.

'*Yebo*, Mkhulu,' said Vusi. 'There was a big swelling right at the top of the tusk, deep inside. I cut it open. It was rotten.'

I whistled again, for now everything made perfect sense. Poor Mnumzane had been in so much pain for so long that he just couldn't stand it any more. That's why he became so evil-tempered. And, I suddenly realized, that's exactly why he went berserk and flipped the Land Rover over. When I reversed I jarred his excruciatingly sensitive tusk on the edge of the Landy's window. He must have seen blinding stars in his agony. It took the gunshots from my pistol just to yank him out of it.

I sat down on the lawn and put my head in my hands. Although unusual to do with a wild elephant, all it would have taken was a dart of sedative, a good vet and some antibiotics and we could probably have taken his pain away. And he would have still been with us. A picture of him contentedly browsing before me during our 'chats' flashed through my mind. He basically had been a happy creature – despite the tragedies he had witnessed in his short life.

I shook myself out of it, forced myself to focus and then stood up. There was nothing I could do about it now.

'Let's get the tusk cleaned and then store it in a safe place,' I said to Vusi. 'Now at last we know what happened to him and why he went crazy.'

'*Yebo*, Mkhulu.'

'And let's find that other tusk!'

I walked away astonished that one of my own staff could even think of stealing Mnumzane's tusk at a time like this. I had wanted them mounted as a pair in the lodge as a commemoration of his life.

We never found the tusk. But that doesn't mean I'm not still looking.

That afternoon I received a surprise phone call from *Nkosi* Biyela. We had been in regular contact, but more often than not through his *izindunas*, headmen, as intermediaries.

'I would like to meet with you,' he said cheerfully. 'I will come to Thula Thula tomorrow afternoon late.'

'I look forward to it,' I replied heartened by the call, 'and may I make a suggestion? Please bring your wife and stay the night with us at the lodge as our guests.'

'Yes, good idea, thank you. It will give us time to talk about our game-reserve project. I will see you tomorrow then.'

The game reserve, the Royal Zulu, was the main reason I had come to Thula Thula all those years ago. My heart jumped – especially as he had referred to it as 'our project', which was a first since the project had first been presented to his father Nkanyiso Biyela twelve years ago. I had pursued the vision relentlessly but as so often happens in Africa, the delays and complications at times seemed insurmountable. *Nkosi* Biyela was the key to its success as he was by far the most powerful chief in the area and controlled the biggest chunk of the land. And he wanted to talk!

That afternoon he arrived and we drove through the reserve on a late Zululand afternoon, observing the lush wilderness and robust wildlife and talking about the future.

'Whose land is that?' asked the *Nkosi* pointing to a stretch of heavy bush just outside our boundary.

'It is yours.'

'Good! Then I would like to join it with you,' he said. Simple as that.

I realized he wanted to continue and held off a reply. He then got out of the Landy and looked around, pointing to the KZN Wildlife reserve that adjoined Thula Thula to the north.

'That I know is Fundimvelo. It was my grandfather's land. They have offered it to me. I will take it back and join with you. We will then do the joint project you have spoken of for the benefit of my people.' Again, simple as that.

'Thank you, *Nkosi*.'

'Now the Ntambanana land, why are they taking so long in releasing it to us?' he asked, referring to the tract of bush and thorn on my western boundary. Ntambanana was originally land excised by the apartheid government from various tribes some decades ago and was now being returned. The Biyelas had the biggest claim over it, and so for *Nkosi* Biyela to query why this process was taking so long meant that the project was now going to get massive impetus from him.

'I do not know, *Nkosi*. It worries me as well.'

'We must start pushing them now,' he said, referring to the local government. And when *Nkosi* Biyela talks about 'pushing', it certainly gets people's attention.

In those few minutes – completely out of the blue – he had described most of the land that made up my dream African game reserve, but not all of it. There was one last piece of the jigsaw, the most important piece: Mlosheni, an 8,000-acre section which ran north from Ntambanana right up to the White Umfolozi River, the gateway to the world-famous Umfolozi game reserve. Once we had that, we could lower fences with the Umfolozi reserve and have a massive tract of pristine Africa.

'Mlosheni,' I said, then hesitated.

'What of Mlosheni?'

'Mlosheni will join us to the Umfolozi reserve. It is important.'

'Of course! I have spoken with my *izinduna*, it is already agreed,' he said matter-of-factly. 'The animals will migrate as they used to before the apartheid government put up the fences.'

I reached out and we shook hands. I was elated, scarcely able to believe what I was hearing. This project would do more for his people than anything that had ever happened before and my mind raced, assessing the benefits to wildlife as well. *Nkosi* Biyela would lead a coalition of traditional communities into a brave new world.

I knew too that while this agreement represented a fundamental breakthrough that had been twelve years in the making, there was still a lot of work to be done and many lengthy tribal meetings lay ahead. But at long last he was fully committed – now we would win. His word was absolutely crucial; it was without question what we needed most. Everything now could start happening.

That evening in the lodge we continued discussing the Royal Zulu project and what it could do to regenerate our area. I felt the gloom of Mnumzane's death lift; his soaring spirit would be part of a magnificent new reserve that would be Africa as it should be: wild, beautiful, with people and animals living in harmony. Indeed, to me the new reserve would be a monument not only to Mnumzane but to Max and baby Thula as well, who had also shown in spades the qualities most needed in the fight for our last remaining wild lands – courage, loyalty, and above all, perseverance.

It was an evening I will remember for the rest of my days – a vision of what Africa can be. And not least thanks to the cooperation of a remarkable leader, *Nkosi* Biyela. This new reserve, imbued with Zulu history dating from their first king, Shaka Zulu, will kickstart the area both physically with job creation and investment, and spiritually with a true wilderness ethos. One only has to look at the comments in the guestbook at Thula Thula to see how often tourists remark on the spiritual effect the wild has had on them during their stay. Now with *Nkosi* Biyela onside, the final major barrier had been removed. Royal Zulu would at last become a reality and, I hope, a cornerstone of conservation in Africa.

The next morning, after a hefty breakfast with the *Nkosi* during which his enthusiasm for the new project seemed, if anything, even more animated, I switched on the TV news. The looming war against Saddam Hussein in Iraq was being ratcheted up by the hour. It seemed now that an invasion was inevitable. But that morning the news also featured a clip on the Kabul Zoo in Afghanistan and filling the entire screen was a lion, blind in one eye with a tormented face full of shrapnel. A Taliban soldier had thrown a grenade at him. Somehow he'd survived. His name was Marjan. His pock-scabbed face, his baleful, accusing stare seared into my soul. This truly was the reality of animals caught up help-lessly – faultlessly – in the vicious vortex of man's folly. More graphic than any words, that awful image was an indictment of our species. Something snapped in my mind. My anger gnawed corrosively at my innards. I knew I had to get to Iraq and make sure the same thing didn't happen to the creatures at the Baghdad Zoo, the biggest menagerie in the Middle East.

Ten days later, during the coalition invasion, I was in the bomb-blasted Iraqi capital. It didn't long take to grasp the enormity of the task before me and I needed a good man at my side. It took one phone call, and a few weeks later Brendan arrived.

Brendan was with me in those crucial first few months when we saved the last remaining animals in the zoo and elsewhere in Baghdad. He then stayed in the Iraqi capital for more than a year after I left doing absolutely critical work in making sure the animals were well cared for.

After that he went to Kabul where he also did sterling stuff in advising the Afghans on how to improve their zoo. Sadly, Marjan had died long before he arrived. In the process, he left Thula Thula. But I take immense pride in the fact that he had been part of the journey with us, both at Thula Thula and internationally.

Like David, he was integral to what we achieved.

He still comes 'home' to us for regular visits.

chapter forty-two

I returned home nearly six months later. It had been the most intense period of my life – the heat, dust and chaos of Baghdad's war zone matched only by surreal moments of tragedy, exhilaration, hilarity and despair.

The experience taught me one thing for sure, and that is that the innocent, hope-filled days of *Born Free* are long gone. At one stage in Baghdad the zoo staff had kept a pride of desiccated lions and two Bengal tigers alive by manually hauling fetid water from a stinking lake. Hour by torturous hour, we drip-fed the dehydrated cats – a bucket at a time, and that single bucket was all that kept the animals alive – until it was stolen by looters. We in turn brazenly raided kitchens in Saddam's bombed palaces and the city's abandoned hotels for the lion's next meal while fighting raged on around us.

I have never witnessed such selflessness by such a small diverse group of people. From individual American soldiers who, sickened by bureaucracy, sacrificed their rations to feed starving animals, to tough South African 'mercenaries' who acted as self-appointed zoo security guards, and courageous Iraqi zoo workers and civilians who literally put their lives on the line working with Westerners. Baghdad in 2003 was a starkly incongruous snapshot of global good and bad.

The experience fizzed so vividly in my system that I wrote a book about it afterwards called *Babylon's Ark*. The catharsis of putting this adventure down on paper was immense, the lessons learned priceless. I also used this amazing experience to create The Earth Organization, which has grown rapidly. Earth Org is not a typical 'greenie' lobby, we are an organization of common people that targets practical projects to reverse the downward spiral of the dwindling plant and animal kingdoms.

My elephants faced adversity and misfortune in their efforts to survive, and they did so resolutely, always looking after their own, always keeping perspective, never forgetting to squeeze in fun and play when they could. I found the same qualities in the abandoned animals of the Baghdad Zoo. Despite danger and privation in a world turned upside down, I never once saw them give up. These lessons are central to our philosophy.

When I returned from Iraq, the herd was waiting for me at the gate of the reserve itself. This was unusual as I was told they had been in deep bush for most of the time I was away, so much so that the rangers had difficulty finding them for guests. In fact it was so unusual that the gate guard was caught completely unprepared and had to shut himself in the hut near the fence. When I hooted he reluctantly emerged, saw the elephants were still there and hurriedly threw the keys at me and bolted back inside again. I let myself in.

Nana and her family followed me to the main house and milled around outside the fence. I got out of the car and spoke to them, my voice croaking with emotion. There were now fourteen of them, with all the new additions. The original herd of seven had doubled. The four very latest ones were Mnumzane's progeny – his spirit would live on both spiritually and physically.

As they stood there, sniffing the air, something soared in my heart and I knew then just how much this herd meant to me. And even more importantly, the lessons they had individually taught me.

They say you get out of life what you put in, but that is only true if you can understand what it is that you are getting. As Nana's and Frankie's trunks snaked out to me over the fence, it dawned that they had given me so much more than I had given them. In saving their lives, the repayment I have received from them was immeasurable.

From Nana, the glorious matriarch, I learned how much family means. I leaned just how much wise leadership, selfless discipline and tough unconditional love is the core of the family unit. I learned how important one's own flesh and blood actually is when the dice are loaded against you.

From Frankie, the feisty aunt, I learned that loyalty to one's group is paramount. Frankie would have laid down her life in a blink for her herd. To her, nothing was more important – there was no question about this being a 'greater love'. And the love and respect she received in return for her courage was absolute.

From Nandi, I learned about dignity and how much a real mother cares; how she was prepared to stand over her deformed baby for days without food or water, trying right until the end, refusing to surrender until the last breath had been gasped.

From Mandla, I saw how tough it can be for a baby to grow up on the run in a hostile world and how his devoted mother and aunts ensured he made it as best he could. Since Mnumzane's death, he had reached puberty and was about to be kicked out of the herd, as nature decreed, and would have new challenges to face.

From Marula and Mabula, Frankie's children, I saw first-hand what good parenting can achieve despite adverse circumstances. These beautiful, well-behaved children would be what we in human terms would call 'good citizens' – something often in short supply in our world. They saw how their mother and aunt treated me, and in return, they accorded me the respect one would give to a distinguished relative. I loved them for that.

From ET I learned forgiveness. I had managed to reach out to her through her heartbreak and distrust, but only because she had let me. Somewhere along the way she had recovered her life and in the process taught me how to forgive, as she had forgiven humans for the horrors they had visited on her own family before she came to us. She had given birth while I was away and was standing close by looking at me, proudly showing off her baby. I made a special fuss of her.

And, of course, there had been Mnumzane, my big boy who had become one of my dearest friends. Like anyone, there are things I regret in life – and to me the biggest one is that I did not somehow guess that an excruciating tooth infection had been the cause of him going 'rogue'. I console myself knowing that no other game ranger would likely have worked that one out either. Indeed, he would have been shot out of hand a lot earlier on most other reserves.

But perhaps the most important lesson I learned is that there are no walls between humans and the elephants except those we put up ourselves, and that until we allow not only elephants, but all living creatures their place in the sun, we can never be whole ourselves.

I looked at them through the fence, feeling not only the warm peace of being home after six months of mayhem in a war zone, but revelling in the fact that my greater family was now also with me. The rumbling of their stomachs as they gathered at the fence was the most soothing sound I have ever heard. Just as Nana had done to me in the *boma* eight years ago, I felt surrounded by a sense of extraordinary well-being.

Mandla and Mabula were off on the side now. I knew they would go through the same heartache of ostracism as

Mnumzane had and I wished there was something I could do about it. In larger reserves, they would team up with other adolescents forming a loose bachelor association with an adult bull. They're called *askaris* and do what most young groups of men do: hang out, chase girls and test their strength and wits against each other and the world.

The older male becomes the father figure they never had in the matriarchal herd, teaching them masculine etiquette as well as more practical matters of survival in the wild, such as where the best watering holes and the most succulent branches and berries are. These geography lessons they never forget – hence the cliché about elephants' long memories.

In return, the *askaris* treat their father figure with utmost respect and affection. When he is too old to strip the bark off branches, they escort him to marshes or swamps where the leaves are softer. For elephants do not die gracefully of old age, they starve to death after they lose their sixth set of teeth. And when their leader is too weak to stand and dementia sets in, the *askaris* somtimes even guard him as he sags, preventing hyenas or lions from attacking him. Even when he dies, the *askaris* have been known to chase scavengers off the carcass. After he has gone they will visit his bones for as long as they are there, paying respects to a fallen leader. The fact that almost all elephants which perish naturally do so in the soft-food wetlands has led to the myth of secret graveyards and ivory troves where elephants instinctively migrate to die. The truth is they all usually die in the last areas where food is soft enough to ingest.

This is also why those who hunt old bulls don't – or refuse – to understand the harm they are doing. An ageing elephant male is not something surplus to be dispatched by some meagre trophy-gatherer. He is a breathing reference library; he's there for the health and well-being of future elephants. He teaches the youngsters who they really are and imparts priceless bush skills to succeeding generations.

It was now clear that a wise masculine role model is needed in our ever-growing family. With Thula Thula being expanded dramatically into adjoining tribal trust lands as part of the Royal Zulu project, we would be able to import a mature bull to teach the growing number of young males on the reserve the facts of life.

I have subsequently put the word out, and judging by the enthusiastic response, I know that soon we will get a sage patriarch to teach my *askaris* good manners. And I know that Mandla and Mabula will grow up to be fine young males. As soon as the Royal Zulu is established, we will have a piece of Africa as the mother continent was always meant to be, protected and enhanced by the people rooted in the region, people with a stake in the future of their land.

I was mulling over all of this later after spending time in the bush with Bheki and Ngwenya when I noticed the entire herd grazing about half a mile away. The sun glowed on the hills that guard Thula Thula, back-lighting them like golden sentinels, the elephants before them silhouetted on the savannah. It was a vision of this timeless Africa at its most inspiring and I understood once more why elephants are so iconic of this continent.

Nana and Frankie stood together, the matriarch and her deputy. Next to them were their older daughters, Nandi and Marula, both in the prime of womanhood, and with them the first elephants born in the area for more than a century, Mvula and Ilanga. On the periphery, perhaps 400 yards away, I saw the bachelors, Mandla and Mabula. Scattered throughout were the babies.

I will have no interaction with the new generations. The whole idea when I initially adopted the herd was to release them directly into the bush. I never planned to have any connection with them, as to me all wild animals should be just that – wild. Circumstances, such as their escape and their anguish at being relocated and witnessing siblings being shot, made my intervention a reluctant necessity. As I said previously, I only wanted to get Nana the matriarch to trust one human to ease her bitterness over our species as a whole. Once that was achieved, and she knew her family would no longer be molested, my mission was accomplished. I was keenly aware that too much interaction with humans dilutes the feral qualities demanded in the wilderness.

It's working beautifully. Today, when I drive past the herd, Nana and Frankie may still approach me. I will always have that special relationship with them. Nandi, Mabula, Marula and Mandla and of course ET also still know me; although they acknowledge my presence and still may come forward behind Nana they do so with greater reservation.

But the youngsters ignore me as I do them. Totally. I am an outsider. The relationships I had with their grandmothers will never be repeated. They will have no direct contact with humans whatsoever – not with me, nor my rangers. And that's the way it should be.

They are going to grow up just as I wanted my original group to. Wild. If there is one thing I disapprove of it's the unnatural capture and taming of wild animals, whether an elephant or a bird.

To me, the only good cage is an empty cage.

afterword

Graham Spence, January 2017

We got the call at 5 a.m. on 2 March 2012. My wife Terrie, who is also Lawrence's sister, took it. At our age every call at an unusual hour is a heart-stopper. I was instantly awake.

Terrie nodded and put the mobile phone down on the bedside table. She put her head in her hands. I knew what she was going to say.

'Lawrence is dead. He had a heart attack.'

I knew his health hadn't been good. But even so, Lawrence was indestructible – he had the constitution of an ox. I couldn't believe it.

One newspaper called him the Indiana Jones of Conservation, and that about sums him up. He did everything in life as a swashbuckler. That's how I will always remember him.

And yet, how do you explain that enigmatic quality? He had deliberately broken off contact with the elephant herd at Thula Thula as he wanted them to be truly wild. He wouldn't come out to greet them any more at his and Françoise's humble cottage. Eventually they no longer came. After all, it was a bit out of the way of the best grazing, and to cap it all Lawrence wouldn't talk to them now.

But yet, but yet . . . The day after Lawrence died, the elephants, led by Nana, arrived at his house in an eerie vigil that still gives me goosebumps. A ranger took a video of that silent march-past that went viral on YouTube. A Google search for 'elephants mourn Lawrence Anthony' gets over a million results.

There is no doubt about Lawrence's global impact. It was shown in spades at the outpouring of anguish following his death.

His incredible legacy lives on thanks to his wife Françoise and the energetic team at Thula Thula. And perhaps the most vivid symbol of that legacy is the amazing expansion of the elephant herd he loved so much.

They came to him as a rogue group of just seven agitated animals in 1999. When he died in 2012, the number had multiplied to twenty-one happy members of a settled pachyderm community. A remarkable growth rate when you consider that an African elephant's gestation period is twenty-two months. Even more significant is the fact that a reproducing herd is a sign of a happy herd.

However, this did pose a problem. Soon after Lawrence's tragic death, the conservation authority for Zululand, Ezemvelo KZN Wildlife, told Françoise that the maximum carrying capacity on Thula Thula was twenty-four elephants. It was a gentle reminder that, the way things were going, the herd's numbers would soon surpass the land's ability to sustain these magnificent giants.

There were two solutions; relocating some of the elephants to another area, or reversible male fertility control, where bull elephants are darted with contraception medicine.

The decision for Françoise and her team was an easy one. No one at Thula Thula would even fleetingly consider the notion of any of their precious elephants being uprooted and moved elsewhere.

The first contraception project was started in September 2012, six months after Lawrence died, with a veterinary surgeon coming to the reserve at six-month intervals to dart the four reproductive males – Gobisa (introduced as the patriarch after Mnumzane died), Mabula, Mandla and Ilanga. If not administered at those intervals, the bull becomes fertile again. It is as simple as that; it's completely reversible and doesn't harm either the animals or the environment.

Since the first contraception dart was fired, there have been nine more elephant babies, bringing the number to thirty! In fact, the last baby born on Thula Thula was actually discovered by the vet while doing birth-control darting. No one is quite sure why the system hasn't worked on the reserve, as it has proved effective elsewhere.

'Maybe we missed the fertility window by a few days,' said Françoise. 'Maybe we misjudged the virility of some of the younger bulls that we believed still to be at a pre-puberty stage. We just don't know.'

However, while delighted with the new arrivals, this growth is not sustainable and the darting programme has now been extended to include some of the younger males.

There is, of course, a plus side.

As Françoise says, 'We have a very happy herd full of playful babies which are a delight for our guests to observe and admire.'

There are currently new studies being carried out to include female contraception, which may be more effective, but this is a long process and extremely expensive. And although contraception does not adversely affect the elephants physically or trigger any behavioural side effects, questions do remain as to how continued contraception might influence such a highly sociable species.

So this brings us to the 'first-prize' solution for the Thula Thula herd; getting more land for it to flourish. That was Lawrence's dream when he bought the reserve – to establish a vast biosphere that links to the world-famous Hluhluwe-Imfolozi Park boundary some twenty-five miles away, which would be called the Royal Zulu.

371

Although plans are still on the drawing board, that dream is coming closer to fruition. Thanks to the local communities who own much of the adjacent land, Thula Thula now has the immediate opportunity to add a further 3,500 hectares to the elephants' range. It will come at a hefty operational price, though. Installing an extra twenty-five miles of electric fencing alone will cost £250,000. Not to mention expanding the road network, employing extra rangers, buying additional security equipment and vehicles, as well as providing training in conservation and land management.

However, not acquiring the land would be short-sighted. Community projects such as this not only support wildlife, but also provide local employment and education. This is critical for the future of the area. Game reserves cannot exist as isolated islands; they have to benefit local people in the surrounding deprived areas and give all a stake in the future.

To help achieve this, Françoise has created a non-profit animal welfare organization called the South African Conservation Fund. This provides key funds to implement projects such as the Thula Thula Land Expansion Project for Elephants, and the Thula Thula Rhino Fund for anti-poaching operations and protection of wildlife (see http://thulathula.com/conservation-fund).

Those of you who have read the other books in the Lawrence Anthony trilogy (*Babylon's Ark* and *The Last Rhinos*), may also be interested to know that a Thula Thula Rhino Orphanage has been established following the successful rearing of Thabo and Ntombi, the first orphans to arrive at the reserve in 2009. As described in *The Last Rhinos*, it was the brutal slaughter by poachers of a gentle rhino called Heidi that started Lawrence on his quest to save the northern white rhino.

The orphans on Thula Thula, all of whom have seen their mothers murdered by poachers, have had their horns infused with indelible dye and are guarded by armed rangers from the Anti-Poaching Unit around the clock. Thabo and Ntombi have also been dehorned, which is one of the front line deterrents against poachers. A rhino horn grows like a fingernail. It can be cut off every eighteen months or so without harming the animal.

As Lawrence said to me before his death, 'This is sadly what modern conservation will come to.'

Indeed, but at least the legacy survives. In fact, at Thula Thula, it flourishes.

A true testament to a truly great man.

Read on for the first chapter from

The Elephant in My Kitchen

by Françoise Malby-Anthony and Katja Willemsen,
which will be published in 2018

With Lawrence gone, Françoise was left to face the tough reality of running Thula Thula without him, even though she knew very little about the conservation/animal side of the reserve. She was short on money, poachers were capitalizing on the chaos of Lawrence's death, and even Mabula was stroppy – charging Land Rovers on game drives and terrifying guests. There was no time to mourn when Thula Thula's human and animal family were depending on her.

How Françoise survived and Thula Thula thrived is beautifully described in this charming, funny and poignant book. As well as keeping us up to date with old friends such as elephant matriarch Nana, Françoise introduces us to many new characters, including the abandoned hippo baby Charlie who hates water and German Shepherd Duma who is nursemaid, coach and best friend to all the traumatized rhino, hippo and elephant orphans. And of course we learn more about the herd, from the day baby Tom became separated from the others and found his way into Françoise's kitchen to the desperate race against time to save Marula's baby who had a snare wrapped around his little face and couldn't open his mouth to suckle. If you loved *The Elephant Whisperer* then you won't want to miss this sparkling sequel.

chapter one

Violent weather always unsettled our elephants and the predicted gale-force winds meant there was a dangerous risk of broken trees causing breaks in Thula Thula's perimeter fence. The cyclone had threatened for days and while we desperately needed water after a scorching summer, we definitely didn't need a tropical storm. We were worried about the animals but my husband Lawrence and I were confident that, somewhere in the vast expanse of our game reserve, the herd was safe under the watchful eye of their wise matriarch Nana.

We hadn't seen them near the house in a while and I missed them. The minute they arrived, their trunks immediately curled up to 'read' our house. Were we home? Where were the dogs? Was that a whiff of new bougainvillea?

Bijou, my Maltese poodle and sovereign princess of the reserve, hated losing her spot centre stage and always yapped indignantly at them. The adult elephants ignored her, but the babies were as cocky as she was, and would gleefully charge her along the length of the wire fence that bordered our garden, their bodies a gangly bundle of flapping ears and tiny swinging trunks.

No matter how much we treasured their visits, we knew it wasn't safe for them to be this comfortable around humans. Poachers took advantage of their trust and so we planned to slowly wean them off us, or to be more accurate, wean *ourselves* off them. Not that Lawrence would dream of giving up his beloved Nana – theirs was a two-way love affair because Nana had no intention of giving him up either.

They met in secret. Lawrence would park his battered Land Rover a good half kilometre away from the herd and wait. Nana would catch his scent in the air, quietly separate from the others and amble towards him through the dense scrubland, trunk high in delighted greeting. He would tell her about his day and she no doubt told him about hers with soft throaty rumbles and trunk-tip touches.

What a difference she made to the distressed creature that had arrived at Thula Thula back in 1999!

We had only just bought the reserve the year before and elephants weren't part of our plan. So when a representative of an animal welfare organization asked us to adopt a rogue herd of elephants, we were flabbergasted. We knew nothing about keeping elephants, nor did we have the required *boma* – secure enclosure – within the reserve where they could stay until they adjusted to their new environment.

'The woman must know we don't have any experience,' I said to Lawrence. 'Why *us*?'

'Probably because no one else is stupid enough, but Françoise, if we say no, they're going to be shot, even the two babies.'

I was horrified. 'Phone her and say yes. We'll make a plan somehow. We always do.'

Two weeks later, in the middle of a night of torrential rains, three huge articulated trucks brought them to us. When I saw the size of the vehicles, the full impact of what was arriving hit me. Two adult females, three sub-adults, an adolescent bull and two babies. We knew enough about elephants by then to know that if there were going to be problems, they'd come from the older ones. Lawrence and I exchanged glances. *Let the* boma *hold*.

Just as they pulled up at the game reserve, a tyre exploded

and the vehicle tilted dangerously in the mud. My heart froze at the elephants' terrified trumpeting and screeching. It was only at dawn that we managed to get them into the safety of the new enclosure.

They weren't there for long.

By the next day, they had figured out a way to avoid the electric fence's brutal 8,000 volts by pushing a nine metre high tambotie tree onto it. The wires shorted and off they went, heading northwards in the direction of their previous home. Hundreds of villages dot the hills and valleys around our game reserve so it was a code-red disaster.

We struggled to find them. You'd think it would be easy to find a herd of elephants but it isn't. Animals big and small instinctively know how to make themselves disappear in the bush and disappear they did. Trackers on foot, 4x4s and helicopters couldn't find them. Frustrated with doing nothing, I jumped into my little Tazz and hit the dirt roads to look for them, with Penny, our feisty bull terrier, as my assistant.

'*Sawubona*, have you seen seven elephants?' I asked everyone I passed in my best Zulu.

But with a French accent that butchered their language, they just stared at the gesticulating blonde in front of them and politely shook their heads.

It took ten days to get the herd back to Thula Thula. Ten long, exhausting days. We survived on adrenalin, coffee and very little sleep. How Lawrence managed to stop them from being shot was a miracle. The local wildlife authority had every right to demand that the elephants be put down. They had human safety issues to consider and besides, they knew only too well that the chances of rehabilitating the group were close to zero. We were warned that if they escaped again, they would definitely be shot.

The pressure to settle them down was terrible and my life changed overnight from worrying about cobras or scorpions in my bedroom to lying awake, waiting for Lawrence to come home, scared stiff he was being trampled to death in his desperation to persuade the elephants to accept their new home. Night after night, he stayed as close to the *boma* as he dared, singing to them, talking to them and telling them stories until he was hoarse. With tender determination and no shortage of madness, Lawrence breached Nana's terror of man and gained her trust.

One hot afternoon, he came home and literally bounced up the steps towards me.

'You won't believe what happened,' he said, still awestruck. 'Nana put her trunk through the fence and touched my hand.'

My eyes widened in shock. Nana could have slung her trunk around his body and yanked him through the wires.

'How did you know she wouldn't hurt you?'

'You know when you can sense someone's mood without a word being spoken? That's what it was like. She isn't angry any more and she isn't frightened. In fact, I think she's telling me they're ready to explore their new home.'

'Please get out of this alive,' I begged.

'We're over the worst. I'm going to open the *boma* at daybreak.'

That night, Lawrence and I sat on our verandah under a star-flung sky and clinked champagne glasses.

'To Nana,' I sighed.

'To my baba,' Lawrence grinned.

The herd had become family over the past thirteen years so we were extremely worried when the storm warnings worsened and the risk of the cyclone smashing into us increased with every passing hour. Lawrence was away on business and I was on my own. He called me non-stop. *How bad are the winds now? Has it started raining yet? Are the rangers patrolling the fence?* It was the worst possible time for him to be away. Cyclones are rare in Zululand but when they strike, their devastation can be catastrophic. I found out afterwards that he called our insurance company from Johannesburg to double our weather-damage cover. That's how alarmed he was. I couldn't wait for him to get back.

Then, in the middle of this chaos, at seven in the morning I received a call telling me that my indestructible husband had died in the night. I didn't believe it. Lawrence had survived war-torn Baghdad and savage Congolese violence, and now I wouldn't be fetching him from Durban International Airport and bringing him home. I sank onto the bed, numb with shock.

The game reserve fell silent in disbelief.

'It was as if somebody switched off the plugs of life,' said Mabona, our lodge manageress.

Like a robot, I kept going. The storm was still raging and the KwaZulu-Natal emergency services had warned us that it was heading our way. I made sure the guests were safe and instructed the rangers to secure the tented camp with extra ropes and wire. Then Mother Nature gave us an incredible reprieve and Cyclone Irena veered offshore. The crisis was over. We let out a collective groan of relief and prepared to stare grief in the face.

How was I going to survive without Lawrence at Thula Thula? It felt impossible, for me and for our staff. Many thought I would take refuge in France. He and I had run the game reserve as a rock-solid team. Lawrence, or *Lolo*, as I called him, took on everything to do with the animals and their safety, and I handled hospitality, marketing and finance. We learnt on the hop, adapted to things we knew nothing about and simply tackled each out-of-the-blue challenge that flew our way. Like adopting a herd of emotionally deranged elephants. What were we thinking?

But we managed, more than managed, with courage and craziness and plenty of laughter. We loved each other and we loved the oasis we had built in the African bush. Protecting animals, especially elephant and rhino, was the focus of our life together.

And now, from one day to the next, my partner in everything was gone. It was unthinkable, and because he was away when it happened, his death didn't feel real. Word spread like bushfire and emails, calls and messages poured in from around the world. It wasn't just my grief, it was everyone's grief. Still it didn't sink in. I kept expecting a call from him.

'Françoise, I'm at the airport! Where *are* you?'

I stumbled through that first weekend in a daze. Very early on Sunday morning, I received a call informing me that the herd had surfaced and was on the move.

'They're heading south,' crackled the radio. 'Direction main house.'

That was a surprise. The last sighting of them had been during the worst of the storm alerts when they had been a good twelve hours' walk from us, and remember, that's twelve hours powered by mammoth muscles. Now they were a mere fifteen minutes away. But to be honest, I really didn't give it any more thought. Life was a blur and I could hardly breathe for the things I had to do. Our guests didn't know what had happened and somehow I had to keep the lodge running for them.

Promise Dlamini, one of our game rangers, was the first to see the herd and almost drove into them. They were right at the main gate, making it impossible for him to drive through. He immediately noticed something odd.

'Even the bulls are here,' he reported.

Bachelor elephants tend to stay away from the others or, if they are close by, they stay out of sight. That morning, all twenty-one members of the herd jostled about at the gate, clearly agitated. This was highly unusual because their visits were usually so serene.

382

Sometimes, if Lawrence had returned from being away, they would pop by, mill about and graze patiently while they waited for him to come out and say hello. Or if there was a baby to introduce, they would stand along the fence, radiating peace, and gently nudge the new arrival forward to meet him.

The Sunday after he died was completely different. They were restless and pacing. They walked in a disorganized jumble to the front of the house, stayed there for a few minutes then shouldered their way to the back again, never grazing, always moving.

'They were disturbed but I had no idea why. I thought maybe they had had a run-in with poachers. When I got closer, I saw the telltale streaks of stress on the sides of their faces, even the babies,' Promise said afterwards, rubbing his own cheek in amazement.

An elephant's temporal gland sits between its eye and ear, and secretes liquid when the animal is stressed, which can create the mistaken image that they're crying. The elephants at our entrance weren't crying but the dark moist lines running down their massive cheeks showed they were deeply stressed. After about forty minutes, they lined up at the fence separating the lodge from the bush and their gentle communication started.

Solemn rumbles rolled through the air, the same low-frequency language they always used with Lawrence. Mabula, the herd's dominant bull, paced up and down with the others; just Nana stood by silently, as if waiting for Lawrence to appear but knowing he wasn't going to.

We hadn't seen them in months. Why now? Why this exact weekend? And why were they so anxious? No science book can explain why our herd came to the house *that* weekend, and why they came for many years afterwards on the anniversary of his death.

But to me, it makes perfect sense. When my husband's

heart stopped, something stirred in theirs, and they crossed the miles and miles of wilderness to mourn with us, to pay their respects, like they do when one of their own has died.

I didn't always understand the mysterious wonders of animals. Far from it. I grew up in France a city girl, a Parisian through and through. I could tell you the quickest way to Saint-Germain-des-Prés but I knew nothing about animals. Our family never had pets, although we did once have a tortoise in our garden. Living and working in a city, even a beautiful one like Paris, there's no time to notice nature like you do in the bush. It's *metro, boulot, dodo*, as they say in France, when life is a relentless treadmill of *commute, work, sleep*. Yet even as I pounded the Parisian treadmill, somewhere deep inside me I always knew I would end up in a foreign country.

But living in the sticks in Africa? Not *that* foreign.

And yet, there I was, in the sticks, alone, and burying my husband. I didn't know where to begin. I asked Vusi and Promise, Lawrence's trusted right-hand men, to come to the house to talk about the scattering of his ashes.

'We should move Mnumzane's bones to the dam. I want Lawrence and him to be together,' I murmured.

Mkhulu Dam was Lawrence's favourite spot at Thula. He and Vusi had built it themselves and it's where he went to clear his mind, fill his soul. And Mnumzane was his favourite boy elephant who had come to us as part of Nana's group, a distraught youngster whose mother and sister had been shot before his eyes. Even though he was only a teenager when he arrived, just a kid really, and a troubled one, he understood the responsibility of being the oldest male, and the very first thing he did was charge Lawrence to stop him from getting too close to his new family. Lawrence admired his gutsiness so much that he named him *Mnumzane*, Zulu for *Sir*, and it became one of his favourite stories.

'He must have been terrified,' Lawrence loved to recount. 'He'd just travelled eighteen hours in a rattling, iron prison on wheels and once out of it, everything was foreign. No familiar smells, no safe hiding place to run to, just a bunch of exhausted human beings who would have represented extreme danger to him, but he still bloody well charged us. If I'd been wearing a hat, I would have raised it to him.'

Some months afterwards, Mnumzane was ousted from the herd. It's how elephants bring up their boys – they separate them and their growing testosterone levels from the teenage girls. This ensures genes are spread far and wide, and stops inbreeding, but of course, poor Mnumzane was an orphan and had no genetic links at all to the female youngsters. But Nana was a strict matriarch and there would be no hanky-panky on her watch. It was heartbreaking how he suffered. He had already lost his mother and sister, and now he was losing his foster mum and siblings too. He barely ate and became so thin that we had to tempt him with special snacks of alfalfa and thorny acacia branches, which he guzzled with the same relish a human teenager guzzles burgers.

I'll never forget the day Mnumzane decided to let Lawrence know exactly how he felt about him. This great big four-ton elephant lumbered up to his Land Rover and stood in front of him, stopping him from going further.

'I got the fright of my life,' Lawrence told me later, 'but then he fixed me with those old-soul eyes of his and lolled his giant head from side to side, as if to say *no need to be so jumpy, old man*, and I just *knew* he was telling me that he loved being with me.'

'He's looking for a new *papa*,' I teased.

'You're probably right and it's something we have to think about. He's getting to the age where he'll need to be kept in line by someone who can pack a bigger punch than me!'

From then on, Mnumzane regularly sought out Lawrence

for father–son bush chats. I don't know who loved those get-togethers more. Lawrence, the proud foster father, watching his boy grow up, or Mnumzane, the rejected teenager, flourishing under Lawrence's love and acceptance.

So it was devastating for Lawrence when this gentle giant suddenly turned violent. Unbeknown to anyone, mind-blowing pain from an abscess was literally driving Mnumzane crazy and when he killed a rhino then utterly wrecked a broken-down 4x4, Lawrence knew it was time. Putting him down was one of the most traumatic decisions he ever faced. He withdrew with grief and I didn't know how to console him. He even stopped joining guests at the bar, something he loved to do. Often he disappeared for hours on end and I knew he was visiting the site where his boy had fallen. We went for long drives in the bush. We sat on the edge of Mkhulu Dam and reminisced about all the things Mnumzane had done in his short time with us.

'A bloody *abscess*. A jab of antibiotics would have fixed it. I should have *known*.'

'You couldn't have. Not even you, Lolo,' I said countless times.

They were kindred spirits, those two – brave, unpredictable, funny and tender. I knew with all my heart that reuniting them in death was exactly what Lawrence would have wanted.

Only snatches of memory remain of the day we scattered his ashes. I remember the convoy of cars that seemed as long as the road itself. I remember the clouds of dust from the dirt track when we headed north to where the dam was. I remember we stood in a half moon at the water's edge. I remember anecdotes and stories. I remember tears and laughter. I remember dark ripples in the water.

By then, I had been in South Africa for twenty-five years and I loved and embraced its melting pot of traditions and cultures, but for a few moments that day, I yearned for the busy familiarity of Montparnasse where I had lived in Paris. It was the one and only time I longed for France because my life was in South Africa, and like Nana, my family was now the animals and people at Thula Thula.

Living in the bush teaches you that life is a magnificent cycle of birth and death, and nothing showed me that more powerfully than when Nana gave birth to a beautiful baby boy around the time of Lawrence's passing.

Of course I named him *Lolo*.